OPENING DOORS:
A Presentation of Laws Protecting Filipino Child Workers

Third Edition

**International Labour Organisation –
International Program on the
Elimination of Child Labour**
6th floor, Neda sa Makati Bldg.
106 Amorsolo St., Legaspi Village
Makati City, 1209 Philippines

in cooperation with

**Ateneo Human Rights Center –
Adhikain Para sa Karapatang Pambata**
G/F Ateneo Professional Schools,
Rockwell Drive, Rockwell Center
Makati City, 1200 Philippines

INTERNATIONAL PROGRAMME ON THE ELIMINATION OF CHILD LABOR (IPEC)

IPEC'S OBJECTIVES

The aim of IPEC is the progressive elimination of child labor by strengthening the capability of countries to deal with the problem and by promoting a worldwide movement to combat child labor.

Child labor is a vast, complex, multi-faceted phenomenon. In the long term, it can be solved only from within the countries themselves. That is why ILO-IPEC strives to:

- support national efforts to combat child labor and to build up a permanent capacity to tackle the problem; and,
- give priority to the eradication of the most hazardous and exploitative types of child labor.

Poverty is the main cause, but not the only cause, of child labor. Many poor societies do not tolerate it, while it flourishes in others. Child labor exists also because of unawareness, tolerance or indifference; this needs to change.

THE PHILIPPINE CHILD LABOUR PROGRAM AND THE ILO

The Government of the Philippines signed a Memorandum of Understanding (MOU) with the ILO in June 1994. Following the recommendations of a National Planning Workshop, an Indicative Framework of Philippine ILO Action established priority target groups:

- children working under forced labor conditions and victims of trafficking and bonded labor; and,

- children in hazardous working conditions and occupations in mining and quarrying, in home-based work, especially under sub-contracting arrangements, in the fireworks industry, in deep-sea diving, in domestic service, in vegetable and sugar production, and the children trapped in prostitution.

Within these groups, working girls who are particularly vulnerable to exploitation and abuse, are a special focus of attention.

IPEC'S STRATEGY

The starting point for implementing ILO-IPEC's strategy in participating countries is the will and commitment of individual governments to address child labor in cooperation and consultation with employers' organizations, workers' organizations, NGOs and relevant partners in society, such as universities and the media. They are aided to adopt measures, which aim at:

- preventing child labor;
- withdrawing children from exploitative and hazardous work and providing alternatives; and,
- improving working conditions as a transitional measure towards the elimination of child labor.

IPEC has supported partner organizations in various initiatives involving direct services, awareness-raising and advocacy, law and policy reform, capability-building through training and action-oriented research.

IPEC'S PARTNERS

In the Philippines, the **Department of Labor and Employment** leads the national child labor program. Other executive departments are equally involved, including the Department of Education, Culture and Sports, the Department of Social Welfare and Development, the Department of Justice, and the Department of Interior and Local Government. Child labor committees are active at the regional and provincial levels in close coordination with local governments.

ILO's tripartite partners, **the employers and the workers' organizations,** have also become important IPEC partners in raising awareness among members and child workers, in lobbying for policy- and program-reform and in monitoring children's working conditions. The Employers Confederation of the Philippines, the Trade Union Congress of the Philippines and the Federation of Free Workers are implementing child labor programs in the Philippines.

Non-governmental organizations (NGOs) are among the most effective partners in the campaign against child labor. IPEC has worked with the Kamalayan Development Center, Visayan Forum, Philippine Center for Investigative Journalism, and STOP Trafficking of Pilipinos, Inc. and the Ateneo Human Rights Center, among others.

Atty. Janet F. Sunga
Opening Doors, A Presentation of Laws Protecting Filipino Child Workers
2002Edition
Makati City, International Labour Office, 2002

ISBN 92-2-113314-1

Compiled, edited and published by

**Adhikain Para sa Karapatang Pambata —
Ateneo Human Rights Center**

Atty. Ana Janet F. Sunga
Author

Atty. Tricia Clare A. Oco
Editor

Atty. Sedfrey M. Candelaria
Atty. Aleli Domingo
Advisory Board

with the support of

**International Labour Organization —
International Program on the Elimination of Child Labor**

Preface to the 2002 Edition

With the current developments of child labor policies in the Philippines we found it necessary to publish the third edition of this book. Particularly significant is the ratification by the Philippines of ILO Convention No.182 where the country binds itself to take immediate and effective measures to secure the prohibition and elimination of the worst forms of child labor. We have also included in this edition national laws, department orders and circulars recently issued by different government agencies addressing the issues on child labor in the light of the provisions of ILO Convention No. 182 and related international instruments dealing with the worst forms. It is with hope that this book would provide an updated and comprehensive compilation of international instruments and laws and their implementing rules and regulations related to the rights and special protection of child workers.

Acknowledgments

I wish to thank Atty. Ana Janet F. Sunga for her invaluable assistance and support while this book was being updated; Atty. Rea Chiongson for the important input she provided; Miss Claire Clementir for her administrative help and for proofreading the final draft of the text; Atty Roselle Tenefrancia, for the layout of this edition and Atty. Ronaldo Romey Gutierrez for the design of the cover illustration.

Atty. Tricia Clare. A. Oco
Child Labour, Program Coordinator
AKAP-Ateneo Human Rights Center

Preface to the Revised Edition (1997)

Since the first publication of this book in 1996, there were significant laws, department orders, circulars, and rules and regulations that were issued which impelled us to make revisions. Among the new laws that were included in this edition is Republic Act No. 8369 or the "Family Courts Act of 1997." Ordinances issued by different local government units, and new department orders and circulars during the interval were incorporated as well.

Furthermore, the demand for more copies of the first edition encouraged us to reprint this book and develop it further both in form and content..

In this regard, I wish to recognize the invaluable contribution of Atty. Ana Janet Suñga for her untiring effort in producing the first edition and helping us in updating it. The generous assistance of Generose Mislang and Amanda Abrera in lay-outing and editing this revised edition is likewise acknowledged.

Atty. Ma. Aleli R. Domingo
Coordinator, AKAP-Ateneo
Human Rights Center

ACKNOWLEDGMENTS

The author gratefully acknowledges the following:

The generous support of **ILO-IPEC**;

Atty. Maria Paz Angeles, Racquel Constantino, Ethel Mercado, Racquel Ros and Myra Ann Salvador for their invaluable assistance in doing the research for this project;

ILO-IPEC Philippines, Department of Labor and Employment, Institute for Labor Studies (DOLE ILS), DOLE Child Labor Project Management Team, STOP Trafficking of Pilipinos Foundation, Inc., and Trade Union Congress of the Philippines for sharing their research materials on child labor;

Ma. Alcestis Abrera-Mangahas for her assistance and advice;

Ronaldo Romey Gutierrez for the cover illustration; and,

The staff and friends of the Ateneo Human Rights Center.

Atty. Ana Janet F. Sunga
Author
(1996)

FOREWORD

Child Labor is a phenomenon that exists throughout the world. In the Philippines, millions of children can be found working in poor and unsafe conditions, risking their life and health for little, or no remuneration in order to survive. Majority of these children are abused and exploited, their futures threatened by work, which inhibits their physical, intellectual and moral development. The problem of child labor can be traced to major societal and economic factors, such as overpopulation, poverty, unemployment, cultural beliefs, failures in the educational system, and political instability, among others. It is evident, therefore, that the problem requires both immediate and long-term solutions -- immediate measures to put an end to intolerable work, and gradual measures to act on the root causes of child labor and to change cultural attitudes towards it.

The law can be an effective tool in combating child labor by providing child workers with sufficient rights, and providing effective sanctions against those who abuse or exploit them. The Philippines is replete with these laws and is in fact considered to have some of the strictest laws on child labor. Yet, the incidence of child labor in the country has continued to increase unabatedly and the exploitation of children at work persists. It is significant to note that, to this date, no employer has ever been successfully prosecuted under the child labor laws, which have been in existence since the 1920s. It must be emphasized that legislation is not an end in itself but only a means among many. The more important goal is to have a collective will to enforce these laws. It is unfortunate that, in the Philippines, very few people possess the proper knowledge and understanding of the laws protecting child workers. This lack of awareness and comprehension of the laws actually render these laws inutile in protecting the country's children.

This book aims to promote awareness and understanding of child labor laws and the legal procedures involved in their enforcement. It attempts to present in one publication all the existing laws, which may be invoked in protecting the rights of Filipino child workers. It is fervently hoped that this will provide the much-needed assistance to all those involved in law enforcement -- labor inspectors, policemen, prosecutors, judges, social workers, governmental and non-governmental organizations — so they may open the doors for the children who are waiting to be saved.

TABLE OF CONTENTS

Page number

FOREWORD

TABLE OF CONTENTS . . . . *i*

PART ONE – UNDERSTANDING CHILD LABOR

I. DEFINITION OF CHILD LABOR 1

II. CHILD LABOR SITUATION IN THE PHILIPPINES 5

III. THE REASONS WHY CHILDREN WORK 9

IV. STRATEGIES IN ADDRESSING CHILD LABOR 11

PART TWO –
THE LEGAL PROTECTION OF CHILD WORKERS

INTRODUCTION 16

I. GENERAL POLICY CONSIDERATIONS 27

    A. INTERNATIONAL INSTRUMENTS
        1. International Covenant On
           Economic, Social And Cultural
           Rights (Art. 10) 27
        2. Convention On The Rights
           Of The Child (Art. 32 & 34). 28

    B. NATIONAL LAWS
        1. Philippine Constitution 29
        2. Child and Youth Welfare Code (P.D. 603) 30

II. MINIMUM AGE OF EMPLOYMENT
   - EXCEPTIONS/DUTIES OF EMPLOYER   32

   A. INTERNATIONAL CONVENTIONS
      1. ILO Convention No. 59   32
         Convention Fixing The
         Minimum Age For Admission
         Of Children To Industrial
         Employment (Revised 1937)
      2. ILO Convention No. 138   35
         Minimum Age Convention,
         1973 Convention Concerning
         Minimum Age For Admission
         To Employment
      3. Recommendation No. 146 48
         Recommendation Concerning
         Minimum Age For Admission To
         Employment

   B. NATIONAL LAWS
      1. Minimum Age: Principal Policy
         1.1 R.A. 7658   56
            An Act Prohibiting The
            Employment Of Children
            Below 15 Years Of Age
            In Public And Private
            Undertakings, Amending
            For This Purpose Section
            12, Article VIII Of R.A. 7610
         1.2 Labor Code (Art. 139)   59
         1.3 Omnibus Rules Implementing
            The Labor Code   59
            Book III, Rule XII, Section 2
      2. Minimum Age: Hazardous Work   60
         2.1 Labor Code (Art. 139)   60
         2.2 Omnibus Rules Implementing

The Labor Code   60

Book III, Rule XII, Section 3

2.3 Department Order No. 4   61

Hazardous Work And

Activities To Persons

Below 18 Years of Age

2.4 Occupational Safety And
Health Standards   65

Rule 1013, Hazardous

Workplaces

3. Minimum Age: Modeling In
Commercials/Advertisements
Promoting Alcoholic Beverages,
Tobacco, Violence, Etc.   66

R.A. 7610, Section 14

4. Minimum Age: Apprentices   67

4.1 Labor Code, Title II, Chapter I   67

4.2 Omnibus Rules Implementing

The Labor Code   68

5. Minimum Age: The Child And
Youth Welfare Code   69

P.D. 603, Title VI, Chapter II

6. Minimum Age: Opinion of the Secretary   70

III. WORST FORMS OF CHILD LABOR   72

A. INTERNATIONAL CONVENTIONS

1. ILO Convention No. 182   72

Convention Concerning The

Prohibition And Immediate Action

For The Elimination of the Worst

Forms of Child Labour

1.1 ILO Recommendation No. 190   80

Recommendation Concerning

The Prohibition And Immediate Action

*For The Elimination Of The Worst
Forms of Child Labour*

2. Optional Protocol to the Convention on the
   Rights of the Child on the Involvement of
   Children in Armed Conflict   88

3. Optional Protocol to the Convention on the
   Rights of the Child on the Sale of Children,
   Child Prostitution and Child Pornography   97

4. Protocol to Prevent, Suppress and Punish
   Trafficking in Persons, Especially Women
   and Children, Supplementing the
   United Nations Convention against
   Transnational Organized Crime   111

5. Convention on the Suppression of Traffic in
   Persons and of the Exploitation of the
   Prostitution of Others   127

B. NATIONAL LAWS
   1. Worst Form: All Forms of Slavery
      or Practices   139
         1.1 Slavery: 139
         1.2 Forced or Compulsory Labor   139
         1.3 Debt Bondage   140
         1.4 Sale of Children and Trafficking
             in Children   149
         1.5 Children in Armed Conflict   149
   2. Worst Form: Child Prostitution and
      Other Sexual Abuse   162
   3. Worst Form: Child Pornography   168
   4. Worst Form: Production and Trafficking
      of Drugs   170
   5. Other Worst Forms   172

IV. TERMS AND CONDITIONS OF EMPLOYMENT   175

  A. INTERNATIONAL CONVENTIONS
     1. ILO Convention No. 77   175
       Convention Concerning
       Medical Examination For
       Fitness For Employment
       In Industry Of Children
       And Young Persons
     2. ILO Convention No. 90   184
       Convention Concerning
       The Night Work Of Young
       Persons Employed In
       Industry (Revised 1948)

  B NATIONAL LAWS
     1. Non-Discrimination   195
     2. Employer's Reportorial Duties   195
     3. Hours of Work, Night Work and
       Physical Examination of Children   196
     4. Children Below 15 Years   198
       ANNEXES TO R.A. 7658
       Minor's Work Permit   203
       CL-DOLE Form No. 2   204
       CL-DOLE Form No. __   206
     5. Children in the Movie, Television, Radio
       And Entertainment Industry   208
     6. Children in Apprentice Work   212
       6.1 Labor Code   212
       6.2 Omnibus Rules Implementing
         The Labor Code   213
     7. Children in Domestic Work   216
       7.1 Labor Code   217
       7.2 Omnibus Rules Implementing

The Labor Code   219
7.3 The New Civil Code   220
8. Children in Homework   222
9. Children in Sub-contracting and
   Labor-only Contracting   225
   9.1. D.O. No. 18-02   227
10. Workers in General   239
   10.1 Working Hours and Rest Periods. . .   239
   10.2 Wages   240
      10.2.1   Labor Code   241
      10.2.2   13th Month Pay   246
   10.3   Occupational Safety and Health . . .   246
      10.3.1   Labor Code   246
      10.3.2   Omnibus Rules
               Implementing the
               Labor Code   248
   10.4 Social Security Benefits   248
      10.4.1 R.A. 1161, Social Security
              Law   249
      10.4.2 Employers' Compensation
              and State Insurance Fund. . . .   251
      10.4.3 Medicare Act / Health
              Insurance Act   252
   10.5 Security of Tenure   253

V. RIGHTS AND PRIVILEGES OF WORKING CHILDREN . . .   254

A. THE SAMAHAN   255

B. NON-FORMAL EDUCATION   258

C. SUMMER EMPLOYMENT   258
   1. R.A. 7323   258

*An Act To Help Poor But Deserving
Students Pursue Their Education
By Encouraging Their Employment
During Summer And/Or Christmas
Vacations, Through Incentives
Granted To Employers*

2. Implementing Rules of R.A. 7323   261

**VI. REMEDIES AGAINST ABUSE, EXPLOITATION AND
DISCRIMINATION**   269

A. ILLEGAL RECRUITMENT
UNDER THE LABOR CODE
   1. Prosecute Under Art. 39 of the Labor Code . . .   269
   2. Order Suspension/Cancellation of
      License or Closure of Establishment   273
   3. Prosecute Under R.A. 8042   273

B. VIOLATION OF THE LABOR CODE PROVISIONS.
   1. Order Stoppage of Work or Suspension
      Of Operation   277
   2. Prosecute Under Art. 288 of the Labor Code . .   278

C. NON-PAYMENT OF MINIMUM MONTHLY WAGE
   1. File Money Claim with DOLE Regional
      Director or Labor Arbiter   279
   2. Prosecute for Violation of R.A. 6640,
      R.A. 6726, R.A. 7655   279

D. SOCIAL SECURITY NON-PAYMENT OF CLAIMS,
NON-REMITTANCE OF CONTRIBUTIONS
   1. File Money Claims with the SSS   280
   2. Prosecute For Violation of R.A. 1161   280
   3. Prosecute For Violation of R.A. 7875   281

    4. Prosecute for Violation of R.A. 7655   282

E. INHUMANE TREATMENT
    1. Sue for Damages Under the Civil Code   282
    2. Sue for Violation of The Revised Penal Code,
        R.A. 7610, and Other Criminal Laws   283

F. CRIMES AGAINST CHILDREN UNDER THE
    REVISED PENAL CODE, AS AMENDED
    1. Offenses Against Decency And
        Good Customs   284
            Art. 200. *Grave Scandal*
            Art. 201. *Immoral Doctrines, Obscene*
                       Publications and Exhibitions,
                       and Indecent Shows
            ART. 202. *Vagrants and Prostitutes*
    2. Physical Injuries   286
            Art. 262. *Mutilation*
            Art. 263. *Serious Physical Injuries*
            Art. 265. *Less Serious Physical*
                       Injuries
            Art. 266. *Slight Physical Injuries And*
                       Maltreatment
    3. Rape   289
    4. Crimes Against Chastity   293
            Art. 336. *Acts of Lasciviousness*
            Art. 337. *Qualified Seduction*
            Art. 338. *Simple Seduction*
            Art. 339. *Acts of Lasciviousness with*
                       The Consent of the
                       Offended Party
            Art. 340. *Corruption of Minors*
            Art. 341. *White Slave Trade*
            Art. 342. *Forcible Abduction*
            Art. 343. *Consented Abduction*

5. Crimes Against Liberty And Security 295
    Art. 267. *Kidnapping and Serious Illegal Detention*
    Art. 268. *Slight Illegal Detention*
    Art. 270. *Kidnapping and Failure to Return a Minor*
    Art. 271. *Inducing a Minor to Abandon His Home*
    Art. 272. *Slavery*
    Art. 273. *Exploitation of Child Labor*
    Art. 274. *Services Rendered Under Compulsion in Payment of Debts*
    Art. 276. *Abandoning A Minor*
    Art. 277. *Abandoning Of Minor By Person Entrusted With His Custody; Indifference of Parents*
    Art. 278. *Exploitation of Minors*
6. Threats And Coercions 299
    Art. 282. *Grave Threats*
    Art. 283. *Light Threats*
    Art. 285. *Other Light Threats*
    Art. 286. *Grave Coercions*
    Art. 287. *Light Coercions*
    Art. 288. *Other Similar Coercions*
7. Swindling And Other Deceits 302
    Art. 317. *Swindling A Minor*
    Art. 318. *Other Deceits*

G. LIABILITIES AND RESPONSIBILITIES OF PARENTS
    1. Child and Youth Welfare Code, P.D. 603 302
    2. Family Code 304

H. CHILD ABUSE, EXPLOITATION
    AND DISCRIMINATION
      An Act Providing For Stronger
      Deterrence And Special Protection
      Against Child Abuse, Exploitation
      And Discrimination, Providing
      Penalties For Its Violation, And For
      Other Purposes (R.A. 7610)   306

I. CHILD TRAFFICKING   322

J. DRUG ABUSE
      Dangerous Drugs Law (R.A. 6425)   323

K. ORDINANCES ON CHILD LABOR AND
    CHILD PROSTITUTION   326
          1. S.P. Resolution 192-96 (Butuan City)
          2. Resolution No. 4 (Region VIII)
          3. Ordinance No. 06 (Hinigaran, Neg. Occ.)
          4. S.P. Ord. No. 1025-94 (Butuan City)
          6. Ordinance No. 201 (Lapu-lapu City)
          7. Ordinance No. 7789 (Manila City)
          8. Ordinance No. 7791 (Manila City)
          9. Ordinance No. 92-012 (Zamboanga City)
          10. MMC Ordinance No. 83-04 (Metro Manila)

L. LIABILITIES OF HOTEL/MOTEL OWNERS
          1. Department of Tourism A.O. No. 95-17   348
          2. Bureau of Tourism Services Circular No. 11 . .   349

PART THREE -
LEGAL PROCEDURES FOR THE ENFORCEMENT
OF RIGHTS

I. DETECTION AND REPORTING 351

    A. SPECIAL AGENCIES AND COMMITTEES

        1. Local Council For The
           Protection Of Children 352

        2. Committee For The Special
           Protection Of Children 353

        3. Child Labor Project Management
           Team 355

        4. Agencies To Investigate Sex Tours 357

        5. "*Sagip Batang Manggagawa*":
           Inter-Agency Quick Action Team
           On Handling Of Exploitative/
           Hazardous Child Labor Cases 358

        6. Department of Justice –
           Task Force on the Protection
           Of Children 363

        7. National Bureau of Investigation -
           VAWCD 364

        8. Commission on Human Rights –
           Child Rights Center 365

    B. DUTY TO REPORT 370

    C. PROCEDURES IN REPORTING
        AND INVESTIGATION 371

II. INFORMATION VERIFICATION 380

    A. VISITORIAL AND INSPECTION POWERS OF
        THE DOLE 380
        Labor Code, Art. 128

B. INSPECTION PRIORITIES 381

C. INVESTIGATION BY THE DEPARTMENT
   OF SOCIAL WELFARE AND DEVELOPMENT 382

III. **REMOVAL AND RESCUE** 383

A. APPLICATION FOR WARRANTS OF
   ARREST, SEARCH AND SEIZURE
     1. Who Issues the Warrant 383
     2. Requisites For a Valid Search Warrant
        And/Or Warrant of Arrest 384
     3. When Warrant Is Not Needed 385
        3.1 Lawful Arrest Without Warrant 385
        3.2 Lawful Search and Seizure
            Without Warrant 386

B. ASSEMBLY OF RESCUE TEAM 386

C. RESCUE 387

IV. **CUSTODY/REHABILITATION** 389

A. R.A. 7610, SECTION 28 389

B. RULES AND REGULATION S IN THE
   INVESTIGATION AND REPORTING OF
   CHILD ABUSE CASES, SECTIONS 9-15 389

C. E.O. NO. 56 390
   Authorizing The Ministry Of Social
   Services And Development To Take
   Protective Custody Of Child
   Prostitutes And Sexually Exploited
   Children, And For Other Purposes

D. LEGAL PROCEDURES FOR THE CUSTODY OF DEPENDENT, ABANDONED, NEGLECTED CHILDREN
   P.D. 603, Arts. 141-164 390
E. SUSPENSION/TERMINATION OF PARENTAL AUTHORITY
   Family Code, Arts. 230-232 398

V. **RECOVERY OF WAGES AND OTHER MONETARY BENEFITS UNDER THE LABOR CODE** 399

   A. PERIOD WITHIN WHICH TO FILE 399

   B. WHERE TO FILE / JURISDICTION
      1. DOLE Regional Director 399
      2. Labor Arbiters And The NLRC 400

   C. PROCEDURES WITH DOLE REGIONAL DIRECTOR .. 400

   D. PROCEDURES WITH LABOR ARBITERS AND NLRC 401

   E. AMICABLE SETTLEMENT/COMPROMISES 402

VI. **ADMINISTRATIVE SANCTIONS** 404

   A. DOLE 404

   B. DSWD 404

   C, LGUs 404

   D. DOT 406

VI. CRIMINAL PROSECUTION 407

   A. JURISDICTION OVER CRIMINAL CASES
      1. Katarungang Pambarangay 407
      2. Family Courts 408

   B. WHO MAY FILE COMPLAINT
      1. Crimes Under R.A. 7610 414
      2. Crimes Under The Revised
         Penal Code 415

   C. WHERE TO FILE COMPLAINTS
      1. Offenses Subject to the
         Katarungang Pambarangay 416
      2. Offenses Under the Jurisdiction
         Of the RTC or Family Courts 416
         2.1. Compromise Agreements 416

   D. PROCEDURE IN KATARUNGANG PAMBARANGAY .. 417

   E. SUMMARY PROCEDURES IN THE FAMILY COURTS... 419

   F. PROCEDURES IN PRELIMINARY INVESTIGATION
      BEFORE THE FISCAL/PROSECUTOR. 421

   G. ORDINARY PROCEDURE IN RTC OR FAMILY COURTS
      1. ARREST OF ACCUSED 423
      2. BAIL 423
      3. ARRAIGNMENT AND PLEA 424
      4. TRIAL 424

         4.1 R.A. 7610, Sections 29-30 424
         4.2 Administrative Circular No. 23-95 ... 425
         4.3 Rule on Examination of Child Witness . 426

5. JUDGMENT 448
6. MOTION FOR RECONSIDERATION
   NEW TRIAL/APPEAL 449

BIBLIOGRAPHY 450

PART ONE

UNDERSTANDING CHILD LABOR

"There is one dream that all Filipinos share: that our children may have a better life than we have had . . . there is one vision that is distinctly Filipino: the vision to make this country, our country, a nation for our children."

- Jose W. Diokno

I.   DEFINITION OF CHILD LABOR

Before one can even begin to grasp the issue of child labor, its definition should first be examined to acquire a better understanding of the problem.

In the Philippines, a child is defined as a person below the age of emancipation, which is 18 years.[1]   As soon as a person reaches 18 years of age, he/she is no longer considered a child and becomes automatically entitled to do all acts of civil life, such as contracting marriage or transacting business deals with corresponding legal effects.   The term "child" recently acquired a new meaning upon the enactment of R.A. 7610 in 1992, otherwise known as the Child Protection Law.   The new law, which devotes

---

[1]   Pursuant to R.A. 6809, An Act Lowering the Age of Majority from Twenty-One to Eighteen Years.

an entire chapter on working children, expanded the definition of children to mean "persons below eighteen (18) years of age or those over but are unable to fully take care of themselves or protect themselves from abuse, neglect, cruelty, exploitation or discrimination because of a physical or mental disability or condition."[2]

While there is a clear-cut definition of the term "child", the same cannot be said about "child labor" which has been defined and interpreted in many different ways. Child labor, in its general sense, is the participation of children in a wide variety of work situations, on a more or less regular basis, to earn a livelihood for themselves or for others.[3] There is a need, however, to distinguish "child labor" from "child work". Not all types of child work are considered child labor. Child labor refers only to economic activities or "those activities which are socially useful and remunerable, requiring manual and/or intellectual effort, which result in the production of goods or performance of services."[4] Thus, child labor excludes household chores for one's own family since such is not remunerable. It also excludes mendicancy because such is not a socially useful means of livelihood and does not entail the production of goods or services.[5]

In its strict sense, however, child labor does not refer merely to any form of economic activity, as described above, but to a form of economic exploitation damaging to the child. In this light, the International Labour Organization - International Programme on the Elimination of Child Labour (ILO-IPEC) defines child labor as "work situations where children are compelled to work on a regular basis to earn a living for themselves and their families, and as a result are disadvantaged educationally and socially; where children work in conditions that are exploitative and damaging to their health and to their physical and mental

---

[2] R.A. 7610, Special Protection of Children Against Abuse, Exploitation and Discrimination Act, Sec. 3 (a).

[3] Comprehensive Study on Child Labor in the Philippines (Institute for Labor Studies, DOLE, Intramuros, Manila), 1994, at 4.

[4] R. Ballescas, The Institutional Context of Child Labor (U.P. Department of Sociology, Quezon City), 1987.

[5] *Id.*

development; where children are separated from their families, often deprived of educational and training opportunities; where children are forced to lead prematurely adult lives."[6] This stricter definition throws caution to those child advocates who tend to equate all forms of child labor with exploitation, thereby hiding the real issues, through playing more on emotions rather than on reason.[7] The types of child labor which are really exploitative should first be identified instead of lumping all forms of child labor and in the process, lose sight of the forms of child labor that should be fought.[8]

What is economically exploitative, however, is essentially a cultural decision depicted in the community's daily practices. The State formalizes this decision through the formulation of national standards, which become part of its laws.[9]

The State, through the Department of Labor and Employment, defines "child labor" as "the illegal employment of children below the age of fifteen (15), where they are not directly under the sole responsibility of their parents or legal guardian, or the latter employs other workers apart from their children, who are not members of their families, or their work endangers their life, safety, health and morals or impairs their normal development including schooling. It also includes the situation of children below the age of eighteen (18) who are employed in hazardous occupations."[10] This definition was taken from the existing child labor statutes of the country and clearly pertains only to the work situations of children, which under Philippine laws are considered illegal. Accordingly, children above 15 years old but below 18 years of age who are employed in non-hazardous undertakings, and children below 15 years old who are employed in exclusive family undertakings where their safety, health,

---

[6]   Datasets on Child Labour in the Philippines (ILO-IPEC, Makati, Philippines), 1995.

[7]   V. del Rosario, Child Labor Phenomenon in the Philippines: Problems and Policy Thrusts, Philippine Journal of Industrial Relations (U.P., 1986), at 43.

[8]   *Id.*

[9]   Datasets on Child Labour, *supra* note 6.

[10] "Child Labor Program, Questions and Answers", unpublished reports, Child Labor Project Management Team, Department of Labor and Employment.

schooling and normal development are not impaired, are not considered as "child labor" under the law.

In this book, unless defined by the law presented, the term "child labor" shall be used in its strict sense as defined by the ILO-IPEC. On the other hand, the terms "child worker" and/or "working children" shall be used in their general sense to refer to all children below 18 years old who are engaged in an economic activity on a more or less regular basis to earn a living for themselves, for their families, or for others, whether or not such children work in the formal (or informal) sector of the economy, and whether or not such children are legally (or illegally) employed.

II. CHILD LABOR SITUATION IN THE PHILIPPINES

The authorities on minors are one in the appraisal that child labor exists worldwide in astronomical figures. No one knows exactly how many child workers exist in the world today because they are statistically hidden even in the modern sector. Moreover, many governments and employers deny that they exist. ILO also identified the absence of an appropriate survey methodology for probing into the work of children as a reason for scarce data on child labor. As a result, ILO came up with a special survey designed to produce estimates on the size of working children at regional and global levels for the year 1995.[11] "According to the new estimates, there are some 250 million children 5-14 years old who are toiling in economic activity in developing countries. For close to one-half of them (or 120 million), this work is carried out on a full time basis, while for the remaining one-half it is combined with schooling or other non-economic activities (part time). Among school going children, up to one-third of the boys (33%) and more than two-fifths (42%) of the girls are also engaged in economic activities on a part-time basis. The overall estimates of 250 million working children are exclusive of children who are engaged in regular non-economic activities, including those who provide services of domestic nature on a full-time basis in their own parents' or guardians' households." [12]

Although child labor can be found in almost every country, it is more prevalent in developing countries, especially in the Asian Region.[13] Out of 250 million children between the ages of 4 and 14 working in the developing countries, some 61 per cent of this total, or nearly 150 million, are found in Asia; 32 per cent, or 80 million, are in Africa and 7 per cent, or 17.5 million, live in Latin America.[14] In the Philippines, which is reputed to have the worst

---

[11]   Kebebew Ashagrie, International Labour Office, Geneva. First Published in 1997, revised April 1998. *Statistics on Working Children and Hazardous Child Labour in Brief,* (visited October 9, 2001) <http://www.ilo.org/public/english/standards/ipec/simpoc/stats/child/stats.htm>

[12]   *Id.*

[13]   264th Session of the Governing Body, Committee on Employment and Social Policy, ILO (International Labour Office, Geneva, November 1995), at 4.

[14]   *Statistics: Revealing a Hidden Tragedy*
<http"//www.ilo.org/publish/English/standards/ipec/simpoc/stats/4stt.htm>

poverty incidence among ASEAN countries, the phenomenon of child labor is prevalent and is still spreading. In a 1995 survey, the National Statistics Office (NSO) reveals that 2.1 million children from the ages 10-17 years participate in the country's labor force. In the summer months, when the children leave school, the number of child workers rises to as much as 5.1 million.[15] Since 1989, the incidence of child labor in the country has been steadily increasing at an average rate of 3.8 percent annually over a ten-year period.[16] Another calculation places the number of working children between the ages of 5 and 14 years at 5 million, or 19 per cent of the total labor force. Of the 5 million working children in the Philippines between 5 and 14 years of age, about 3.9 million (or 77 per cent) live in rural and 1.1 million (23 percent) in urban areas."[17]

Working children may be found in diverse sectors of the Philippine economy. Of the country's working children, 67% are in agriculture, fishing and forestry, 20% are in services, and 7% are in industry.[18] The major areas in the formal sector[19] of the economy where children can be found working are the garments industry, wood-based industry and the food industry. Hiring of apprentices in these industries is common. The rest of the children are in the metal and mining industry.[20] In the informal sector of the economy, the magnitude of working children is virtually unknown because many of the establishments are not registered with the proper government regulatory agencies. Nevertheless, studies show that in this sector, children are mostly found in agriculture, in the garments and handicraft sectors working for subcontractors, in the street-vending trade, in illegal

---

[15] National Statistics Office, as quoted in Datasets on Child Labour in the Philippines, (ILO-IPEC, Philippines), 1995.

[16] T. Cruz, *Pact Signed on Protection of Child Labor*, Philippine Times Journal, August 15 1992.

[17] V. Rialp, *Children and Hazardous Work in the Philippines,* ILO-Child Labour Collection (International Labour Office - ILO, Geneva, 1993), at 1.

[18] National Statistics Office, *supra* note 15.

[19] The formal sector is characterized by firms or entities registered or licensed by government regulatory agencies.

[20] Philippine National Monograph on Child Labor (Bureau of Women and Young Workers, DOLE, Manila, 1987), at 3.

trade such as prostitution, and in domestic or bonded labor wherein children are pledged to landlords in payment of debt.[21]

Most of the country's working children are exposed to very poor working conditions. Children in agriculture are exposed to heavy loads, chemicals used for fertilizers and pesticides, and to natural elements such as rain, sun and strong winds. Those in fishing suffer from ruptured eardrums and shark attacks. On board the fishing vessels, they have to endure congested, unsanitary conditions and poor food, which often lead to illnesses.[22]

Factory child workers risk cuts and other injuries from accidents caused by modern machineries and from the lack of protective mechanisms such as gloves and masks. Children in garment factories and in wood industries suffer from back strain, hand cramps, eyestrain, headaches and allergies due to dust. Those in the pyrotechnics-manufacturing run the additional risk of injury or death caused by the accidental explosion of their products. [23]

Aside from the substandard working conditions suffered by children at work, they face exploitation by their employers in terms of long hours of work, insufficient rest periods and extremely low wages. On the average, children work from 4 to 6 hours a day, earn below P1,000 per month, and are paid in "pakyaw" or piece rate. A significant number do not even get paid since their contribution to the total production efforts of their families are not recognized by employers. It is estimated that 55.7% of the country's working children are unpaid family workers, 38.2% are wage and salary workers, and 7.1% work on their own account.[24]

Of the children in the informal sector who work on their own account, those involved in street trades suffer not only from

---

[21]   *Id.*

[22]   Comprehensive Study on Child Labor, *supra* note 3, at 43-45.

[23]   *Id.*

[24]   Datasets on Child Labour, *supra* note 6.

sickness due to exposure to heat, rain, dust and fumes, but also from the risk of vehicular accidents and from frequent molestation and harassment by peers, adult syndicates and even law enforcers. In addition to these, the child scavengers suffer from tetanus infections, while those engaged in prostitution get constantly exposed to sexually transmitted diseases and maltreatment from sadistic customers.[25]

Child labor not only entails physical repercussions such as stunted growth and diseases, but also certain psycho-social effects. The work, in which many children are engaged in, distorts their values, leads to loss of dignity and self-confidence, and exposes them to anti-social behavior. Due to long hours of work, their emotional and personal development is retarded and their creative thinking limited. [26]

Child labor also takes its toll on the education of the working children. Although more than 75% of the country's working children are still able to go to school, a number have experienced being repeaters (36%) and drop-outs (9%-15%). Many have poor grades and are never able to study their lessons at home.[27]

---

[25] Comprehensive Study on Child Labor. *supra* note 3, at 44-45.

[26] Children in Especially Difficult Circumstances (CEDC-1), (UNICEF, Thailand, January 1989), at 18.

[27] Datasets on Child Labour, *supra* note 6.

III. THE REASONS WHY CHILDREN WORK

Child labor is rooted in poverty and the lack of economic opportunities. It is often a response by the household to the need to satisfy basic requirements. Children with unemployed parents or whose parents do not have social security must work to help in their family's struggle for survival.[28] The satisfaction of these children's basic needs in life takes precedence over their other needs such as education and recreation.[29]

Children are also impelled to work from an early age because of the centuries-old tradition that the child must work through solidarity with the family group, so as to compensate as much as possible for the economic burden that he/she represents and to share in the maintenance of his/her family, which is usually a very large one.[30] In the Philippines, families particularly value helpfulness and responsibility-sharing. Philippine culture especially in rural areas, "considers child work as a phase of socialization where future roles are learned and working to share in the family is seen as a training. [T]he transmission of skills from parents and the evolution of proper attitudes to work are some of the considered social contributions of child labor."[31]

Another reason why children work is the failure in the education system. Many parents prefer to send their children out to work rather than to school, either because there is no school within a reasonable distance of the family home, or because they cannot do without the income the working child brings in, or because they cannot meet the costs of sending the child to school, or again because they cannot see what use schooling would be to him.[32] Poor schooling has little credibility for many families since it does not promote economic improvement. For so long as

[28]   A. Bequele and J. Boyden, Combating Child Labour (ILO Geneva, 1988), at 85.
[29]   V. del Rosario, *supra* note 7, at 42-43.
[30]   E. Mendelievich, Children at Work (ILO, Geneva, 1979), at 8.
[31]   V. del Rosario, *supra* note 7, at 43, citing Bekombo, 1981.
[32]   *Still So Far to Go: Child Labor in the World Today,* International Labor Office Special Report on the Occasion of the 10th Anniversary of the International Year of the Child (ILO, Geneva, 1989), at 23.

developing countries cannot successfully maintain their commitment to a decent quality universal education, increased child participation in the labor market is to be expected.[33]

Another major factor in the increase in the number of working children is the demand for child workers. Employers know all too well the advantages of employing children. They represent a docile work force, which could be hired and replaced at a fraction of adult wages. They do not join labor unions and very seldom complain. Above all, employers who hire children gain a competitive advantage in both national and international markets due to the low wages they pay children. [34]

---

[33] *Id.*

[34] M. Longford, Seminar on Ways and Means of Achieving the Elimination of Child Labour in All Parts of the World (Geneva, Switzerland, 1985), at 10.

IV. STRATEGIES IN ADDRESSING THE CHILD LABOR PROBLEM

Despite the government's prohibition on child labor since the 1920s, as embedded in Philippine laws, the problem continues to persist to this day. Child labor is a major economic and societal problem that requires a far more vigorous stance from the government. Because child labor jeopardizes the children's potential to become productive adults, it undermines the government's economic and social development objectives for the country's future.[35] More importantly, because the children have but one childhood to live, they cannot afford to wait. For the sake of the country and its children, something has to be done now. Exactly what is to be done and how it is to be done, however, are questions that have been constantly debated upon.

Admittedly, the perennial problem of child labor is one that cannot be solved overnight. Although poverty is not a worthy excuse for child labor, the fact remains that child labor is rooted in the economic structure of the country itself and in underdevelopment.[36] Given the economic realities in many low-income countries, the objective of the abolition of child labor cannot be attained right away. "Child labor is embedded in poverty and it is through sustained increases in standards of living that it will be abolished."[37] The ILO, in recognition of this fact, has adopted a "two-pronged approach" to the child labor problem. Its main objective remains the eventual elimination of child labor. However, until this goal can be achieved, commitment is given to improving the conditions under which children work.[38]

The government, however, is still confronted with a nagging dilemma: Given its limited resources, the government cannot simply remove all illegally employed children from their current

---

[35]   264th Session of the Governing Body, *supra* note 13, at 11.

[36]   Longford, *supra* note 34.

[37]   *Excerpt from the Report of the Director-General,* Child Labour: A Briefing Manual (ILO, Geneva, 1986), at 55.

[38]   A. Bequele, Questions and Answers in Child Labour: A Briefing Manual (ILO Geneva, 1986), at 11.

employment or work situations without a ready alternative for their survival. On the other hand, given the other option of providing these children with protective work conditions, the government is faced with another predicament. How can it give protection to these children within their very workplaces when the law prohibits their employment in the first place? In the latter case, the government would be violating its own law. This enigma is one that does not have a definitive solution. Clearly, a careful and deliberate strategizing is required to determine the most viable and effective national action in controlling child labor and in eventually eliminating it.

Current actions to address the child labor problem evolved from a variety of special projects designed to address specific needs, to a national concerted programme and plan of action to combat child labor. It was in the year 1986, right after the people's revolution, when projects for street children and child scavengers began to emerge. In 1988, the government, through the auspices of UNICEF, launched the "Breaking Ground for Community Action on Child Labor" project to identify and assist communities in regions with a high concentration of child labor. Activities under the project focused on provision of basic health and education services to children, on provision of livelihood and entrepreneurial skills to children's parents, and on advocacy work to convince parents and employers to remove children from heavy or dangerous work.[39] Significantly, in 1989, the government promulgated the Philippine Plan of Action for children which set specific goals for children in especially difficult circumstances, among which is the banning of children from hazardous occupations/situations by 80% by the year 2000.[40] The year 1991 saw the creation of the National Child Labor Program Committee, which expanded the original implementors of the project "Breaking Ground..." to involve 14 governmental and non-governmental agencies.[41]

---

[39] Comprehensive Study on Child Labor, *supra* note 3, at 100-104.

[40] *Id.*

[41] *Id.*

In 1994, the Philippine government became a participating country in the ILO-International Programme on the Elimination of Child Labor (ILO-IPEC) after which an agenda of action for attacking child labor in the Philippines was formulated by representatives of various government agencies, NGOs, employers' and workers' organizations, local government officials and academics from the different regions of the country.[42] The resulting agenda which was adopted by the Philippines, set out priority target groups for action, among which are victims of trafficking and bonded labor, children in home-based industries, children in mining and quarrying, and children trapped in prostitution. Priority areas of action for the IPEC programme were also identified as follows: direct action on protection, removal and rehabilitation of children from dangerous occupations; awareness-raising; legislation and law enforcement; and capability building.[43]

Today, the focus of actions in the country is on the elimination of risk to children rather than on ending their participation in all forms of work. Such approach is needed to accommodate the poverty element in child labor and allow the families flexibility in maintaining their essential survival mechanisms while protecting the children involved.[44] Thus, among the emerging strategies now being pursued by the government is the focusing of rescue efforts on the most exploitative forms of child labor or the high-risk children such as the very young (below age 12 or 13), those in hazardous working conditions, or those in bonded labor. For the rest of the working children, however, until alternatives for survival are set in place, heightened efforts should be exerted to assure that they are in jobs that are not harmful to their health and physical and mental development, that they have opportunities for education and recreation, and that they receive the same conditions of employment and protection as ordinary workers in addition to

---

[42] Attacking Child Labour in the Philippines, *An Indicative Framework for Philippine-ILO Action* (International Labour Office, Geneva, 1994).

[43] *Id.*

[44] J. Boyden and W. Myers. *Exploring Alternative Approaches to Child Labour: Case Studies from Developing Countries*, Innocenti Occasional Papers, Child Rights Series. Number 8 (UNICEF, International Child Development Center, Florence, Italy, February, 1995), at 18.

their rights as children. The protection of existing labor legislation, standards, as well as welfare schemes designed to protect workers' well being, should be extended to them. At the same time, sufficient and effective programs of rehabilitation are needed to complement the said strategy.

To realize the foregoing objectives in the area of law enforcement, community groups and local government units have been mobilized to immediately respond to complaints of child abuse and exploitation and to assist the concerned children in obtaining redress for the violation of their rights. Nevertheless, to assure them complete and adequate relief throughout the entire judicial process, the training of significant actors such as labor inspectors, prosecutors, judges, social workers and NGOs for a better comprehension of the laws and legal procedures on children, and for a deeper sensitization on children's rights still need to be intensified.

The immediate measures required for the protection of child workers, as suggested above, would be ineffective unless accompanied by schemes to address the root causes of child labor. Thus, aside from existing social welfare services to needy families, income generating or community livelihood projects must be strengthened to increase the families' earning power. In like manner, educational programs that are free, relevant to the needs of the child workers and flexible enough to allow them enough time to carry on traditional but non-hazardous work should be made accessible to them.[45]

As a preventive approach to the problem of child labor, activities aimed to educate the general public, policy-makers, employers, workers, families, and children themselves on the evils of child labor and to improve their understanding of the problem should, likewise, be intensified.

In the area of legislation, the possibility of ratifying international conventions or of amending existing child labor laws to make them conform to international standards, as well as of

---

[45] 264th Session of the Governing Body, *supra* note 13, at 13 and 20.

enacting new laws, which are realistic and enforceable, is sincerely being considered by the government. The formulation of simplified rules and regulations to guide law enforcers and the general public in the correct interpretation and proper implementation of existing laws should, however, be fast-tracked.

Although a host of other strategies and activities to combat child labor are already being effected in the country, they are evidently inadequate when weighed against the magnitude of the problem. Definitely, an enormous task still lies ahead for those willing to stake their time and efforts to save the country's children. The following chapters aim to assist all concerned government agencies, non-governmental organizations and other groups or individuals in their efforts to protect and promote the rights of child workers, by empowering them with knowledge on the laws and legal procedures involved in this complex issue of child labor.

PART TWO

THE LEGAL PROTECTION OF CHILD WORKERS

INTRODUCTION:
HISTORICAL EVOLUTION OF CHILD LABOR LAWS IN THE PHILIPPINES

Laws, which restrict the employment of children sprung largely from social reform movements of the late nineteenth century. Although work had traditionally been seen as essential to a child's upbringing, the growth of industrialism gradually changed the nature of the work and attitudes toward it. Children who were sent to meet the increasing demand for workers in factories suffered in economic terms and were no longer being trained in a vocation but typically learned only how to do small tasks. It was becoming apparent that work in factories was physically harmful to children who were being given the unhealthiest work. The increasing awareness of the abuse and exploitation accompanying child labor, thereupon, produced demands for reform. Pressure for child labor laws began to grow at the same time as pressure for compulsory education, and the two movements developed alongside in the years from 1830 to 1930.[46]

Act. No. 3071

In the Philippines, the concern for the plight of working children started as early as March 16, 1923, during the American

---

[46] R. Mnookin and D. Weisberg, Child, Family and State: Problems and Materials on Children and the Law (Little Brown and Company, Canada, 1989), at 825-826.

Regime, when Act No. 3071, "An Act to Regulate the Employment of Women and Children in Shops, Factories, Industrial, Agricultural and Mercantile Establishments, and Other Place of Labor in the Philippine Islands, to Provide Penalties for Violations Hereof and for Other Purposes" was enacted into law. The Woman and Child Labor Section of the Inspection Division of the then Bureau of Labor, was assigned to enforce this Act in 1925.

Act No. 3071 prohibited the employment of persons below certain ages, depending on the type of work or establishment involved. For example, the employment of persons in mines or in places where explosives are used or manufactured was prohibited for persons below 14 years of age.[47] Work in connection with the preparation of any poisonous, noxious, explosive or infectious substance was prohibited for persons below 16 years of age.[48] Act No. 3071 also set the minimum age of employment at 16 years for the following types of work: operator of elevators; motorman or fireman; cleaning of machinery; underground work;[49] work in billiard rooms, cockpits or other places where games are being played with stakes of money; work in dance halls, stadiums or race courses as bailarinas, boxers or jockeys;[50] and sale of medicines and drugs in a pharmacy or for any work that may affect the health of the public.[51] Work in bars was likewise prohibited for males under 16 years of age and for females under 18 years of age.[52] In the case of other acts not specified in Act No. 3071, which involves serious danger to the life of the laborer, the minimum age of employment was set at 18 years.[53]

Act No. 3071 also prescribed the conditions of work of children. The employer was required to provide proper seats for women and children, to allow them not less than 60 minutes for

---

[47] Act No. 3071, Sec. 1.
[48] Act No. 3071, Sec. 7.
[49] Act No. 3071, Sec. 10.
[50] Act No. 3071, Sec. 11.
[51] Act No. 3071, Sec. 14.
[52] Act No. 3071, Sec. 5.
[53] Act No. 3071, Sec. 8.

their noon meal, [54] and to have in his establishment a duly certified copy of the birth certificates of each of his laborers below 18 years of age.[55] Moreover, the written consent of the children's parents or guardians is a prerequisite to their employment. Children below 16 years of age may not be employed to work before 6:00 a.m. or after 6:00 p.m., and may not work for more than 7 hours daily or 42 hours weekly.[56] The employment of persons below 14 years of age on school days was also prohibited, unless such children know how to read and write.[57]

Revised Penal Code

In 1932, the Revised Penal Code (RPC), a codification of the country's penal laws, was enacted into law. The RPC, which remains in effect up to this day, contains several provisions prohibiting certain types of child work, such as "Exploitation of Child Labor" (Art. 273) and "Exploitation of Minors" (Art. 278). The former prohibits the retaining of a minor in one's service against his/her will under the pretext of reimbursing a debt incurred by the minor's ascendants. The latter prohibits the employment of a minor under 16 years of age as an acrobat, gymnast, diver, wild-animal tamer, and in other dangerous exhibitions. Other provisions in the RPC relating to slavery, prostitution, corruption of minors, illegal detention and kidnapping of minors, are equally applicable to child workers depending on their particular situation.

R.A. 679

In 1946, the Philippines proclaimed its independence from American Rule and became a Republic. Gradually, the existing laws enacted under the former regime were replaced by Republic Acts. Thus, on April 15, 1952, Act No. 3071 was repealed by

---

[54] Act No. 3071, Sec. 2.
[55] Act No. 3071, Sec. 4.
[56] Act No. 3071, Sec. 3.
[57] Act No. 3071, Sec. 4.

Republic Act (R.A.) No. 679, "An Act to Regulate the Employment of Women and Children, to Provide Penalties for Violation Hereof, and for Other Purposes". The implementation of R.A. 679 was entrusted to the Women and Minors Division of the former Bureau of Labor Standards, in 1957.

Under R.A. 679, children below 14 years of age may only be employed to perform light work which is not harmful to their health or normal development, and which is not such as to prejudice their attendance in school. Likewise, no child below 14 years of age may be employed on school days unless such child knows how to read and write. Nevertheless, these requisites need not be present for children below 14 years old employed in the following permissible instances: 1) domestic work; 2) establishments in which only members of the family are employed, except employment which is harmful or dangerous; 3) work done in vocational, technical or professional schools, not intended for commercial profit; and 4) employment as gymnast, acrobat or circus performer, or in any dancing, theatrical or musical exhibition.[58]

R.A. 679 retained the previous age limit of 16 years set by Act No. 3071 for the following types of work: operator of elevators, motorman, or fireman; operator/cleaner of machinery; underground work; and work in billiard rooms, cockpits, other place where games are played with stakes of money, or in a bar, night club, dance hall, stadium or race track, as waiter, boxer or jockey.[59] In addition, R.A. 679 prohibited the employment of persons below 16 years in the following types of work: work in mines, quarries, etc.; undertakings in which articles are manufactured, transformed, altered, repaired, demolished, etc.; undertakings engaged in shipbuilding or in the generation or transmission of electricity or motive power; undertakings engaged in building and civil engineering works; undertakings engaged in the transport of passengers or goods, or in the handling of goods at docks, wharves or airports; etc..[60] However, R.A. 679 raised to 18

---

[58] R.A. 679, Sec. 1.
[59] R.A. 679, Sec. 2.
[60] R.A. 679, Sec. 2.

years the previous age limit of 16 years, set by Act No. 3071 for work in any pharmacy for the preparation of drugs, and for work done in connection with the preparation of or involves contamination with any noxious, poisonous, infectious or explosive substances,. Eighteen years remained the age limit for other types of work involving serious danger to the life or health of the employee.[61]

Of particular significance in R.A. 679 is the power of the Secretary of Labor to grant a special work permit for the employment of a child whose employment is otherwise prohibited, "whenever in his judgment, the economic necessity of the family to which such child belongs requires his assistance for increasing the family income".[62]

The conditions of work of children required by Act No. 3071 were reproduced in R.A. 679. However, the new law added a few more requirements such as the "medical examination of children for fitness for employment" before actual employment and every 6 months thereafter or oftener,[63] and the prohibition on night work, from 10:00 p.m. to 6:00 a.m., of persons between 16 and 18 years of age.[64]

ILO Convention Nos. 59, 77 & 90

In the years 1953 and 1960, respectively, the Philippines ratified three international conventions adopted by the International Labour Organization (ILO), relating to child labor. These are: ILO Convention No. 59, "Minimum Age for Admission of Children to Industrial Employment"; ILO Convention No. 77, "Medical Examination for Fitness for Employment in Industry of Children and Young Persons; and ILO Convention No. 90, "Night Work of Young Persons Employed in Industry". The conventions ratified by Member States create binding obligations upon them.

---

[61]   R.A. 679, Sec. 3.
[62]   R.A. 679, Sec. 10.
[63]   R.A. 679, Sec. 4.
[64]   R.A. 679, Sec. 5.

ILO Convention No. 90, ratified by the country in May 1953, prohibits the employment of children in industry during night time. The term night signifies a period of at least 12 consecutive hours which includes the interval between 10:00 p.m. and 6:00 a.m. for children below 16 years of age, and a period which includes the interval of at least 7 consecutive hours between 10:00 p.m. and 7:00 a.m. for children between 16 and 18 years old.[65]

ILO Convention No. 59, which the country ratified in May 1960, fixes the minimum age of employment for industry at 15 years but allows younger children to be employed in undertakings in which only members of the employer's family are employed, provided that such work are not dangerous to the life, health or morals of the children employed therein.[66]

ILO Convention No. 77, which the country ratified also in May 1960, requires the medical examination of children as a pre-requisite to employment and their subsequent re-examinations therein. It also contains medical examination guidelines for different types of work for children.

R.A. 2714

On June 18, 1960, R.A. 2714, "An Act to Establish in the Department of Labor a Bureau to be Known as Women and Minors Bureau" was passed into law. This Bureau replaced the former Women and Minors Division of the Bureau of Labor Standards and was tasked, among others, to administer and enforce, the woman and child labor laws. The Bureau of Women and Minors was renamed Bureau of Women and Young Workers in 1987.

---

[65] ILO Convention No. 90, Art. 2.
[66] ILO Convention No. 59, Art. 2.

P.D. 148

The failure of the successive administrations to cope with the economic crises that befell the country after the war, to arrest the increasing gross imbalances in societal structures, and to curb the rapid increase in population, led to the onslaught of poverty in the 1960s to the 1970s. This propelled the sudden upsurge in the number of children who began to work in order to augment their families' income. The resulting discontent stirred by the rampant graft and corruption in the government impelled the growth of student activism, which forced the Marcos government to place the entire country under martial law in 1972. The legislative body was abolished and the President's decrees partook of the nature of laws. During the Martial Law era, several Presidential Decrees (P.D.s) were issued resulting in the amendment of the child labor laws.

On March 13, 1973, P.D. No. 148 amended R.A. 679, The Woman and Child Labor Law. P.D. 148 simplified the complex provisions of R.A. 679, which provided confusing age limits for different types of undertakings. Under the new law, P.D. 148, "no child below 14 years of age shall be employed by any employer, except where the child works directly under the sole responsibility of his parent or guardian, involving activities which are not hazardous in nature and which do not in any way interfere with his schooling."[67] Under the same Act, "any person between 14 and 18 years of age may be employed in any non-hazardous undertaking."[68]

Noticeably, this law repealed the previous exceptions to the minimum age of employment allowed by R.A. 679, such as light work, domestic work, work done in schools, work demanded by economic necessity, etc., leaving only one type of exception as stated above. It is also worth noting that P.D. 148 contravened ILO Convention No. 59, which fixes the minimum age of employment in industry at 15 years. Nevertheless, the conditions of work of children prescribed by R.A. 679 were not repealed by the new law.

---

[67] P.D. 148, Sec. 1.
[68] P.D. 148, Sec. 2.

P.D. 442 - Labor Code

After only one year from its enactment, P.D. 148 was amended by the passage of P.D. 442, the Labor Code of the Philippines, on November 1, 1974. The Labor Code raised the minimum age of employment from 14 years to 15 years, thereby complying with the requirements of ILO Convention No. 59. Article 139 of the Labor Code prohibits the employment of a child below 15 years "except when he works directly under the sole responsibility of his parents or guardian, and his employment does not in any way interfere with his schooling".

The Labor Code retained the previous minimum age for hazardous undertakings at 18 years. It also added a minimum age requirement for apprentices, which is 14 years. Unfortunately, the terms and conditions of employment of children, provided by R.A. 679, as amended by P.D. 148, were not reproduced in the Labor Code, thus creating a serious gap in the new law.

P.D. 603 - Child and Youth Welfare Code

On December 10, 1974, one month after the Labor Code was passed, P.D. 603 or the Child and Youth Welfare Code was enacted into law. The new law, which took effect on June 5, 1975, is a codification of different provisions for the well-being of all children. P.D. 603 permits the employment of children below 16 years of age for "light work which is not harmful to their safety, health or normal development and which is not prejudicial to their studies." This provision should, however, be read in conjunction with the Labor Code, which allows the employment of children below 15 years, only if under the direct and sole responsibility of their parents or guardian.

The Child and Youth Welfare Code includes a host of other benefits for working children such as the duty of employers to submit reports and to keep a register of employed children, the right of working children to self-organization, welfare programs, etc..

U.N. Convention on the Rights of the Child

Despite the existing laws banning child labor, no serious efforts were exerted by the Marcos government and its predecessors to resolve the growing problem. In 1986, after the people's revolution brought about the peaceful change of government, revelations about the abuses and exploitation suffered by the country's children started to unfold. At the same time, demands for reforms in government policies, legislation and programs affecting children gradually intensified. The new government responded by ratifying the United Nations Convention on the Rights of the Child (CRC) on July 26, 1990. The U.N. CRC entered into force as an international agreement on September 2, 1990.

Unlike the ILO Conventions on child labor, the U.N. CRC does not provide a specific age limit for the employment of children, leaving it up to the ratifying countries to set their own policies on the matter. Nevertheless, it directs the ratifying countries to protect the children from economic exploitation and from performing work which is hazardous or which is harmful to the child's health, education, and development. It further obliges countries to provide for a minimum age of employment, for regulation of the hours and conditions of employment of children, and for proper penalties or sanctions against the violators of children's rights.[69]

R.A. 7610 - The Child Protection Law

On June 17, 1992, to comply with the mandate of the U.N. CRC, the government enacted R.A. 7610, "An Act Providing for Stronger Deterrence and Special Protection Against Child Abuse, Exploitation and Discrimination, Providing Penalties for Its Violation and For Other Purposes". Although, R.A. 7610 was lauded for the innovative provisions it introduced for the protection of children in especially difficult circumstances, it was nevertheless severely criticized for its provisions on working

---

[69] U.N. Convention on the Rights of the Child. Art. 32.

children, which abruptly changed the entire Philippine policy of prohibiting child labor. Article VIII, Section 12, of R.A. 7610 legalized the employment of all children below 15 years of age, provided only that the employer first secures a work permit from the Department of Labor and Employment and ensures the protection of the child.

R.A. 7658

Upon pressure from the Department of Justice, non-governmental organizations, and international bodies such as the ILO and UNICEF, the Philippine Congress, realizing that Article VIII, Section 12, of R.A. 7610 is a flagrant violation of ILO Convention No. 59, enacted a new law to amend such section after only one year from its passage. R.A. 7658, "An Act Prohibiting the Employment of Children Below 15 Years of Age in Public and Private Undertakings" was passed into law in October, 1993, thereby restoring the erstwhile prohibition on the employment of children below 15 years of age.

R.A. 7658 allows only two exceptions to the prohibition on employment below the minimum age: 1) "work directly under the sole responsibility of the child's parents or legal guardian and where only members of the employer's family are employed", and 2) "where a child's employment in public entertainment or information through cinema, theater, radio or television is essential".[70] The first exception is merely a reproduction of those contained in previous laws (Labor Code and ILO Convention No. 59), with the added requisite that the guardian be a legally appointed one. The second exception is something new brought about by the practical consideration that only children can realistically perform children's roles required in the entertainment and information industry. In both exceptions, the employment should neither endanger the child's life, safety, health, morals, and normal development, nor prejudice the child's education. It is also mandatory for the employers to first secure for the child a

---

[70] R.A. 7658, Sec. 1.

work permit from the Department of Labor and Employment before the child can even begin to work.[71]

ILO Convention 182

On November 28, 2000 the Senate through a resolution ratified ILO Convention 182. The Convention shall come into force 12 months after the date on which its ratification has been registered.[72] As a Member that ratified the Convention, the Philippines undertakes to take immediate and effective measures to secure the prohibition and elimination of the worst forms of child labour as a matter of urgency.[73] The necessary actions range from a reform of laws and their enforcement, to practical and direct help to children and their families.[74]

To date, despite the series of amendments to the past laws on child labor, the present state policies and legislation governing the protection and promotion of the rights of child workers still remain scattered among the different laws of the country. This chapter attempts to present all these laws in a manner that will assist the reader in better understanding the legal protection available to the country's child workers.

---

[71] R.A. 7658, Sec. 1.

[72] ILO Convention 182, Art. 10 (3)

[73] ILO Convention 182, Art. 1

[74] *The Convention on the Worst Forms of Child Labour (No. 182) Comes into Force: What Does this Mean?* (Visited October 10, 2001)
<http://www.ilo.org/public/english/standards/ipec/about/factsheet/facts23pr.htm>.

I. GENERAL POLICY CONSIDERATIONS

The general policies of the State with respect to children are enshrined in the Philippine Constitution and in the Child and Youth Welfare Code. The International Covenant on Economic, Social and Cultural Rights, as well as the Convention on the Rights of the Child, both ratified by the country, also contain principles relevant to child workers.

Principles and policies declared in the Constitution of the State and in International Conventions ratified by the country serve as mandates to the Government to undertake measures to give them vitality and force. The details of these principles and policies are provided for by laws passed by the Congress and are further strengthened by rules and regulations promulgated by the executive department. The policies presented below may be invoked to advocate for the further protection of the rights of child workers.

A. INTERNATIONAL INSTRUMENTS

1. International Covenant On Economic, Social And Cultural Rights
[Ratified by the Philippines on June 7, 1974]

Article 10

The States Parties to the present Covenant recognize that:

x x x

3.   Special measures of protection and assistance should be taken on behalf of all children and young persons without any discrimination for reasons of parentage or other conditions. Children and young persons should be protected from economic and social exploitation. Their employment in work harmful to their morals or health or dangerous to life or likely to hamper their normal development should be punishable by law. States should also set age limits below which the

paid employment of child labour should be prohibited and punishable by law.

2. Convention On The Rights Of The Child
[Ratified by the Philippines on July 26, 1990]

Article 32

1. States Parties recognize the right of the child to be protected from economic exploitation and from performing any work that is likely to be hazardous or to interfere with the child's education, or to be harmful to the child's health or physical, mental, spiritual, moral or social development.

2. States Parties shall take legislative, administrative, social and educational measures to ensure the implementation of the present article. To this end, and having regard to the relevant provisions of other international instruments, States Parties shall in particular:

(a) Provide for a minimum age or minimum ages for admission to employment;
(b) Provide for appropriate regulation of the hours and conditions of employment; and
(c) Provide for appropriate penalties or other sanctions to ensure the effective enforcement of the present article.

Article 34

States Parties shall undertake to protect the child from all forms of sexual exploitation and sexual abuse. For these purposes, States Parties shall in particular take all appropriate national, bilateral and multilateral measures to prevent:

(a) The inducement or coercion of a child to engage in unlawful sexual activity;

(b)   The exploitative use of children in prostitution or other unlawful activity;

(c)   The exploitative use of children in pornographic performances and materials.

Article 35

States Parties shall take all appropriate national, bilateral and multilateral measures to prevent the abduction of, sale of or traffic in children for any purpose or in any form.

B. NATIONAL LAWS

1. Philippine Constitution

Art. II. Declaration of Principles and State Policies.

Sec. 13. The State recognizes the vital role of the youth in nation-building and shall promote and protect their physical, moral, spiritual, intellectual, and social well-being. It shall inculcate in the youth patriotism and nationalism, and encourage their involvement in public and civic affairs.

Art. XV. The Family

Sec. 3. The State shall defend:

x x x

(2)   The right of children to assistance, including proper care and nutrition, and special protection from all forms of neglect, abuse, cruelty, exploitation, and other conditions prejudicial to their development.

2. Child And Youth Welfare Code (P.D. 603)

Art. 1. Declaration of Policy. - The Child is one of the most important assets of the nation. Every effort should be exerted to promote his welfare and enhance his opportunities for a useful and happy life.

x x x

Art. 3. Rights of the Child.

(1) Every child is endowed with the dignity and worth of a human being from the moment of his conception, as generally accepted in medical parlance, and has, therefore, the right to be born well.

(2) Every child has the right to a wholesome family life that will provide him with love, care and understanding, guidance and counselling, and moral and material security.

The dependent or abandoned child shall be provided with the nearest substitute for a home.

(3) Every child has the right to a well-rounded development of his personality to the end that he may become a happy, useful and active member of society.

The gifted child shall be given opportunity and encouragement to develop his special talents.

The emotionally disturbed or socially maladjusted child shall be treated with sympathy and understanding, and shall be entitled to treatment and competent care.

The physically or mentally handicapped child shall be given the treatment, education and care required by his particular condition.

(4) Every child has the right to a balanced diet, adequate clothing, sufficient shelter, proper

medical attention, and all the basic physical requirements of a healthy and vigorous life.

(5) Every child has the right to be brought up in an atmosphere of morality and rectitude for the enrichment and the strengthening of his character.

(6) Every child has the right to an education commensurate with his abilities and to the development of his skills for the improvement of his capacity for service to himself and to his fellowmen.

(7) Every child has the right to full opportunities for safe and wholesome recreation and activities, individual as well as social, for the wholesome use of his leisure hours.

(8) Every child has the right to protection against exploitation, improper influences, hazards and other conditions or circumstances prejudicial to his physical, mental, emotional, social and moral development.   [*Underscoring supplied.*]

(9) Every child has the right to live in a community and a society that can offer him an environment free from pernicious influences and conducive to the promotion of his health and the cultivation of his desirable traits and attributes.

(10) Every child has the right to the care, assistance, and protection of the State, particularly when his parents or guardians fail or are unable to provide him with his fundamental needs for growth, development, and improvement.

(11) Every child has the right to an efficient and honest government that will deepen his faith in democracy and inspire him with the morality of the constituted authorities both in their public and private lives.

(12) Every child has the right to grow up as a free individual, in an atmosphere of peace, understanding, tolerance, and universal brotherhood, and with the determination to contribute his share in the building of a better world.

II. MINIMUM AGE OF EMPLOYMENT -- EXCEPTIONS

A. INTERNATIONAL CONVENTIONS

1. ILO Convention No. 59

CONVENTION FIXING THE MINIMUM AGE
FOR ADMISSION OF CHILDREN
TO INDUSTRIAL EMPLOYMENT
(REVISED 1937)
[Ratified by the Philippines in May, 1960]

The General Conference of the International Labour Organisation,

Having been convened at Geneva by the Governing Body of the International Labour Office, and having met in its Twenty-third Session on 3 June 1937, and

Having decided upon the adoption of certain proposals with regard to the partial revision of the Convention fixing the minimum age for admission of children to industrial employment adopted by the Conference at its First Session, which is the sixth item on the agenda of the Session, and

Considering that these proposals must take the form of an international Convention, adopts this twenty-second day of June of the year one thousand nine hundred and thirty-seven, the following Convention, which may be cited as the Minimum Age (Industry) Convention (Revised), 1937:

PART I. GENERAL PROVISIONS

Article 1

1. For the purpose of this Convention, the term "industrial undertaking" includes particularly-

(a) mines, quarries, and other works for the extraction of minerals from the earth;

(b) industries in which articles are manufactured, altered, cleaned, repaired, ornamented, finished, adapted for sale, broken up or demolished, or in which materials are transformed; including shipbuilding, and the generation, transformation, and transmission of electricity and motive power of any kind;

(c) construction, reconstruction, maintenance, repair, alteration, or demolition of any building, railway, tramway, harbour, dock, pier, canal, inland waterway, road, tunnel, bridge, viaduct, sewer, drain, well, telegraphic or telephonic installation, electrical undertaking, gas work, waterwork, or other work of construction, as well as the preparation for or laying the foundations of any such work or structure; and,

(d) transport of passengers or goods by road or rail or inland waterway, including the handling of goods at docks, quays, wharves, and warehouses, but excluding transport by hand.

2. The competent authority in each country shall define the line of division which separates industry from commerce and agriculture.

Article 2

1. Children under the age of fifteen years shall not be employed or work in any public or private industrial undertaking, or in any branch thereof.

2.   Provided that, except in the case of employment which, by their nature or the circumstances in which they are carried on, are dangerous to the life, health or morals of the persons employed therein, national laws or regulations may permit such children to be employed in undertakings in which only members of the employer's family are employed.

Article 3

The provisions of this Convention shall not apply to work done by children in technical schools, provided that such work is approved and supervised by public authority.

Article 4

In order to facilitate the enforcement of the provisions of this Convention, every employer in an industrial undertaking shall be required to keep a register of all persons under the age of eighteen years employed by him, and of the dates of their births.

Article 5

1. In respect of employments which, by their nature or the circumstances in which they are carried on, are dangerous to the life, health or morals of the persons employed therein, national laws shall either -

(a)   prescribe a higher age or ages than fifteen years for the admission thereto of young persons or adolescents; or

(b)   empower an appropriate authority to prescribe a higher age or ages than fifteen years for the admission thereto of young persons or adolescents.

2. The annual reports to be submitted under Article 22 of the Constitution of the International Labour Organisation shall include full information concerning the age or ages prescribed by national laws in pursuance of subparagraph (a) of the preceding paragraph or concerning the action taken by the appropriate authority in exercise of the powers conferred upon it in pursuance of subparagraph (b) of the preceding paragraph, as the case may be.

2. ILO Convention No. 138

In 1973, the International Labour Conference decided to establish ILO Convention No. 138, a general instrument on child labor which would gradually replace those applicable to limited economic sectors such as ILO Convention No. 59, Minimum Age (Industry); ILO Convention No. 10, Minimum Age (Agriculture); ILO Convention No. 58, Minimum Age (Sea); ILO Convention No. 123 (Underground Work); etc.. ILO Convention No. 138 is general in scope, and in principle covers all economic sectors and all employment or work, whether or not such are performed under a contract of employment. It allows flexibility in the formulation of national laws by providing sufficient exceptions to the minimum age of employment, conditioned by national circumstances and the level of the standards already achieved in each country. Having ratified this Convention the Philippines, as enunciated in Article 1, shall now undertake to pursue national policies and legislation designed to ensure the effective abolition of child labor and to raise progressively the minimum age of employment consistent with the fullest physical and mental development of the child.

MINIMUM AGE CONVENTION, 1973
CONVENTION CONCERNING MINIMUM AGE
FOR ADMISSION TO EMPLOYMENT
[Ratified by the Philippines on April 6, 1998]

The General Conference of the International Labour Organisation,

Having been convened at Geneva by the Governing Body of the International Labour Office and having met in its Fifty-eighth Session on 6 June 1973, and

Having decided upon the adoption of certain proposals with regard to minimum age for admission to employment, which is the fourth item on the agenda of the session, and

Noting the terms of the Minimum Age (Industry) Convention, 1919, the Minimum Age (Sea) Convention, 1920, the Minimum Age (Agriculture) Convention, 1921, the Minimum Age (Trimmers and Stokers) Convention, 1921, the Minimum Age (Non-Industrial Employment) Convention, 1932, the Minimum Age (Sea) Convention (Revised), 1936, the Minimum Age (Industry) Convention (Revised), 1937, the Minimum Age (Non-Industrial Employment) Convention (Revised), 1937, the Minimum Age (Fishermen) Convention, 1959, and the Minimum Age (Underground Work) Convention, 1965, and

Considering that the time has come to establish a general instrument on the subject, which would gradually replace the existing ones applicable to limited economic sectors, with a view to achieving the total abolition of child labour, and

Having determined that this instrument shall take the form of an international Convention, adopts this twenty-sixth day of June of the year one thousand nine hundred and seventy-three the following Convention, which may be cited as the Minimum Age Convention, 1973:

Article 1

Each Member for which this Convention is in force undertakes to pursue a national policy designed to ensure the effective abolition of child labour and to raise progressively the minimum age for admission to employment or work to a level consistent with the fullest physical and mental development of young persons.

Article 2

1. Each Member which ratifies this Convention shall specify, in a declaration appended to its ratification, a minimum age for admission to employment or work within its territory and on means of transport registered in its territory; subject to Articles 4 to 8 of this Convention, no one under that age shall be admitted to employment or work in any occupation.

2. Each Member which has ratified this Convention may subsequently notify the Director-General of the International Labour Office, by further declarations, that it specifies a minimum age higher than that previously specified.

3. The minimum age specified in pursuance of paragraph 1 of this Article shall not be less than the age of completion of compulsory schooling and, in any case, shall not be less than 15 years.

4. Notwithstanding the provisions of paragraph 3 of this Article, a Member whose economy and educational facilities are insufficiently developed may, after consultation with the

organisations of employers and workers concerned, where such exist, initially specify a minimum age of 14 years.

5. Each Member which has specified a minimum age of 14 years in pursuance of the provisions of the preceding paragraph shall include in its reports on the application of this Convention submitted under Article 22 of the Constitution of the International Labour Organisation a statement:

(a) that its reason for doing so subsists; or
(b) that it renounces its right to avail itself of the provisions in question as from a stated date.

Article 3

1. The minimum age for admission to any type of employment or work which by its nature or the circumstances in which it is carried out is likely to jeopardize the health, safety or morals of young persons shall not be less than 18 years.

2. The types of employment or work to which paragraph 1 of this Article applies shall be determined by national laws or regulations or by the competent authority, after consultation with the organisations of employers and workers concerned, where such exist.

3. Notwithstanding the provisions of paragraph 1 of this Article, national laws or regulations or the competent authority may, after consultation with the organisations of employers and workers concerned, where such exist, authorize employment or work as from the age of 16 years on condition that the health, safety and morals of the young persons concerned are fully protected and that the young persons have received adequate

specific instruction or vocational training in the relevant branch of activity.

Article 4

1.   In so far as necessary, the competent authority, after consultation with the organisations of employers and workers concerned, where such exist, may exclude from the application of this Convention limited categories of employment or work in respect of which special and substantial problems of application arise.

2.   Each Member which ratifies this Convention shall list in its first report on the application of the Convention submitted under Article 22 of the Constitution of the International Labour Organisation any categories which may have been excluded in pursuance of paragraph 1 of this Article, giving the reasons for such exclusion, and shall state in subsequent reports the position of its law and practice in respect of the categories excluded and the extent to which effect has been given or is proposed to be given to the Convention in respect of such categories.

3. Employment or work covered by Article 3 of this Convention shall not be excluded from the application of the Convention in pursuance of this Article.

Article 5

1.   A Member whose economy and administrative facilities are insufficiently developed may, after consultation with the organisations of employers and workers concerned, where such exist, initially limit the scope of application of this Convention.

2. Each Member which avails itself of the provisions of paragraph 1 of this Article shall specify, in a declaration appended to its ratification, the branches of economic activity or types of undertakings to which it will apply the provisions of the Convention.

3. The provisions of the Convention shall be applicable as a minimum to the following: mining and quarrying; manufacturing; construction; electricity, gas and water; sanitary services; transport, storage and communication; and plantations and other agricultural undertakings mainly producing for commercial purposes, but excluding family and small-scale holdings producing for local consumption and not regularly employing hired workers.

4. Any Member which has limited the scope of application of this Convention in pursuance of this Article:

(a) shall indicate in its reports under Article 22 of the Constitution of the International Labour Organisation the general position as regards the employment or work of young persons and children in the branches of activity which are excluded from the scope of application of this Convention and any progress which may have been made towards wider application of the provisions of the Convention; and

(b) may at any time formally extend the scope of application by a declaration addressed to the Director-General of the International Labour Office.

Article 6

This Convention does not apply to work done by children and young persons in schools for general, vocational or technical education or in other training institutions, or to work done by persons at least 14 years of age in undertakings, where such work is carried out in accordance with conditions prescribed by the competent authority, after consultation with the organisations of employers and workers concerned, where such exist, and is an integral part of:

(a) a course of education or training for which a school or training institution is primarily responsible;

(b) a programme of training mainly or entirely in an undertaking, which programme has been approved by the competent authority; or

(c) a programme of guidance or orientation designed to facilitate the choice of an occupation or of a line of training.

Article 7

1. National laws or regulations may permit the employment or work of persons 13 to 15 years of age on light work which is:

(a) not likely to be harmful to their health or development; and

(b) not such as to prejudice their attendance at school, their participation in vocational orientation or training programmes approved by the competent authority or their capacity to benefit from the instruction received.

2. National laws or regulations may also permit the employment or work of persons who are at least 15 years of age but have not yet completed their compulsory schooling or work which meets the requirements set forth in subparagraphs (a) and (b) of paragraph 1 of this Article.

3. The competent authority shall determine the activities in which employment or work may be permitted under paragraphs 1 and 2 of this Article and shall prescribe the number of hours during which and the conditions in which such employment or work may be undertaken.

4. Notwithstanding the provisions of paragraphs 1 and 2 of this Article, a Member which has availed itself of the provisions of paragraph 4 of Article 2 may, for as long as it continues to do so, substitute the ages 12 and 14 for the ages 13 and 15 in paragraph 1 and the age 14 for the age 15 in paragraph 2 of this Article.

Article 8

1. After consultation with the organisations of employers and workers concerned, where such exist, the competent authority may, by permits granted in individual cases allow exceptions to the prohibition on employment or work provided for in Article 2 of this Convention, for such purposes as participation in artistic performances.

2. Permits so granted shall limit the number of hours during which and prescribe the conditions in which employment or work is allowed.

Article 9

1. All necessary measures, including the provision of appropriate penalties, shall be taken by the competent authority to ensure the effective enforcement of the provisions of this Convention.

2 National laws or regulations or the competent authority shall define the persons responsible for compliance with the provisions giving effect to the Convention.

3.   National laws or regulations or the competent authority shall prescribe the registers or other documents which shall be kept and made available by the employer; such registers or documents shall contain the names and ages or dates of birth, duly certified wherever possible, of persons whom he employs or who work for him and who are less than 18 years of age.

Article 10

1. This Convention revises, on the terms set forth in this Article, the Minimum Age (Industry) Convention, 1919, the Minimum Age (Sea) Convention, 1920, the Minimum Age (Agriculture) Convention, 1921, the Minimum Age (Trimmers and Stokers) Convention, 1921, the Minimum Age (Non-Industrial Employment) Convention, 1932, the Minimum Age (Sea) Convention (Revised), 1936, the Minimum Age (Industry) Convention (Revised), 1937, the Minimum Age (Non-Industrial Employment) Convention (Revised), 1937, the Minimum Age (Fishermen) Convention, 1959, and the Minimum Age (Underground Work) Convention, 1965.

2. The coming into force of this Convention shall not close the Minimum Age (Sea) Convention (Revised), 1936, the Minimum Age (Industry) Convention (Revised), 1937, the Minimum Age (Non-Industrial Employment) Convention (Revised), 1937, the Minimum Age (Fishermen) Convention, 1959, and the Minimum Age (Underground Work) Convention, 1965, to further ratification.

3. The Minimum Age (Industry) Convention, 1919, the Minimum Age (Sea) Convention, 1920, the Minimum Age (Agriculture) Convention, 1921, and the Minimum Age (Trimmers and Stokers)

Convention, 1921, shall be closed to further ratification when all the parties thereto have consented to such closing by ratification of this Convention or by a declaration communicated to the Director-General of the International Labour Office.

4. When the obligations of this Convention are accepted:

(a) by a Member which is a party to the Minimum Age (Industry) Convention (Revised), 1937, and a minimum age of not less than 15 years is specified in pursuance of Article 2 of this Convention, this shall *ipso jure* involve the immediate denunciation of that Convention;

(b) in respect of non-industrial employment as defined in the Minimum Age (Non-Industrial Employment) Convention, 1932, by a Member which is a party to that Convention, this shall *ipso jure* involve the immediate denunciation of that Convention;

(c) in respect of non-industrial employment as defined in the Minimum Age (Non-Industrial Employment) Convention, (Revised), 1937, by a Member which is a party to the Convention, and a minimum age of not less than 15 years is specified in pursuance of Article 2 of this Convention, this shall *ipso jure* involve the immediate denunciation of that Convention;

(d) in respect of maritime employment, by a Member which is a party to the Minimum Age (Sea) Convention (Revised), 1936, and a minimum age of not less than 15 years is specified in pursuance of Article 2 of this Convention or the Member specifies that Article 3 of this Convention applies to maritime employment, this shall *ipso jure* involve the immediate denunciation of that Convention;

(e) in respect of employment in maritime fishing, by a Member which is a party to the

Minimum Age (Fishermen) Convention, 1959, and a minimum age of not less than 15 years is specified in pursuance of Article 2 of this Convention or the Member specifies that Article 3 of this Convention applies to maritime fishing, this shall *ipso jure* involve the immediate denunciation of that Convention;

(f) by a Member which is a party to the Minimum Age (Underground Work) Convention, 1965, and a minimum age of not less than the age specified in pursuance of that Convention is specified in pursuance of Article 2 of this Convention or the Member specifies that such an age applies to employment underground in mines in virtue of Article 3 of this Convention, this shall *ipso jure* involve the immediate denunciation of that Convention; if and when this Convention shall have come into force.

5. Acceptance of the obligations of this Convention:

(a) shall involve the denunciation of the Minimum Age (Industry) Convention, 1919, in accordance with Article 12 thereof;

(b) in respect of agriculture shall involve the denunciation of the Minimum Age (Agriculture) Convention, 1921, in accordance with Article 9 thereof;

(c) in respect of maritime employment shall involve the denunciation of the Minimum Age (Sea) Convention, 1920, in accordance with Article 10 thereof, and of the Minimum Age (Trimmers and Stokers) Convention, 1921, in accordance with Article 12 thereof; if and when this Convention shall have come into force.

Article 11

The formal ratifications of this Convention shall be communicated to the Director-General of the International Labour Office for registration.

Article 12

1. This Convention shall be binding only upon those Members of the International Labour Organisation whose ratifications have been registered with the Director-General.

2. It shall come into force twelve months after the date on which the ratifications of two Members have been registered with the Director-General.

3. Thereafter, this Convention shall come into force for any Member twelve months after the date on which its ratification has been registered.

Article 13

1. A Member which has ratified this Convention may denounce it after the expiration of ten years from the date on which the Convention first comes into force, by an act communicated to the Director-General of the International Labour Office for registration. Such denunciation shall not take effect until one year after the date on which it is registered.

2. Each Member which has ratified this Convention and which does not, within the year following the expiration of the period of ten years mentioned in the preceding paragraph, exercise the right of denunciation provided for in this Article, will be bound for another period of ten years and, thereafter, may denounce this Convention at the

expiration of each period of ten years under the terms provided for in this Article.

Article 14

1. The Director-General of the International Labour Office shall notify all Members of the International Labour Organisation of the registration of all ratifications and denunciations communicated to him by the Members of the Organisation.

2. When notifying the Members of the Organisation of the registration of the second ratification communicated to him, the Director-General shall draw the attention of the Members of the Organisation to the date upon which the Convention will come into force.

Article 15

1. The Director-General of the International Labour Office shall communicate to the Secretary-General of the United Nations for registration in accordance with Article 102 of the Charter of the United Nations full particulars of all ratifications and acts of denunciation registered by him in accordance with the provisions of the preceding Articles.

Article 16

At such times as it may consider necessary the Governing Body of the International Labour Office shall present to the General Conference a report on the working of this Convention and shall examine the desirability of placing on the agenda of the Conference the question of its revision in whole or in part.

Article 17

1.   Should the Conference adopt a new Convention revising this Convention in whole or in part, then, unless the new Convention otherwise provides:

(a) the ratification by a Member of the new revising Convention shall *ipso jure* involve the immediate denunciation of this Convention, notwithstanding the provisions of Article 13, above, if and when the new revising Convention shall have come into force;

(b) as from the date when the new revising Convention comes into force this Convention shall cease to be open to ratification by the Members.

2. This Convention shall in any case remain in force in its actual form and content for those Members which have ratified it but have not ratified the revised Convention.

Article 18

The English and French versions of the text of this Convention are equally authoritative.

2.1   ILO Recommendation No. 146

Recommendations of the ILO are intended to offer guidelines for action by member States. ILO Recommendation No. 146 has the same value as ILO Convention No. 138 in that it provides a framework for drawing-up national laws, regulations and programs of practical action on child labor.

RECOMMENDATION CONCERNING
MINIMUM AGE
FOR ADMISSION TO EMPLOYMENT

The General Conference of the International Labour Organisation,

Having been convened at Geneva by the Governing Body of the International Labour Office, and having met in its Fifty-eighth Session on 6 June 1973, and

Recognising that the effective abolition of child labour and the progressive raising of the minimum age for admission to employment constitute only one aspect of the protection and advancement of children and young persons, and

Noting the concern of the whole United Nations system with such protection and advancement, and

Having adopted the Minimum Age Convention, 1973, and

Desirous to define further certain elements of policy which are the concern of the International Labour Organisation, and

Having decided upon the adoption of certain proposals regarding minimum age for admission to employment, which is the fourth item on the agenda of the session, and

Having determined that these proposals shall take the form of a Recommendation supplementing the Minimum Age Convention, 1973:

I. NATIONAL POLICY

1. To ensure the success of the national policy provided for in Article 1 of the Minimum Age Convention, 1973, high priority should be given to planning for and meeting the needs of children and youth in national development policies and programmes and to the progressive extension of the inter-related measures necessary to provide the best possible conditions of physical and mental growth for children and young persons.

2. In this connection special attention should be given to such areas of planning and policy as the following:

(a) firm national commitment to full employment, in accordance with the Employment Policy Convention and Recommendation, 1964, and the taking of measures designed to promote employment-oriented development in rural and urban areas;

(b) the progressive extension of other economic and social measures to alleviate poverty wherever it exists and to ensure family living standards and income which are such as to make it unnecessary to have recourse to the economic activity of children;

(c) the development and progressive extension, without any discrimination, of social security and family welfare measures aimed at ensuring child maintenance, including children's allowances;

(d) the development and progressive extension of adequate facilities for education and vocational orientation and training appropriate in form and content to the needs of the children and young persons concerned;

(e) the development and progressive extension of appropriate facilities for the protection and welfare of children and young persons, including employed young persons, and for the promotion of their development.

3. Particular account should as necessary be taken of the needs of children and young persons who do not have families or do not live with their own families. Measures taken to that end should include the provision of fellowships and vocational training.

4. Full-time attendance at school or participation in approved vocational orientation or training programmes should be required and effectively ensured up to an age at least equal to that specified for admission to employment in accordance with Article 2 of the Minimum Age Convention, 1973.

5. (1) Consideration should be given to measures such as preparatory training, not involving hazards, for types of employment or work in respect of which the minimum age prescribed in accordance with Article 3 of the Minimum Age Convention, 1973, is higher than the age of completion of compulsory full-time schooling.

(2) Analogous measures should be envisaged where the professional exigencies of a particular occupation include a minimum age for admission which is higher than the age of completion of compulsory full-time schooling.

II. MINIMUM AGE

6. The minimum age should be fixed at the same level for all sectors of economic activity.

7. (1) Members should take as their objective the progressive raising to 16 years of the minimum age for admission to employment or work

specified in pursuance of Article 2 of the Minimum Age Convention, 1973.

(2) Where the minimum age for employment or work covered by Article 2 of the Minimum Age Convention, 1973, is still below 15 years, urgent steps should be taken to raise to that level.

8. Where it is not immediately feasible to fix a minimum age for all employment in agriculture and in related activities in rural areas, a minimum age should be fixed at least for employment on plantations and in the other agricultural undertakings referred to in Article 5, paragraph 3, of the Minimum Age Convention, 1973.

III. HAZARDOUS EMPLOYMENT OR WORK

9. Where the minimum age for admission to types of employment or work which are likely to jeopardise the health, safety or morals of young persons is below 18 years, immediate steps should be taken to raise to that level.

10. (1) In determining the types of employment or work to which Article 3 of the Minimum Age Convention, 1973, applies, full account should be taken of relevant international labour standards, such as those concerning dangerous substances, agents or processes (including ionising radiations), the lifting of heavy weights and underground work.

(2) The list of the types of employment or work in question should be re-examined periodically and revised as necessary, particularly in the light of advancing scientific and technological knowledge.

11. Where, by reference to Article 5 of the Minimum Age Convention, 1973, a minimum age is not immediately fixed for certain branches of

economic activity or types of undertakings, appropriate minimum age provisions should be made applicable therein to types of employment or work presenting hazards for young persons.

IV. CONDITIONS OF EMPLOYMENT

12. (1) Measures should be taken to ensure that the conditions in which children and young persons under the age of 18 years are employed or work reach and are maintained at a satisfactory standard. These conditions should be supervised closely.

(2) Measures should likewise be taken to safeguard and supervise the conditions in which children and young persons undergo vocational orientation and training within undertakings, training institutions, and schools for vocational or technical education, and to formulate standards for their protection and development.

13. (1) In connection with the application of the preceding Paragraph, as well as in giving effect to Article 7, Paragraph 3, of the Minimum Age Convention, 1973, special attention should be given to:

(a) the provision of fair remuneration and its protection, bearing in mind the principle of equal pay for equal work;

(b) the strict limitation of the hours spent at work in a day and in a week, and the prohibition of overtime, so as to allow enough time for education and training (including the time needed for homework related thereto), for rest during the day and for leisure activities;

(c) the granting, without possibility of exception save in genuine emergency, of a minimum consecutive period of 12 hours' night rest, and of customary weekly rest days;

(d) the granting of an annual holiday with pay of at least four weeks and, in any case, not shorter than that granted to adults;

(e) coverage by social security schemes, including employment injury, medical care and sickness benefit schemes, whatever the conditions of employment or work may be;

(f) the maintenance of satisfactory standards of safety and health and appropriate instruction and supervision.

(2) Subparagraph (1) of this paragraph applies to young seafarers in so far as they are not covered in respect of the matters dealt with therein by international labour Conventions or Recommendations specifically concerned with maritime employment.

V. ENFORCEMENT

14. (1) Measures to ensure the effective application of the Minimum Age Convention, 1973, and of this Recommendation should include:

(a) the strengthening as necessary of labour inspection and related services, for instance by the special training of inspectors to detect abuses in the employment or work of children and young persons and to correct such abuses; and

(b) the strengthening of services for the improvement and inspection of training in undertakings.

(2) Emphasis should be placed on the role which can be played by inspectors in supplying information and advice on effective means of complying with relevant provisions as well as in securing their enforcement.

(3) Labour inspection and inspection of training in 99undertakings should be closely co-ordinated to provide the greatest economic efficiency and, generally, the labour administration services should work in close co-operation with the services responsible for the education, training, welfare and guidance of children and young persons.

15. Special attention should be paid:

(a) to the enforcement of provisions concerning employment in hazardous types of employment or work; and

(b) in so far as education or training is compulsory, to the prevention of the employment or work of children and young persons during the hours when instruction is available.

16. The following measures should be taken to facilitate the verification of ages:

(a) the public authorities should maintain an effective system of birth registration, which should include the issue of birth certificates;

(b) employers should be required to keep and to make available to the competent authority registers or other documents indicating the names and ages or dates of birth, duly certified wherever possible, not only of children and young persons employed by them but also of those receiving vocational orientation or training in their undertakings;

(c) children and young persons working in the streets, in outside stalls, in public places, in itinerant occupations or in other circumstances which make the checking of employers' records impracticable should be issued licences or other documents indicating their eligibility for such work.

B. NATIONAL LAWS

Today, the basic minimum age of employment in the Philippines is contained in R.A. 7658.   The minimum age of employment for hazardous work, on the other hand, is contained in the Labor Code. These two laws are complemented by other national laws containing some provisions relevant to the minimum age of employment.   All of these laws are presented hereunder.

1. Minimum Age: Principal Policy

1.1 R.A. 7658

AN ACT PROHIBITING THE EMPLOYMENT OF
CHILDREN BELOW 15 YEARS OF AGE
IN PUBLIC AND PRIVATE UNDERTAKINGS,
AMENDING FOR THIS PURPOSE
SECTION 12, ARTICLE VIII OF R.A. 7610

Be it enacted by the Senate and House of Representatives of the Philippines in Congress assembled:

Sec. 1. Section 12, Article VIII of R.A. 7610 otherwise known as the "Special Protection of Children Against Child Abuse Exploitation and Discrimination Act" is hereby amended to read as follows:

"*Sec. 12.* Employment of Children - Children below fifteen (15) years of age shall not be employed except:

1) When a child works directly under the sole responsibility of his parents or legal guardian and where only members of the employer's family are employed: Provided, however, That his employment neither

endangers his life, safety, health and morals, nor impairs his normal development: Provided, further, That the parent or legal guardian shall provide the said minor child with the prescribed primary and/or secondary education; or

2) Where a child's employment or participation in public entertainment or information through cinema, theater, radio or television is essential: Provided, The employment contract is concluded by the child's parents or legal guardian, with the express agreement of the child concerned, if possible, and approval of the Department of Labor and Employment: and Provided, That the following requirements in all instances are strictly complied with:

(a) The employer shall ensure the protection, health, safety, morals and normal development of the child;
(b) The employer shall institute measures to prevent the child's exploitation or discrimination taking into account the system and level of remuneration and the duration and arrangement of working time; and
(c) The employer shall formulate and implement, subject to the approval and supervision of competent authorities, a continuing program for training and skills acquisition of the child.

In the above exceptional cases where any such child may be employed, the employer shall first secure, before engaging such child, a work permit from the Department of Labor and Employment which shall ensure observance of the above requirements.

The Department of Labor and Employment shall promulgate rules and regulations necessary for the effective implementation of this Section.

Sec. 2. All laws, decrees, executive orders, rules and regulations or parts thereof contrary to, or inconsistent with this Act are hereby modified or repealed accordingly.

Sec. 3. This Act shall take effect fifteen (15) days after its complete publication in the Official Gazette or in at least two (2) national newspapers of general circulation whichever comes earlier.

Approved,

JOSE DE VENECIA, JR.
Speaker of the
House of Representatives

EDGARDO J. ANGARA
President of the
Senate

This bill which is a consolidation of Senate Bill No. 1155 and House Bill No. 8179, was finally passed by the Senate and the House of Representatives on October 7, 1993 and October 6, 1993, respectively.

CAMILO L. SABIO
Secretary General
Senate
House of Representatives

EDGARDO E. TUMANGAN
Secretary of the

Approved: November 9, 1993

FIDEL V. RAMOS
President of the Philippines

1.2 Labor Code

The basic minimum age of employment under the Labor Code has been superseded by R.A. 7658, although the two laws basically contain the same principles. R.A. 7658, however, is more expansive in scope than the Labor Code which provides that:

Art. 139. Minimum Employable Age. -
(a)   No child below fifteen (15) years of age shall be employed, except when he works directly under the sole responsibility of his parents or guardian, and his employment does not in any way interfere with his schooling.

x x x

1.3 Omnibus Rules Implementing The Labor Code

BOOK III
CONDITIONS OF EMPLOYMENT
RULE XII
EMPLOYMENT OF WOMEN AND MINORS

Sec. 2. Employable Age. -   Children below fifteen (15) years of age may be allowed to work under the direct responsibility of their parents or guardians in any non-hazardous undertaking where the work will not in any way interfere with their schooling. In such cases, the children shall not be considered as employees of the employer or their parents or guardians.

2. Minimum Age: Hazardous Work

2.1 Labor Code

Art. 139.

x x x

(b) Any person between fifteen (15) and eighteen (18) years of age may be employed for such number of hours and such periods of the day as determined by the Secretary of Labor in appropriate regulations.

(c) The foregoing provisions shall in no case allow the employment of a person below eighteen (18) years of age in an undertaking which is hazardous or deleterious in nature as determined by the Secretary of Labor.

2.2 Omnibus Rules Implementing The Labor Code

BOOK III
CONDITIONS OF EMPLOYMENT
RULE XII
EMPLOYMENT OF WOMEN AND MINORS

Sec. 3.   Eligibility for Employment. -   Any person of either sex, between 15 and 18 years of age, may be employed in any non-hazardous work. No employer shall discriminate against such person in regard to terms and conditions of employment on account of his age.

For purposes of this Rule, a non-hazardous work or undertaking shall mean any work or activity in which the employee is not exposed to any risk which constitutes an imminent danger to his safety and health. The Secretary of Labor shall from time to time publish a list of hazardous work and activities in which persons 18 years of age and below cannot be employed.

2.3 Department Order No.4

DEPARTMENT OF LABOR AND EMPLOYMENT
DEPARTMENT ORDER NO. 4
Series of 1999

HAZARDOUS WORK AND ACTIVITIES TO PERSONS
BELOW 18 YEARS OF AGE

Sec. 1. Basis – This Guidelines is being issued pursuant to Article 139(c), Book III of the Labour Code of the Philippines, as amended, and its implementing rules and regulations, and Republic Act No. 7658, An Act Prohibiting the Employment of Children Below 15 Years of Age in Public and Private Undertakings, Amending for this Purpose Section 12, Article VIII of Republic Act No. 7610 (otherwise known as the Special Protection of Children Against Child Abuse, Exploitation and Discrimination Act).

Sec. 2. Policy – (a) The employment of a person below eighteen (18) years of age in an undertaking which is hazardous or deleterious in nature as identified in this Guidelines shall be prohibited.

(b) The employment of children below fifteen (15) years of age in any undertaking is likewise prohibited, except only in employment that would not endanger life, safety, health and morals, or impair their normal development, and in any event subject to the requirements of Republic Act No. 7658.

Sec. 3. Coverage – The following work and activities are hereby declared hazardous to persons below 18 years of age without prejudice to Section 14, Article VIII of Republic Act No. 7610; to DOLE Memorandum Circular No.2, Series of 1998 (Technical Guidelines for Classifying Hazardous and Non-Hazardous Establishments, Workplaces and Work Processes) and to other work and activities that may subsequently be declared as such:

1. Work which exposes children to physical, psychological or sexual abuse, such as in:

   - lewd shows (stripteasers, burlesque dancers, and the like)
   - cabarets
   - bars (KTV, karaoke bars)
   - dance halls
   - bath houses and massage clinics
   - escort service
   - gambling halls and places

2. Work underground, under water, at dangerous heights or at unguarded heights of two meters and above, or in confined places, such as in:

   - mining
   - deep sea fishing/diving
   - installing and repairing of telephone, telegraph and electrical lines;
   - cable fitters
   - painting buildings
   - window cleaning
   - fruit picking involving climbing

3. Work with dangerous machinery, equipment and tools, or which involves manual handling or transport or heavy loads, such as in:

- logging
- construction
- quarrying
- operating agricultural machinery in mechanized farming
- metal work and welding
- driving or operating heavy equipment such as payloaders, backhoes, bulldozers, cranes, pile driving equipment, trailers, road rollers, tractor lifting appliances, scaffold winches, hoists, excavators and loading machines
- operating or setting motor-driven machines such as saws, presses and wood-working machines
- operating power-driven tools such as drills and jack hammers
- stevedoring
- working in airport hangars
- working in warehouses
- working in docks

4. Work in unhealthy environment which may expose children to hazardous processes, to temperatures, noise levels or vibrations damaging to their health, to toxic, corrosive, poisonous, noxious, explosive, flammable and combustible substances or composites, to harmful biological agents, or to other dangerous chemicals including pharmaceuticals, such as in:

- manufacture or handling of pyrotechnics
- tanning
- pesticide spraying
- blacksmithing, hammersmiths, forging
- extracting lard and oil
- tiling and greasing of heavy machinery
- fiber and plastic preparing
- bleaching, dyeing, and finishing of textiles using chemicals

- embalming and as undertakers
- painting or as finishers in metal craft industries
- applying of adhesive/solvent in footwear, handicraft and woodwork industries
- brewing and distilling or alcoholic beverages
- recycling of batteries and containers or materials used or contaminated with chemicals
- working in abattoirs or slaughterhouses
- garbage collecting
- handling of animal manure in poultry houses or as fertilizers (compost and other decaying matter included) in farming
- working in hospitals or other health care facilities
- assisting in laboratories and x-ray work
- welding
- working in furnaces or kilns
- working in discotheques
- working in video arcades

5. Work under particularly difficult conditions such as work for long hours or during the night, or work where the child is unreasonably confined to the premises of the employer.

Sec. 4. Applicability of this Guideline to Domestic or Household Service – Persons between 15 and 18 years of age may be allowed to engage in domestic or household service, subject in all cases to the limitations prescribed in Nos. 1 to 5 of Section 3 herein.

Sec. 5. Enforcement - The labor standards enforcement officers of the Department of Labour and Employment shall use this Guidelines in monitoring of compliance with labour standards and laws related to child labour which provides for only two exceptions allowing children below fifteen (15) years of age to be employed provided such employment would not endanger their life, safety, health and morals, nor impair their normal development.

Sec. 6. Separability Clause – If any part or provision of this Guidelines is declared invalid or unconstitutional, the remaining provisions not affected thereby shall continue in full force and effect.

This Department Order shall take effect fifteen (15) days after its complete publication in two (2) newspapers of general circulation.

Accordingly, Department Order No. 4 approved on June 8, 1973 is hereby superseded.

(Sgd.) BIENVENIDO E. LAGUESMA
Secretary

2.4. OSHS, Rule 1013

OCCUPATIONAL SAFETY AND HEALTH STANDARDS

HAZARDOUS WORKPLACES

1. Where the nature of work exposes the workers to dangerous environmental elements, contaminants or work conditions including ionizing radiation, chemical, fire, flammable substance, noxious components and the like;

2. Where the workers are engaged in construction work, logging, firefighting, mining, quarrying, blasting, stevedoring, dockwork, deep-sea fishing and mechanized farming;

3.   Where the workers are engaged in the manufacture or handling of explosive and other pyrotechnic products;

4.   Where the workers use or are exposed to power-driven or explosive power-actuated tools; and

5.   Where the workers are exposed to biological agents such as bacteria, fungi, viruses, protozoans, hematodes and other parasites.

3. Minimum Age: Modeling In Commercials/Advertisements Promoting Alcoholic Beverages, Tobacco, Violence, Etc.

The minimum age for modeling in commercials or advertisements which promote alcoholic beverages, tobacco, violence and the like, is 18 years old. This is implicit in the prohibition contained in R.A. 7610 which took effect on June 17, 1992, as follows:

R.A. 7610
THE CHILD PROTECTION CODE

Article VIII
Working Children

Sec.. 14.   Prohibition on the Employment of Children in Certain Advertisements. - No person shall employ child models in all commercials or advertisements promoting alcoholic beverages, intoxicating drinks, tobacco and its by-products, and violence.

4. Minimum Age: Apprentices

The law on apprenticeship is governed by the Labor Code which sets the minimum age for apprentices at 14 years. However, the Omnibus Rules Implementing the Labor Code prescribes a 15-year age requirement for apprentices and not 14 years. Moreover, considering that both Article 139 of the Labor Code and R.A. 7658 prescribe a minimum employable age of 15 years without including apprentices among the exceptions, the laws taken together could be construed to mean that the minimum age for apprentices is actually 15 years. This issue remains to be settled by competent authorities.

4.1 Labor Code

TITLE II
TRAINING AND EMPLOYMENT OF SPECIAL WORKERS
CHAPTER I
APPRENTICES

Art. 58. Definition of Terms. - As used in this Title:

(a) "Apprenticeship" means practical training on the job supplemented by related theoretical instruction.

(b) An "apprentice" is a worker who is covered by a written apprenticeship agreement with an individual employer or any of the entities recognized under this Chapter.

(c) An "apprenticeship occupation" means any trade, form of employment or occupation which requires more than three (3) months of practical training on the job supplemented by related theoretical instruction.

(d) "Apprenticeship agreement" is an employment contract wherein the employer binds himself to train the apprentice and the apprentice in turn accepts the terms of training.

Art. 59. Qualifications of Apprentice. - To qualify as an apprentice, a person shall:
(a) Be at least fourteen (14) years of age;
(b) Possess vocational aptitude and capacity for appropriate tests; and
(c) Possess the ability to comprehend and follow oral and written instructions.
Trade and industry associations may recommend to the Secretary of Labor appropriate educational requirements for different occupations.

Art. 60. Employment of Apprentices. - Only employers in the highly technical industries may employ apprentices and only in apprenticeable occupations approved by the Secretary of Labor and Employment.

4.2. Omnibus Rules Implementing The Labor Code

BOOK II
NATIONAL MANPOWER DEVELOPMENT PROGRAM
RULE VI
APPRENTICESHIP TRAINING AND EMPLOYMENT OF
SPECIAL WORKERS

Sec. 11. Qualifications of apprentices. - To qualify as an apprentice, an applicant shall:

(a) Be at least fifteen years of age; provided those who are at least fifteen years of age but less than eighteen may be eligible for apprenticeship only in non-hazardous occupations;
(b) Be physically fit for the occupation in which he desires to be trained;

(c) Possess vocational aptitude and capacity for the particular occupation as established through appropriate tests; and

(d) Possess the ability to comprehend and follow oral and written instructions.

5. Minimum Age: Child And Youth Welfare Code

The Child and Youth Welfare Code (P.D. 603) took effect in 1975, shortly after the Labor Code's own effectivity. P.D. 603 does not directly prescribe a minimum age of employment. Rather, it permits light work for persons under the age of 16 years. This does not mean, however, that all children below 16 years old are allowed to perform light work. P.D. 603 states that it adopts the Labor Code provisions relating to employable age as part of it. Thus, under P.D. 603, the minimum age of employment is still 15 years as prescribed by the Labor Code.' But with respect to those under 15 years old who are allowed by the Labor Code to work under the direct responsibility of their parents, they are permitted to perform only light work as defined by P.D. 603.

TITLE VI
CHILD AND YOUTH WELFARE
AND THE SAMAHAN
CHAPTER 2
WORKING CHILDREN

Art. 107. Employment of Children Below Sixteen Years. - Children below sixteen years of age may be employed to perform light work which is not harmful to their safety, health or normal development and which is not prejudicial to their studies.

The provisions of the Labor Code relating to employable age and conditions of employment of children are hereby adopted as part of this Code insofar as not inconsistent herewith.

6. Minimum Age: Opinion Of The Secretary Of Labor

OPINION OF THE SECRETARY OF LABOR
DATED SEPT. 3, 1991

Children below 18 years of age may be allowed to work subject to the following conditions:

a. Those from 16 to below 18 years of age are subject to Art. 139 (b), Labor Code (LC) as amended, and by Art. 107 of the Child and Youth Welfare Code (CYWC), that is, they may be employed for such number of hours and such periods of the day as determined by the Secretary of Labor and Employment in appropriate legislation.

b. Those from 15 to below 16 years of age are subject to Art. 107 of the CYWC and Art. 139 (b) of the LC, hence they may be employed to perform light work which is not harmful to their safety, health or normal development and which is not prejudicial to their studies (Art. 107, CYWC), for such number of hours and such periods of the day as determined by the Secretary of Labor and Employment in appropriate regulations [Art. 139 (b), LC].

c. Those who are below 15 are subject to Art. 139 (a) of the LC and Art. 107 of the CYWC, that is, they may be employed when they work directly under the sole responsibility of their parents or guardian and their employment does not in any way interfere with their schooling [Art. 139 (a), LC] and to perform light work which is not harmful to their safety, health or normal development and which is not prejudicial to their studies [Art. 107, CYWC].

Article 139(a) was amended by RA No. 7610 and which was later amended by RA No. 7658 which now provides that a child under this bracket may be employed when he works directly under the sole responsibility of his parents or legal guardian and where only members of the employer's family are employed: Provided, however, that his employment neither endangers his life, safety, health and morals, nor impairs his normal development: Provided, further that the parent or legal guardian shall provide the said minor child with the prescribed primary and/or secondary education.

d. All of the above, that is below 18 years are subject to Art. 139 (c) of the LC, hence, all of them may not be employed in an undertaking which is hazardous or deleterious in nature as determined by the Secretary of Labor and Employment.

III. WORST FORMS OF CHILD LABOR

A. INTERNATIONAL CONVENTIONS

The Philippines is a signatory to the following international instruments and has ratified "ILO Convention No. 182", "Optional Protocol to the Convention on the Rights of the Child on the Involvement of Children in Armed Conflict", "Optional Protocol to the Convention on the Rights of the Child on the Sale of Children, Child Prostitution and Child Pornography" and "Convention on the Suprression of Traffic in Persons and of the Exploitation of the Prostitution of Others". These Conventions now form part of Philippines laws by virtue of the 'doctrine of incorporation'. As regards "Protocol to Prevent, Suppress and Punish Trafficking in Persons, Especially Women and Children, Supplementing the United Nations Convention Against Transnational Organized Crime", although a signature alone does not make the treaty binding, the State signing it is obliged to refrain from acts which would defeat the object of the treaty until it shall have made its intention clear not to become a party to the treaty. [75]

1. ILO Convention No. 182

The total abolition of child labor is a gradual process. International consensus, however, stressed the urgency for prohibition and immediate action to eliminate the worst forms of child labor, consequently the adoption of ILO Convention 182 to strengthen ILO Convention 138. The main provisions of the ILO Convention 182 aim to clarify which situations should be classified as the worst forms of child labor and to specify what governments must do to prohibit and eliminate them. [76] *ILO Convention 138 remains the focal policy in combating child labor.*

---

[75] Art. 18 Vienna Convention on the Law on Treaties U.N. Doc. A/CONF. 39/27, (1969).

[76] Geneva NGO Group for the Convention on the Rights of the Child Sub-Group on Child Labour, *The New ILO Worst Forms of Child Labour Convention 1999*, (visited June 18, 2001) <http://www.antislavery.org/homepage/resources/ILOeng.pdf>

CONVENTION CONCERNING THE PROHIBITION
AND IMMEDIATE ACTION FOR THE ELIMINATION
OF THE WORST FORMS OF CHILD LABOUR
[Ratified by the Philippines on November 28, 2000]

The General Conference of the International Labour Organization,

Having been convened at Geneva by the Governing Body of the International Labour Office, and having met in its 87th Session on 1 June 1999, and

Considering the need to adopt new instruments for the prohibition and elimination of the worst forms of child labour, as the main priority for national and international action, including international cooperation and assistance, to complement the Convention and the Recommendation concerning Minimum Age for Admission to Employment, 1973, which remain fundamental instruments on child labour, and

Considering that the effective elimination of the worst forms of child labour requires immediate and comprehensive action, taking into account the importance of free basic education and the need to remove the children concerned from all such work and to provide for their rehabilitation and social integration while addressing the needs of their families, and

Recalling the resolution concerning the elimination of child labour adopted by the International Labour Conference at its 83rd Session in 1996, and

Recognizing that child labour is to a great extent caused by poverty and that the long-term solution lies in sustained economic growth leading to social progress, in particular poverty alleviation and universal education, and

Recalling the Convention on the Rights of the Child adopted by the United Nations General Assembly on 20 November 1989, and

Recalling the ILO Declaration on Fundamental Principles and Rights at Work and its Follow-up, adopted by the International Labour Conference at its 86th Session in 1998, and

Recalling that some of the worst forms of child labour are covered by other international instruments, in particular the Forced Labour Convention, 1930, and the United Nations Supplementary Convention on the Abolition of Slavery, the Slave Trade, and Institutions and Practices Similar to Slavery, 1956, and

Having decided upon the adoption of certain proposals with regard to child labour, which is the fourth item on the agenda of the session, and

Having determined that these proposals shall take the form of an international Convention; adopts this seventeenth day of June of the year one thousand nine hundred and ninety-nine the following Convention, which may be cited as the Worst Forms of Child Labour Convention, 1999.

Article 1

Each Member which ratifies this Convention shall take immediate and effective measures to secure the prohibition and elimination of the worst forms of child labour as a matter of urgency.

Article 2

For the purposes of this Convention, the term "child" shall apply to all persons under the age of 18.

Article 3

For the purposes of this Convention, the term "the worst forms of child labour" comprises:

(a) all forms of slavery or practices similar to slavery, such as the sale and trafficking of children, debt bondage and serfdom and forced or compulsory labour, including forced or compulsory recruitment of children for use in armed conflict;

(b) the use, procuring or offering of a child for prostitution, for the production of pornography or for pornographic performances;

(c) the use, procuring or offering of a child for illicit activities, in particular for the production and trafficking of drugs as defined in the relevant international treaties;

(d) work which, by its nature or the circumstances in which it is carried out, is likely to harm the health, safety or morals of children. *[Underscoring supplied]*

Article 4

1. The types of work referred to under Article 3(d) shall be determined by national laws or regulations or by the competent authority, after consultation with the organizations of employers and workers concerned, taking into consideration relevant international standards, in particular Paragraphs 3 and 4 of the Worst Forms of Child Labour Recommendation, 1999.

2. The competent authority, after consultation with the organizations of employers and workers concerned, shall identify where the types of work so determined exist.

3. The list of the types of work determined under paragraph 1 of this Article shall be periodically examined and revised as necessary, in consultation with the organizations of employers and workers concerned.

Article 5

Each Member shall, after consultation with employers' and workers' organizations, establish or designate appropriate mechanisms to monitor the implementation of the provisions giving effect to this Convention.

Article 6

1. Each Member shall design and implement programmes of action to eliminate as a priority the worst forms of child labour.

2. Such programmes of action shall be designed and implemented in consultation with relevant government institutions and employers' and workers' organizations, taking into consideration the views of other concerned groups as appropriate.

Article 7

1. Each Member shall take all necessary measures to ensure the effective implementation and enforcement of the provisions giving effect to this Convention including the provision and application of penal sanctions or, as appropriate, other sanctions.

2. Each Member shall, taking into account the importance of education in eliminating child labour, take effective and time-bound measures to:

(a) prevent the engagement of children in the worst forms of child labour;

(b) provide the necessary and appropriate direct assistance for the removal of children from the worst forms of child labour and for their rehabilitation and social integration;

(c) ensure access to free basic education, and, wherever possible and appropriate, vocational training, for all children removed from the worst forms of child labour;

(d) identify and reach out to children at special risk; and

(e) take account of the special situation of girls.

3. Each Member shall designate the competent authority responsible for the implementation of the provisions giving effect to this Convention.

Article 8

Members shall take appropriate steps to assist one another in giving effect to the provisions of this Convention through enhanced international cooperation and/or assistance including support for social and economic development, poverty eradication programmes and universal education.

Article 9

The formal ratifications of this Convention shall be communicated to the Director-General of the International Labour Office for registration.

Article 10

1. This Convention shall be binding only upon those Members of the International Labour Organization whose ratifications have been

registered with the Director-General of the International Labour Office.

2. It shall come into force 12 months after the date on which the ratifications of two Members have been registered with the Director-General.

3. Thereafter, this Convention shall come into force for any Member 12 months after the date on which its ratification has been registered.

Article 11

1. A Member which has ratified this Convention may denounce it after the expiration of ten years from the date on which the Convention first comes into force, by an act communicated to the Director-General of the International Labour Office for registration. Such denunciation shall not take effect until one year after the date on which it is registered.

2. Each Member which has ratified this Convention and which does not, within the year following the expiration of the period of ten years mentioned in the preceding paragraph, exercise the right of denunciation provided for in this Article, will be bound for another period of ten years and, thereafter, may denounce this Convention at the expiration of each period of ten years under the terms provided for in this Article.

Article 12

1. The Director-General of the International Labour Office shall notify all Members of the International Labour Organization of the registration of all ratifications and acts of denunciation communicated by the Members of the Organization.

2. When notifying the Members of the Organization of the registration of the second ratification, the Director-General shall draw the attention of the Members of the Organization to the date upon which the Convention shall come into force.

Article 13

The Director-General of the International Labour Office shall communicate to the Secretary-General of the United Nations, for registration in accordance with article 102 of the Charter of the United Nations, full particulars of all ratifications and acts of denunciation registered by the Director-General in accordance with the provisions of the preceding Articles.

Article 14

At such times as it may consider necessary, the Governing Body of the International Labour Office shall present to the General Conference a report on the working of this Convention and shall examine the desirability of placing on the agenda of the Conference the question of its revision in whole or in part.

Article 15

1. Should the Conference adopt a new Convention revising this Convention in whole or in part, then, unless the new Convention otherwise provides --

(a) the ratification by a Member of the new revising Convention shall *ipso jure* involve the immediate denunciation of this Convention, notwithstanding the provisions of Article 11 above, if and when the new revising Convention shall have come into force;

(b) as from the date when the new revising Convention comes into force, this Convention shall cease to be open to ratification by the Members.

2. This Convention shall in any case remain in force in its actual form and content for those Members which have ratified it but have not ratified the revising Convention.

Article 16

The English and French versions of the text of this Convention are equally authoritative.

1.1. ILO Recommendation No. 190

The Recommendation provides guidelines for national action that the government should consider in the implementation of ILO Convention 182.[77]

RECOMMENDATION CONCERNING THE PROHIBITION AND IMMEDIATE ACTION FOR THE ELIMINATION OF THE WORST FORMS OF CHILD LABOR

The General Conference of the International Labour Organization,

Having been convened at Geneva by the Governing Body of the International Labour Office, and having met in its 87th Session on 1 June 1999, and

---

[77] *Id.*

Having adopted the Worst Forms of Child Labour Convention, 1999, and

Having decided upon the adoption of certain proposals with regard to child labour, which is the fourth item on the agenda of the session, and

Having determined that these proposals shall take the form of a Recommendation supplementing the Worst Forms of Child Labour Convention, 1999; adopts this seventeenth day of June of the year one thousand nine hundred and ninety-nine the following Recommendation, which may be cited as the Worst Forms of Child Labour Recommendation, 1999.

1. The provisions of this Recommendation supplement those of the Worst Forms of Child Labour Convention, 1999 (hereafter referred to as "the Convention"), and should be applied in conjunction with them.

I. Programmes of action

2. The programmes of action referred to in Article 6 of the Convention should be designed and implemented as a matter of urgency, in consultation with relevant government institutions and employers' and workers' organizations, taking into consideration the views of the children directly affected by the worst forms of child labour, their families and, as appropriate, other concerned groups committed to the aims of the Convention and this Recommendation. Such programmes should aim at, inter alia:

(a) identifying and denouncing the worst forms of child labour;
(b) preventing the engagement of children in or removing them from the worst forms of child

labour, protecting them from reprisals and providing for their rehabilitation and social integration through measures which address their educational, physical and psychological needs;

(c) giving special attention to:

(i) younger children;

(ii) the girl child;

(iii) the problem of hidden work situations, in which girls are at special risk;

(iv) other groups of children with special vulnerabilities or needs;

(d) identifying, reaching out to and working with communities where children are at special risk;

(e) informing, sensitizing and mobilizing public opinion and concerned groups, including children and their families.

II. Hazardous work

3. In determining the types of work referred to under Article 3(d) of the Convention, and in identifying where they exist, consideration should be given, inter alia, to:

(a) work which exposes children to physical, psychological or sexual abuse;

(b) work underground, under water, at dangerous heights or in confined spaces;

(c) work with dangerous machinery, equipment and tools, or which involves the manual handling or transport of heavy loads;

(d) work in an unhealthy environment which may, for example, expose children to hazardous substances, agents or processes, or to temperatures, noise levels, or vibrations damaging to their health;

(e) work under particularly difficult conditions such as work for long hours or during the night or work where the child is unreasonably confined to the premises of the employer.

4. For the types of work referred to under Article 3(d) of the Convention and Paragraph 3 above, national laws or regulations or the competent authority could, after consultation with the workers' and employers' organizations concerned, authorize employment or work as from the age of 16 on condition that the health, safety and morals of the children concerned are fully protected, and that the children have received adequate specific instruction or vocational training in the relevant branch of activity.

III. Implementation

5. (1) Detailed information and statistical data on the nature and extent of child labour should be compiled and kept up to date to serve as a basis for determining priorities for national action for the abolition of child labour, in particular for the prohibition and elimination of its worst forms as a matter of urgency.

(2) As far as possible, such information and statistical data should include data disaggregated by sex, age group, occupation, branch of economic activity, status in employment, school attendance and geographical location. The importance of an effective system of birth registration, including the issuing of birth certificates, should be taken into account.

(3) Relevant data concerning violations of national provisions for the prohibition and elimination of the worst forms of child labour should be compiled and kept up to date.

6. The compilation and processing of the information and data referred to in Paragraph 5 above should be carried out with due regard for the right to privacy.

7. The information compiled under Paragraph 5 above should be communicated to the International Labour Office on a regular basis.

8. Members should establish or designate appropriate national mechanisms to monitor the implementation of national provisions for the prohibition and elimination of the worst forms of child labour, after consultation with employers' and workers' organizations.

9. Members should ensure that the competent authorities which have responsibilities for implementing national provisions for the prohibition and elimination of the worst forms of child labour cooperate with each other and coordinate their activities.

10. National laws or regulations or the competent authority should determine the persons to be held responsible in the event of non-compliance with national provisions for the prohibition and elimination of the worst forms of child labour.

11. Members should, in so far as it is compatible with national law, cooperate with international efforts aimed at the prohibition and elimination of the worst forms of child labour as a matter of urgency by:

(a) gathering and exchanging information concerning criminal offences, including those involving international networks;

(b) detecting and prosecuting those involved in the sale and trafficking of children, or in the use, procuring or offering of children for illicit activities, for prostitution, for the production of pornography or for pornographic performances;

(c) registering perpetrators of such offences.

12. Members should provide that the following worst forms of child labour are criminal offences:

(a) all forms of slavery or practices similar to slavery, such as the sale and trafficking of children, debt bondage and serfdom and forced or compulsory labour, including forced or compulsory recruitment of children for use in armed conflict;

(b) the use, procuring or offering of a child for prostitution, for the production of pornography or for pornographic performances; and

(c) the use, procuring or offering of a child for illicit activities, in particular for the production and trafficking of drugs as defined in the relevant international treaties, or for activities which involve the unlawful carrying or use of firearms or other weapons.

13. Members should ensure that penalties including, where appropriate, criminal penalties are applied for violations of the national provisions for the prohibition and elimination of any type of work referred to in Article 3(d) of the Convention.

14. Members should also provide as a matter of urgency for other criminal, civil or administrative remedies, where appropriate, to ensure the effective enforcement of national provisions for the prohibition and elimination of the worst forms of child labour, such as special supervision of enterprises which have used the worst forms of child labour, and, in cases of

persistent violation, consideration of temporary or permanent revoking of permits to operate.

15. Other measures aimed at the prohibition and elimination of the worst forms of child labour might include the following:

(a) informing, sensitizing and mobilizing the general public, including national and local political leaders, parliamentarians and the judiciary;

(b) involving and training employers' and workers' organizations and civic organizations;

(c) providing appropriate training for the government officials concerned, especially inspectors and law enforcement officials, and for other relevant professionals;

(d) providing for the prosecution in their own country of the Member's nationals who commit offences under its national provisions for the prohibition and immediate elimination of the worst forms of child labour even when these offences are committed in another country;

(e) simplifying legal and administrative procedures and ensuring that they are appropriate and prompt;

(f) encouraging the development of policies by undertakings to promote the aims of the Convention;

(g) monitoring and giving publicity to best practices on the elimination of child labour;

(h) giving publicity to legal or other provisions on child labour in the different languages or dialects;

(i) establishing special complaints procedures and making provisions to protect from discrimination and reprisals those who legitimately expose violations of the provisions of the Convention, as well as establishing helplines or points of contact and ombudspersons;

(j) adopting appropriate measures to improve the educational infrastructure and the training of teachers to meet the needs of boys and girls;

(k) as far as possible, taking into account in national programmes of action:

(i) the need for job creation and vocational training for the parents and adults in the families of children working in the conditions covered by the Convention; and

(ii) the need for sensitizing parents to the problem of children working in such conditions.

16. Enhanced international cooperation and/or assistance among Members for the prohibition and effective elimination of the worst forms of child labour should complement national efforts and may, as appropriate, be developed and implemented in consultation with employers' and workers' organizations. Such international cooperation and/or assistance should include:

(a) mobilizing resources for national or international programmes;

(b) mutual legal assistance;

(c) technical assistance including the exchange of information;

(d) support for social and economic development, poverty eradication programmes and universal education.

2. Optional Protocol To The Convention On The Rights Of The Child On The Involvement Of Children In Armed Conflict
[Ratified by the Philippines in April 2002]

The States Parties to the present Protocol,

Encouraged by the overwhelming support for the Convention on the Rights of the Child, demonstrating the widespread commitment that exists to strive for the promotion and protection of the rights of the child,

Reaffirming that the rights of children require special protection, and calling for continuous improvement of the situation of children without distinction, as well as for their development and education in conditions of peace and security,

Disturbed by the harmful and widespread impact of armed conflict on children and the long-term consequences it has for durable peace, security and development,

Condemning the targeting of children in situations of armed conflict and direct attacks on objects protected under international law, including places that generally have a significant presence of children, such as schools and hospitals,

Noting the adoption of the Rome Statute of the International Criminal Court, in particular, the inclusion therein as a war crime, of conscripting or enlisting children under the age of 15 years or using them to participate actively in hostilities in both international and non-international armed conflicts,

Considering therefore that to strengthen further the implementation of rights recognized in the Convention on the Rights of the Child there is a need to increase the protection of children from involvement in armed conflict,

Noting that article 1 of the Convention on the Rights of the Child specifies that, for the purposes of that Convention, a child means every human being below the age of 18 years unless, under the law applicable to the child, majority is attained earlier,

Convinced that an optional protocol to the Convention that raises the age of possible recruitment of persons into armed forces and their participation in hostilities will contribute effectively to the implementation of the principle that the best interests of the child are to be a primary consideration in all actions concerning children,

Noting that the twenty-sixth International Conference of the Red Cross and Red Crescent in December 1995 recommended, inter alia, that parties to conflict take every feasible step to ensure that children below the age of 18 years do not take part in hostilities,

Welcoming the unanimous adoption, in June 1999, of International Labour Organization Convention No. 182 on the Prohibition and Immediate Action for the Elimination of the Worst Forms of Child Labour, which prohibits, inter alia, forced or compulsory recruitment of children for use in armed conflict,

Condemning with the gravest concern the recruitment, training and use within and across national borders of children in hostilities by armed groups distinct from the armed forces of a State, and recognizing the responsibility of those who recruit, train and use children in this regard,

Recalling the obligation of each party to an armed conflict to abide by the provisions of international humanitarian law,

Stressing that the present Protocol is without prejudice to the purposes and principles contained in the Charter of the United Nations, including Article 51, and relevant norms of humanitarian law,

Bearing in mind that conditions of peace and security based on full respect of the purposes and principles contained in the Charter and observance of applicable human rights instruments are indispensable for the full protection of children, in particular during armed conflicts and foreign occupation,

Recognizing the special needs of those children who are particularly vulnerable to recruitment or use in hostilities contrary to the present Protocol owing to their economic or social status or gender,

Mindful of the necessity of taking into consideration the economic, social and political root causes of the involvement of children in armed conflicts,

Convinced of the need to strengthen international cooperation in the implementation of the present Protocol, as well as the physical and psychosocial rehabilitation and social reintegration of children who are victims of armed conflict,

Encouraging the participation of the community and, in particular, children and child victims in the dissemination of informational and educational programmes concerning the implementation of the Protocol,

Have agreed as follows:

Article 1

States Parties shall take all feasible measures to ensure that members of their armed forces who have not attained the age of 18 years do not take a direct part in hostilities.

Article 2

States Parties shall ensure that persons who have not attained the age of 18 years are not compulsorily recruited into their armed forces.

Article 3

1. States Parties shall raise the minimum age for the voluntary recruitment of persons into their national armed forces from that set out in article 38, paragraph 3, of the Convention on the Rights of the Child, taking account of the principles contained in that article and recognizing that under the Convention persons under the age of 18 years are entitled to special protection.

2. Each State Party shall deposit a binding declaration upon ratification of or accession to the present Protocol that sets forth the minimum age at which it will permit voluntary recruitment into its national armed forces and a description of the safeguards it has adopted to ensure that such recruitment is not forced or coerced.

3. States Parties that permit voluntary recruitment into their national armed forces under the age of 18 years shall maintain safeguards to ensure, as a minimum, that:

(a) Such recruitment is genuinely voluntary;

(b) Such recruitment is carried out with the informed consent of the person's parents or legal guardians;

(c) Such persons are fully informed of the duties involved in such military service;

(d) Such persons provide reliable proof of age prior to acceptance into national military service.

4. Each State Party may strengthen its declaration at any time by notification to that effect addressed to the Secretary-General of the United Nations, who shall inform all States Parties. Such notification shall take effect on the date on which it is received by the Secretary-General.

5. The requirement to raise the age in paragraph 1 of the present article does not apply to schools operated by or under the control of the armed forces of the States Parties, in keeping with articles 28 and 29 of the Convention on the Rights of the Child.

Article 4

1. Armed groups that are distinct from the armed forces of a State should not, under any circumstances, recruit or use in hostilities persons under the age of 18 years.

2. States Parties shall take all feasible measures to prevent such recruitment and use, including the adoption of legal measures necessary to prohibit and criminalize such practices.

3. The application of the present article shall not affect the legal status of any party to an armed conflict.

Article 5

Nothing in the present Protocol shall be construed as precluding provisions in the law of a State Party or in international instruments and international humanitarian law that are more conducive to the realization of the rights of the child.

Article 6

1. Each State Party shall take all necessary legal, administrative and other measures to ensure the effective implementation and enforcement of the provisions of the present Protocol within its jurisdiction.

2. States Parties undertake to make the principles and provisions of the present Protocol widely known and promoted by appropriate means, to adults and children alike.

3. States Parties shall take all feasible measures to ensure that persons within their jurisdiction recruited or used in hostilities contrary to the present Protocol are demobilized or otherwise released from service. States Parties shall, when necessary, accord to such persons all appropriate assistance for their physical and psychological recovery and their social reintegration.

Article 7

1. States Parties shall cooperate in the implementation of the present Protocol, including in the prevention of any activity contrary thereto and in the rehabilitation and social reintegration of persons who are victims of acts contrary thereto, including through technical cooperation and financial assistance. Such assistance and cooperation will be undertaken in consultation with the States Parties

concerned and the relevant international organizations.

2. States Parties in a position to do so shall provide such assistance through existing multilateral, bilateral or other programmes or, inter alia, through a voluntary fund established in accordance with the rules of the General Assembly.

Article 8

1. Each State Party shall, within two years following the entry into force of the present Protocol for that State Party, submit a report to the Committee on the Rights of the Child providing comprehensive information on the measures it has taken to implement the provisions of the Protocol, including the measures taken to implement the provisions on participation and recruitment.

2. Following the submission of the comprehensive report, each State Party shall include in the reports it submits to the Committee on the Rights of the Child, in accordance with article 44 of the Convention, any further information with respect to the implementation of the Protocol. Other States Parties to the Protocol shall submit a report every five years.

3. The Committee on the Rights of the Child may request from States Parties further information relevant to the implementation of this Protocol.

Article 9

1. The present Protocol is open for signature by any State that is a party to the Convention or has signed it.

2. The present Protocol is subject to ratification and is open to accession by any State. Instruments of ratification or accession shall be deposited with the Secretary-General of the United Nations.

3. The Secretary-General, in his capacity as depositary of the Convention and the Protocol, shall inform all States Parties to the Convention and all States that have signed the Convention of each instrument of declaration pursuant to article 3.

Article 10

1. The present Protocol shall enter into force three months after the deposit of the tenth instrument of ratification or accession.

2. For each State ratifying the present Protocol or acceding to it after its entry into force, the Protocol shall enter into force one month after the date of the deposit of its own instrument of ratification or accession.

Article 11

1. Any State Party may denounce the present Protocol at any time by written notification to the Secretary- General of the United Nations, who shall thereafter inform the other States Parties to the Convention and all States that have signed the Convention. The denunciation shall take effect one year after the date of receipt of the notification by the Secretary-General. If, however, on the expiry of that year the denouncing State Party is engaged in armed conflict, the denunciation shall not take effect before the end of the armed conflict.

2. Such a denunciation shall not have the effect of releasing the State Party from its obligations

under the present Protocol in regard to any act that occurs prior to the date on which the denunciation becomes effective. Nor shall such a denunciation prejudice in any way the continued consideration of any matter that is already under consideration by the Committee on the Rights of the Child prior to the date on which the denunciation becomes effective.

Article 12

1. Any State Party may propose an amendment and file it with the Secretary-General of the United Nations. The Secretary-General shall thereupon communicate the proposed amendment to States Parties with a request that they indicate whether they favour a conference of States Parties for the purpose of considering and voting upon the proposals. In the event that, within four months from the date of such communication, at least one third of the States Parties favour such a conference, the Secretary-General shall convene the conference under the auspices of the United Nations. Any amendment adopted by a majority of States Parties present and voting at the conference shall be submitted to the General Assembly of the United Nations for approval.

2. An amendment adopted in accordance with paragraph 1 of the present article shall enter into force when it has been approved by the General Assembly and accepted by a two-thirds majority of States Parties.

3. When an amendment enters into force, it shall be binding on those States Parties that have accepted it, other States Parties still being bound by the provisions of the present Protocol and any earlier amendments they have accepted.

Article 13

1. The present Protocol, of which the Arabic, Chinese, English, French, Russian and Spanish texts are equally authentic, shall be deposited in the archives of the United Nations.

2. The Secretary-General of the United Nations shall transmit certified copies of the present Protocol to all States Parties to the Convention and all States that have signed the Convention.

3. Optional Protocol To The Convention On The Rights Of The Child On The Sale Of Children, Child Prostitution And Child Pornography
[Ratified by the Philippines in April 2002]

The States Parties to the present Protocol,

Considering that, in order further to achieve the purposes of the Convention on the Rights of the Child and the implementation of its provisions, especially articles 1, 11, 21, 32, 33, 34, 35 and 36, it would be appropriate to extend the measures that States Parties should undertake in order to guarantee the protection of the child from the sale of children, child prostitution and child pornography,

Considering also that the Convention on the Rights of the Child recognizes the right of the child to be protected from economic exploitation and from performing any work that is likely to be hazardous or to interfere with the child's education, or to be harmful to the child's health or physical, mental, spiritual, moral or social development,

Gravely concerned at the significant and increasing international traffic in children for the purpose of the sale of children, child prostitution and child pornography,

Deeply concerned at the widespread and continuing practice of sex tourism, to which children are especially vulnerable, as it directly promotes the sale of children, child prostitution and child pornography,

Recognizing that a number of particularly vulnerable groups, including girl children, are at greater risk of sexual exploitation and that girl children are disproportionately represented among the sexually exploited,

Concerned about the growing availability of child pornography on the Internet and other evolving technologies, and recalling the International Conference on Combating Child Pornography on the Internet, held in Vienna in 1999, in particular its conclusion calling for the worldwide criminalization of the production, distribution, exportation, transmission, importation, intentional possession and advertising of child pornography, and stressing the importance of closer cooperation and partnership between Governments and the Internet industry,

Believing that the elimination of the sale of children, child prostitution and child pornography will be facilitated by adopting a holistic approach, addressing the contributing factors, including underdevelopment, poverty, economic disparities, inequitable socio-economic structure, dysfunctioning families, lack of education, urban-rural migration, gender discrimination, irresponsible adult sexual behaviour, harmful traditional practices, armed conflicts and trafficking in children,

Believing also that efforts to raise public awareness are needed to reduce consumer demand for the sale of children, child prostitution and child pornography, and believing further in the importance of strengthening global partnership among all actors and of improving law enforcement at the national level,

Noting the provisions of international legal instruments relevant to the protection of children, including the Hague Convention on Protection of Children and Cooperation in Respect of Intercountry Adoption, the Hague Convention on the Civil Aspects of International Child Abduction, the Hague Convention on Jurisdiction, Applicable Law, Recognition, Enforcement and Cooperation in Respect of Parental Responsibility and Measures for the Protection of Children, and International Labour Organization Convention No. 182 on the Prohibition and Immediate Action for the Elimination of the Worst Forms of Child Labour,

Encouraged by the overwhelming support for the Convention on the Rights of the Child, demonstrating the widespread commitment that exists for the promotion and protection of the rights of the child,

Recognizing the importance of the implementation of the provisions of the Programme of Action for the Prevention of the Sale of Children, Child Prostitution and Child Pornography and the Declaration and Agenda for Action adopted at the World Congress against Commercial Sexual Exploitation of Children, held in Stockholm from 27 to 31 August 1996, and the other relevant decisions and recommendations of pertinent international bodies,

Taking due account of the importance of the traditions and cultural values of each people for the protection and harmonious development of the child,

Have agreed as follows:

Article 1

States Parties shall prohibit the sale of children, child prostitution and child pornography as provided for by the present Protocol.

Article 2

For the purposes of the present Protocol:

(a) Sale of children means any act or transaction whereby a child is transferred by any person or group of persons to another for remuneration or any other consideration;

(b) Child prostitution means the use of a child in sexual activities for remuneration or any other form of consideration;

(c) Child pornography means any representation, by whatever means, of a child engaged in real or simulated explicit sexual activities or any representation of the sexual parts of a child for primarily sexual purposes.

Article 3

1. Each State Party shall ensure that, as a minimum, the following acts and activities are fully covered under its criminal or penal law, whether such offences are committed domestically or transnationally or on an individual or organized basis:

(a) In the context of sale of children as defined in article 2:

(i) Offering, delivering or accepting, by whatever means, a child for the purpose of:

    a. Sexual exploitation of the child;
    b. Transfer of organs of the child for profit;
    c. Engagement of the child in forced labour;

(ii) Improperly inducing consent, as an intermediary, for the adoption of a child in violation of applicable international legal instruments on adoption;

(b) Offering, obtaining, procuring or providing a child for child prostitution, as defined in article 2;

(c) Producing, distributing, disseminating, importing, exporting, offering, selling or possessing for the above purposes child pornography as defined in article 2.

2. Subject to the provisions of the national law of a State Party, the same shall apply to an attempt to commit any of the said acts and to complicity or participation in any of the said acts.

3. Each State Party shall make such offences punishable by appropriate penalties that take into account their grave nature.

4. Subject to the provisions of its national law, each State Party shall take measures, where appropriate, to establish the liability of legal persons for offences established in paragraph 1 of the present article. Subject to the legal principles of the State Party, such liability of legal persons may be criminal, civil or administrative.

5. States Parties shall take all appropriate legal and administrative measures to ensure that all persons involved in the adoption of a child act in conformity with applicable international legal instruments.

Article 4

1. Each State Party shall take such measures as may be necessary to establish its jurisdiction over the offences referred to in article 3, paragraph 1, when the offences are committed in its territory or on board a ship or aircraft registered in that State.

2. Each State Party may take such measures as may be necessary to establish its jurisdiction over the offences referred to in article 3, paragraph 1, in the following cases:

(a) When the alleged offender is a national of that State or a person who has his habitual residence in its territory;
(b) When the victim is a national of that State.

3. Each State Party shall also take such measures as may be necessary to establish its jurisdiction over the aforementioned offences when the alleged offender is present in its territory and it does not extradite him or her to another State Party on the ground that the offence has been committed by one of its nationals.

4. The present Protocol does not exclude any criminal jurisdiction exercised in accordance with internal law.

Article 5

1. The offences referred to in article 3, paragraph 1, shall be deemed to be included as

extraditable offences in any extradition treaty existing between States Parties and shall be included as extraditable offences in every extradition treaty subsequently concluded between them, in accordance with the conditions set forth in such treaties.

2. If a State Party that makes extradition conditional on the existence of a treaty receives a request for extradition from another State Party with which it has no extradition treaty, it may consider the present Protocol to be a legal basis for extradition in respect of such offences. Extradition shall be subject to the conditions provided by the law of the requested State.

3. States Parties that do not make extradition conditional on the existence of a treaty shall recognize such offences as extraditable offences between themselves subject to the conditions provided by the law of the requested State.

4. Such offences shall be treated, for the purpose of extradition between States Parties, as if they had been committed not only in the place in which they occurred but also in the territories of the States required to establish their jurisdiction in accordance with article 4.

5. If an extradition request is made with respect to an offence described in article 3, paragraph 1, and the requested State Party does not or will not extradite on the basis of the nationality of the offender, that State shall take suitable measures to submit the case to its competent authorities for the purpose of prosecution.

Article 6

1. States Parties shall afford one another the greatest measure of assistance in connection with investigations or criminal or extradition proceedings brought in respect of the offences set forth in article 3, paragraph 1, including assistance in obtaining evidence at their disposal necessary for the proceedings.

2. States Parties shall carry out their obligations under paragraph 1 of the present article in conformity with any treaties or other arrangements on mutual legal assistance that may exist between them. In the absence of such treaties or arrangements, States Parties shall afford one another assistance in accordance with their domestic law.

Article 7

States Parties shall, subject to the provisions of their national law:

(a) Take measures to provide for the seizure and confiscation, as appropriate, of:

(i) Goods, such as materials, assets and other instrumentalities used to commit or facilitate offences under the present protocol;
(ii) Proceeds derived from such offences;

(b) Execute requests from another State Party for seizure or confiscation of goods or proceeds referred to in subparagraph (a) (i) and (ii);
(c) Take measures aimed at closing, on a temporary or definitive basis, premises used to commit such offences.

Article 8

1. States Parties shall adopt appropriate measures to protect the rights and interests of child victims of the practices prohibited under the present Protocol at all stages of the criminal justice process, in particular by:

(a) Recognizing the vulnerability of child victims and adapting procedures to recognize their special needs, including their special needs as witnesses;

(b) Informing child victims of their rights, their role and the scope, timing and progress of the proceedings and of the disposition of their cases;

(c) Allowing the views, needs and concerns of child victims to be presented and considered in proceedings where their personal interests are affected, in a manner consistent with the procedural rules of national law;

(d) Providing appropriate support services to child victims throughout the legal process;

(e) Protecting, as appropriate, the privacy and identity of child victims and taking measures in accordance with national law to avoid the inappropriate dissemination of information that could lead to the identification of child victims;

(f) Providing, in appropriate cases, for the safety of child victims, as well as that of their families and witnesses on their behalf, from intimidation and retaliation;

(g) Avoiding unnecessary delay in the disposition of cases and the execution of orders or decrees granting compensation to child victims.

2. States Parties shall ensure that uncertainty as to the actual age of the victim shall not prevent the initiation of criminal investigations, including investigations aimed at establishing the age of the victim.

3. States Parties shall ensure that, in the treatment by the criminal justice system of children who are victims of the offences described in the present Protocol, the best interest of the child shall be a primary consideration.

4. States Parties shall take measures to ensure appropriate training, in particular legal and psychological training, for the persons who work with victims of the offences prohibited under the present Protocol.

5. States Parties shall, in appropriate cases, adopt measures in order to protect the safety and integrity of those persons and/or organizations involved in the prevention and/or protection and rehabilitation of victims of such offences.

6. Nothing in the present article shall be construed to be prejudicial to or inconsistent with the rights of the accused to a fair and impartial trial.

Article 9

1. States Parties shall adopt or strengthen, implement and disseminate laws, administrative measures, social policies and programmes to prevent the offences referred to in the present Protocol. Particular attention shall be given to protect children who are especially vulnerable to such practices.

2. States Parties shall promote awareness in the public at large, including children, through information by all appropriate means, education and training, about the preventive measures and harmful effects of the offences referred to in the present Protocol. In fulfilling their obligations under this article, States Parties shall encourage the participation of the community and, in particular, children and child victims, in such information and

education and training programmes, including at the international level.

3. States Parties shall take all feasible measures with the aim of ensuring all appropriate assistance to victims of such offences, including their full social reintegration and their full physical and psychological recovery.

4. States Parties shall ensure that all child victims of the offences described in the present Protocol have access to adequate procedures to seek, without discrimination, compensation for damages from those legally responsible.

5. States Parties shall take appropriate measures aimed at effectively prohibiting the production and dissemination of material advertising the offences described in the present Protocol.

Article 10

1. States Parties shall take all necessary steps to strengthen international cooperation by multilateral, regional and bilateral arrangements for the prevention, detection, investigation, prosecution and punishment of those responsible for acts involving the sale of children, child prostitution, child pornography and child sex tourism. States Parties shall also promote international cooperation and coordination between their authorities, national and international non-governmental organizations and international organizations.

2. States Parties shall promote international cooperation to assist child victims in their physical and psychological recovery, social reintegration and repatriation.

3. States Parties shall promote the strengthening of international cooperation in order to address the root causes, such as poverty and underdevelopment, contributing to the vulnerability of children to the sale of children, child prostitution, child pornography and child sex tourism.

4. States Parties in a position to do so shall provide financial, technical or other assistance through existing multilateral, regional, bilateral or other programmes.

Article 11

Nothing in the present Protocol shall affect any provisions that are more conducive to the realization of the rights of the child and that may be contained in:
(a) The law of a State Party;
(b) International law in force for that State.

Article 12

1. Each State Party shall, within two years following the entry into force of the present Protocol for that State Party, submit a report to the Committee on the Rights of the Child providing comprehensive information on the measures it has taken to implement the provisions of the Protocol.

2. Following the submission of the comprehensive report, each State Party shall include in the reports they submit to the Committee on the Rights of the Child, in accordance with article 44 of the Convention, any further information with respect to the implementation of the present Protocol. Other States Parties to the Protocol shall submit a report every five years.

3. The Committee on the Rights of the Child may request from States Parties further information relevant to the implementation of the present Protocol.

Article 13

1. The present Protocol is open for signature by any State that is a party to the Convention or has signed it.

2. The present Protocol is subject to ratification and is open to accession by any State that is a party to the Convention or has signed it. Instruments of ratification or accession shall be deposited with the Secretary- General of the United Nations.

Article 14

1. The present Protocol shall enter into force three months after the deposit of the tenth instrument of ratification or accession.

2. For each State ratifying the present Protocol or acceding to it after its entry into force, the Protocol shall enter into force one month after the date of the deposit of its own instrument of ratification or accession.

Article 15

1. Any State Party may denounce the present Protocol at any time by written notification to the Secretary- General of the United Nations, who shall thereafter inform the other States Parties to the Convention and all States that have signed the Convention. The denunciation shall take effect one year after the date of receipt of the notification by the Secretary-General.

2. Such a denunciation shall not have the effect of releasing the State Party from its obligations under the present Protocol in regard to any offence that occurs prior to the date on which the denunciation becomes effective. Nor shall such a denunciation prejudice in any way the continued consideration of any matter that is already under consideration by the Committee on the Rights of the Child prior to the date on which the denunciation becomes effective.

Article 16

1. Any State Party may propose an amendment and file it with the Secretary-General of the United Nations. The Secretary-General shall thereupon communicate the proposed amendment to States Parties with a request that they indicate whether they favour a conference of States Parties for the purpose of considering and voting upon the proposals. In the event that, within four months from the date of such communication, at least one third of the States Parties favour such a conference, the Secretary-General shall convene the conference under the auspices of the United Nations. Any amendment adopted by a majority of States Parties present and voting at the conference shall be submitted to the General Assembly of the United Nations for approval.

2. An amendment adopted in accordance with paragraph 1 of the present article shall enter into force when it has been approved by the General Assembly and accepted by a two-thirds majority of States Parties.

3. When an amendment enters into force, it shall be binding on those States Parties that have accepted it, other States Parties still being bound by

the provisions of the present Protocol and any earlier amendments they have accepted.

Article 17

1. The present Protocol, of which the Arabic, Chinese, English, French, Russian and Spanish texts are equally authentic, shall be deposited in the archives of the United Nations.

2. The Secretary-General of the United Nations shall transmit certified copies of the present Protocol to all States Parties to the Convention and all States that have signed the Convention.

4. Protocol To Prevent, Suppress And Punish Trafficking In Persons, Especially Women And Children, Supplementing The United Nations Convention Against Transnational Organized Crime

Preamble

The States Parties to this Protocol,

Declaring that effective action to prevent and combat trafficking in persons, especially women and children, requires a comprehensive international approach in the countries of origin, transit and destination that includes measures to prevent such trafficking, to punish the traffickers and to protect the victims of such trafficking, including by protecting their internationally recognized human rights,

Taking into account the fact that, despite the existence of a variety of international instruments the exploitation of persons, especially women and children, there is no universal instrument that addresses all aspects of trafficking in persons, Concerned that, in the absence of such an instrument, persons who are vulnerable to trafficking will not be sufficiently protected,

Recalling General Assembly resolution 53/111 of 9 December 1998, in which the Assembly decided to establish an open-ended intergovernmental ad hoc committee for the purpose of elaborating a comprehensive international convention against transnational organized crime and of discussing the elaboration of, inter alia, an international instrument addressing trafficking in women and children,

Convinced that supplementing the United Nations Convention against Transnational Organized Crime with an international instrument for the prevention, suppression and punishment of trafficking in persons, especially women and children, will be useful in preventing and combating that crime,

Have agreed as follows:

I. GENERAL PROVISIONS

Article 1
Relation with the United Nations Convention
against Transnational Organized Crime

1. This Protocol supplements the United Nations Convention against Transnational Organized Crime. It shall be interpreted together with the Convention.

2. The provisions of the Convention shall apply, mutates mutandis, to this Protocol unless otherwise provided herein.

3. The offences established in accordance with article 5 of this Protocol shall be regarded as offences established in accordance with the Convention.

Article 2
Statement of purpose

The purposes of this Protocol are:

(a) To prevent and combat trafficking in persons, paying particular attention to women and children;

(b) To protect and assist the victims of such trafficking, with full respect for their human rights; and

(c) To promote cooperation among States Parties in order to meet those objectives.

Article 3
Use of terms

For the purposes of this Protocol:

(a) "Trafficking in persons" shall mean the recruitment, transportation, transfer, harbouring or receipt of persons, by means of the threat or use of force or other forms of coercion, of abduction, of fraud, of deception, of the abuse of power or of a position of vulnerability or of the giving or receiving of payments or benefits to achieve the consent of a person having control over another person, for the purpose of exploitation. Exploitation shall include, at a minimum, the exploitation of the prostitution of others or other forms of sexual exploitation, forced labour or services, slavery or practices similar to slavery, servitude or the removal of organs;

(b) The consent of a victim of trafficking in persons to the intended exploitation set forth in subparagraph (a) of this article shall be irrelevant where any of the means set forth in subparagraph (a) have been used;

(c) The recruitment, transportation, transfer, harbouring or receipt of a child for the purpose of exploitation shall be considered "trafficking in persons" even if this does not involve any of the means set forth in subparagraph (a) of this article;

(d) "Child" shall mean any person under eighteen years of age.

Article 4
Scope of application

This Protocol shall apply, except as otherwise stated herein, to the prevention, investigation and prosecution of the offences established in accordance with article 5 of this Protocol, where those offences are transnational in nature and involve an organized criminal group, as well as to the protection of victims of such offences.

Article 5
Criminalization

1. Each State Party shall adopt such legislative and other measures as may be necessary to establish as criminal offences the conduct set forth in article 3 of this Protocol, when committed intentionally.

2. Each State Party shall also adopt such legislative and other measures as may be necessary to establish as criminal offences:

(a) Subject to the basic concepts of its legal system, attempting to commit an offence established in accordance with paragraph 1 of this article;

(b) Participating as an accomplice in an offence established in accordance with paragraph 1 of this article; and

(c) Organizing or directing other persons to commit an offence established in accordance with paragraph 1 of this article.

II. PROTECTION OF VICTIMS OF TRAFFICKING IN PERSONS

Article 6
Assistance to and protection of victims of
trafficking in persons

1. In appropriate cases and to the extent possible under its domestic law, each State Party shall protect the privacy and identity of victims of trafficking in persons, including, inter alia, by making legal proceedings relating to such trafficking confidential.

2. Each State Party shall ensure that its domestic legal or administrative system contains measures that provide to victims of trafficking in persons, in appropriate cases:

(a) Information on relevant court and administrative proceedings;
(b) Assistance to enable their views and concerns to be presented and considered at appropriate stages of criminal proceedings against offenders, in a manner not prejudicial to the rights of the defence.

3. Each State Party shall consider implementing measures to provide for the physical, psychological and social recovery of victims of trafficking in persons, including, in appropriate cases, in cooperation with non-governmental organizations, other relevant organizations and other elements of civil society, and, in particular, the provision of:

(a) Appropriate housing;

(b) Counselling and information, in particular as regards their legal rights, in a language that the victims of trafficking in persons can understand;

(c) Medical, psychological and material assistance; and

(d) Employment, educational and training opportunities.

4. Each State Party shall take into account, in applying the provisions of this article, the age, gender and special needs of victims of trafficking in persons, in particular the special needs of children, including appropriate housing, education and care.

5. Each State Party shall endeavour to provide for the physical safety of victims of trafficking in persons while they are within its territory.

6. Each State Party shall ensure that its domestic legal system contains measures that offer victims of trafficking in persons the possibility of obtaining compensation for damage suffered.

Article 7
Status of victims of trafficking in persons
in receiving States

1. In addition to taking measures pursuant to article 6 of this Protocol, each State Party shall consider adopting legislative or other appropriate measures that permit victims of trafficking in persons to remain in its territory, temporarily or permanently, in appropriate cases.

2. In implementing the provision contained in paragraph 1 of this article, each State Party shall give appropriate consideration to humanitarian and compassionate factors.

Article 8
Repatriation of victims of trafficking in persons

1. The State Party of which a victim of trafficking in persons is a national or in which the person had the right of permanent residence at the time of entry into the territory of the receiving State Party shall facilitate and accept, with due regard for the safety of that person, the return of that person without undue or unreasonable delay.

2. When a State Party returns a victim of trafficking in persons to a State Party of which that person is a national or in which he or she had, at the time of entry into the territory of the receiving State Party, the right of permanent residence, such return shall be with due regard for the safety of that person and for the status of any legal proceedings related to the fact that the person is a victim of trafficking and shall preferably be voluntary.

3. At the request of a receiving State Party, a requested State Party shall, without undue or unreasonable delay, verify whether a person who is a victim of trafficking in persons is its national or had the right of permanent residence in its territory at the time of entry into the territory of the receiving State Party.

4. In order to facilitate the return of a victim of trafficking in persons who is without proper documentation, the State Party of which that person is a national or in which he or she had the right of permanent residence at the time of entry into the territory of the receiving State Party shall agree to issue, at the request of the receiving State Party, such travel documents or other authorization as may be necessary to enable the person to travel to and re-enter its territory.

5. This article shall be without prejudice to any right afforded to victims of trafficking in persons by any domestic law of the receiving State Party.

6. This article shall be without prejudice to any applicable bilateral or multilateral agreement or arrangement that governs, in whole or in part, the return of victims of trafficking in persons.

III. PREVENTION, COOPERATION AND OTHER MEASURES

Article 9
Prevention of trafficking in persons

1. States Parties shall establish comprehensive policies, programmes and other measures:

(a) To prevent and combat trafficking in persons; and

(b) To protect victims of trafficking in persons, especially women and children, from revictimization.

2. States Parties shall endeavour to undertake measures such as research, information and mass media campaigns and social and economic initiatives to prevent and combat trafficking in persons.

3. Policies, programmes and other measures established in accordance with this article shall, as appropriate, include cooperation with non-governmental organizations, other relevant organizations and other elements of civil society.

4. States Parties shall take or strengthen measures, including through bilateral or multilateral cooperation, to alleviate the factors that make persons, especially women and children, vulnerable to trafficking, such as poverty, underdevelopment and lack of equal opportunity.

5. States Parties shall adopt or strengthen legislative or other measures, such as educational, social or cultural measures, including through bilateral and multilateral cooperation, to discourage the demand that fosters all forms of exploitation of persons, especially women and children, that leads to trafficking.

Article 10
Information exchange and training

1. Law enforcement, immigration or other relevant authorities of States Parties shall, as appropriate, cooperate with one another by exchanging information, in accordance with their domestic law, to enable them to determine:

(a) Whether individuals crossing or attempting to cross an international border with travel documents belonging to other persons or without travel documents are perpetrators or victims of trafficking in persons;
(b) The types of travel document that individuals have used or attempted to use to cross an international border for the purpose of trafficking in persons; and
(c) The means and methods used by organized criminal groups for the purpose of trafficking in persons, including the recruitment and transportation of victims, routes and links between and among individuals and groups engaged in such trafficking, and possible measures for detecting them.

2. States Parties shall provide or strengthen training for law enforcement, immigration and other relevant officials in the prevention of trafficking in persons. The training should focus on methods used in preventing such trafficking, prosecuting the

traffickers and protecting the rights of the victims, including protecting the victims from the traffickers. The training should also take into account the need to consider human rights and child- and gender-sensitive issues and it should encourage cooperation with non-governmental organizations, other relevant organizations and other elements of civil society.

3. A State Party that receives information shall comply with any request by the State Party that transmitted the information that places restrictions on its use.

Article 11
Border measures

1. Without prejudice to international commitments in relation to the free movement of people, States Parties shall strengthen, to the extent possible, such border controls as may be necessary to prevent and detect trafficking in persons.

2. Each State Party shall adopt legislative or other appropriate measures to prevent, to the extent possible, means of transport operated by commercial carriers from being used in the commission of offences established in accordance with article 5 of this Protocol.

3. Where appropriate, and without prejudice to applicable international conventions, such measures shall include establishing the obligation of commercial carriers, including any transportation company or the owner or operator of any means of transport, to ascertain that all passengers are in possession of the travel documents required for entry into the receiving State.

4. Each State Party shall take the necessary measures, in accordance with its domestic law, to

provide for sanctions in cases of violation of the obligation set forth in paragraph 3 of this article.

5. Each State Party shall consider taking measures that permit, in accordance with its domestic law, the denial of entry or revocation of visas of persons implicated in the commission of offences established in accordance with this Protocol.

6. Without prejudice to article 27 of the Convention, States Parties shall consider strengthening cooperation among border control agencies by, inter alia, establishing and maintaining direct channels of communication.

Article 12
Security and control of documents

Each State Party shall take such measures as may be necessary, within available means:

(a) To ensure that travel or identity documents issued by it are of such quality that they cannot easily be misused and cannot readily be falsified or unlawfully altered, replicated or issued; and

(b) To ensure the integrity and security of travel or identity documents issued by or on behalf of the State Party and to prevent their unlawful creation, issuance and use.

Article 13
Legitimacy and validity of documents

At the request of another State Party, a State Party shall, in accordance with its domestic law, verify within a reasonable time the legitimacy and validity of travel or identity documents issued or purported to have been issued in its name and suspected of being used for trafficking in persons.

IV. FINAL PROVISIONS

Article 14
Saving clause

1. Nothing in this Protocol shall a effect the rights, obligations and responsibilities of States and individuals under international law, including international humanitarian law and international human rights law and, in particular, where applicable, the 1951 Convention and the 1967 Protocol relating to the Status of Refugees and the principle of non-refoulement as contained therein.

2. The measures set forth in this Protocol shall be interpreted and applied in a way that is not discriminatory to persons on the ground that they are victims of trafficking in persons. The interpretation and application of those measures shall be consistent with internationally recognized principles of non-discrimination.

Article 15
Settlement of disputes

1. States Parties shall endeavour to settle disputes concerning the interpretation or application of this Protocol through negotiation.

2. Any dispute between two or more States Parties concerning the interpretation or application of this Protocol that cannot be settled through negotiation within a reasonable time shall, at the request of one of those States Parties, be submitted to arbitration. If, six months after the date of the request for arbitration, those States Parties are unable to agree on the organization of the arbitration, any one of those States Parties may refer the dispute to the International Court of Justice by request in accordance with the Statute of the Court.

3. Each State Party may, at the time of signature, ratification, acceptance or approval of or accession to this Protocol, declare that it does not consider itself bound by paragraph 2 of this article. The other States Parties shall not be bound by paragraph 2 of this article with respect to any State Party that has made such a reservation.

4. Any State Party that has made a reservation in accordance with paragraph 3 of this article may at any time withdraw that reservation by notification to the Secretary-General of the United Nations.

Article 16
Signature, ratification, acceptance,
approval and accession

1. This Protocol shall be open to all States for signature from 12 to 15 December 2000 in Palermo, Italy, and thereafter at United Nations Headquarters in New York until 12 December 2002.

2. This Protocol shall also be open for signature by regional economic integration organizations provided that at least one member State of such organization has signed this Protocol in accordance with paragraph 1 of this article.

3. This Protocol is subject to ratification, acceptance or approval. Instruments of ratification, acceptance or approval shall be deposited with the Secretary-General of the United Nations. A regional economic integration organization may deposit its instrument of ratification, acceptance or approval if at least one of its member States has done likewise. In that instrument of ratification, acceptance or approval, such organization shall declare the extent of its competence with respect to the matters governed by this Protocol. Such organization shall

also inform the depositary of any relevant modification in the extent of its competence.

4. This Protocol is open for accession by any State or any regional economic integration organization of which at least one member State is a Party to this Protocol. Instruments of accession shall be deposited with the Secretary-General of the United Nations. At the time of its accession, a regional economic integration organization shall declare the extent of its competence with respect to matters governed by this Protocol. Such organization shall also inform the depositary of any relevant modification in the extent of its competence.

Article 17
Entry into force

1. This Protocol shall enter into force on the ninetieth day after the date of deposit of the fortieth instrument of ratification, acceptance, approval or accession, except that it shall not enter into force before the entry into force of the Convention. For the purpose of this paragraph, any instrument deposited by a regional economic integration organization shall not be counted as additional to those deposited by member States of such organization. 2. For each State or regional economic integration organization ratifying, accepting, approving or acceding to this Protocol after the deposit of the fortieth instrument of such action, this Protocol shall enter into force on the thirtieth day after the date of deposit by such State or organization of the relevant instrument or on the date this Protocol enters into force pursuant to paragraph 1 of this article, whichever is the later.

Article 18
Amendment

1. After the expiry of five years from the entry into force of this Protocol, a State Party to the Protocol may propose an amendment and file it with the Secretary-General of the United Nations, who shall thereupon communicate the proposed amendment to the States Parties and to the Conference of the Parties to the Convention for the purpose of considering and deciding on the proposal. The States Parties to this Protocol meeting at the Conference of the Parties shall make every effort to achieve consensus on each amendment. If all efforts at consensus have been exhausted and no agreement has been reached, the amendment shall, as a last resort, require for its adoption a two-thirds majority vote of the States Parties to this Protocol present and voting at the meeting of the Conference of the Parties.

2. Regional economic integration organizations, in matters within their competence, shall exercise their right to vote under this article with a number of votes equal to the number of their member States that are Parties to this Protocol. Such organizations shall not exercise their right to vote if their member States exercise theirs and vice versa.

3. An amendment adopted in accordance with paragraph 1 of this article is subject to ratification, acceptance or approval by States Parties.

4. An amendment adopted in accordance with paragraph 1 of this article shall enter into force in respect of a State Party ninety days after the date of the deposit with the Secretary-General of the United Nations of an instrument of ratification, acceptance or approval of such amendment.

5. When an amendment enters into force, it shall be binding on those States Parties which have expressed their consent to be bound by it. Other States Parties shall still be bound by the provisions of this Protocol and any earlier amendments that they have ratified, accepted or approved.

Article 19
Denunciation

1. A State Party may denounce this Protocol by written notification to the Secretary-General of the United Nations. Such denunciation shall become effective one year after the date of receipt of the notification by the Secretary-General.
2. A regional economic integration organization shall cease to be a Party to this Protocol when all of its member States have denounced it.

Article 20
Depositary and languages

1. The Secretary-General of the United Nations is designated depositary of this Protocol.

2. The original of this Protocol, of which the Arabic, Chinese, English, French, Russian and Spanish texts are equally authentic, shall be deposited with the Secretary-General of the United Nations.

IN WITNESS WHEREOF, the undersigned plenipotentiaries, being duly authorized thereto by their respective Governments, have signed this Protocol.

5. Convention On The Suppression Of Traffic In Persons And Of The Exploitation Of The Prostitution Of Others
[Ratified by the Philippines on September 19, 1952]

Whereas prostitution and the accompanying evil of the traffic in persons for the purpose of prostitution are incompatible with the dignity and worth of the human person and endanger the welfare of the individual, the family and the community,

Whereas, with respect to the suppression of the traffic in women and children, the following international instruments are in force:

1. International Agreement of 18 May 1904 for the Suppression of the White Slave Traffic, as amended by the Protocol approved by the General Assembly of the United Nations on 3 December 1948,

2. International Convention of 4 May 1910 for the Suppression of the White Slave Traffic, as amended by the above-mentioned Protocol,

3. International Convention of 30 September 1921 for the Suppression of the Traffic in Women and Children, as amended by the Protocol approved by the General Assembly of the United Nations on 20 October 1947,

4. International Convention of 11 October 1933 for the Suppression of the Traffic in Women of Full Age, as amended by the aforesaid Protocol,

Whereas the League of Nations in 1937 prepared a draft Convention extending the scope of the above-mentioned instruments, and

Whereas developments since 1937 make feasible the conclusion of a convention consolidating the above-mentioned instruments and embodying the substance of the 1937 draft Convention as well as desirable alterations therein;

Now therefore The Contracting Pates Hereby agree as hereinafter provided:

agree as hereinafter provided:

Article I

The parties to the present Convention agree to punish any person who, to gratify the passions of another:

1. Procures, entices or leads away, for purposes of prostitution, another person, even with the consent of that person;

2. Exploits the prostitution of another person, even with the consent of that person.

Article 2

The Parties to the present Convention further agree to punish any person who:

1. Keeps or manages, or knowingly finances or takes part in the financing of a brothel;

2. Knowingly lets or rents a building or other place or any part thereof for the purpose of the prostitution of others.

Article 3

To the extent permitted by domestic law, attempts to commit any of the offences referred to in Articles 1 and 2, and acts preparatory to the commission thereof, shall also be punished.

Article 4

To the extent permitted by domestic law, international participation in the acts referred to in Articles 1 and 2 above shall also be punishable.

To the extent permitted by domestic law, acts of participation shall be treated as separate offences whenever this is necessary to prevent impunity.

Article 5

In cases where injured persons are entitled under domestic law to be parties to proceedings in respect of any of the offences referred to in the present Convention, aliens shall be so entitled upon the same terms as nationals.

Article 6

Each Party to the present Convention agrees to take all the necessary measures to repeal or abolish any existing law, regulation or administrative provision by virtue of which persons who engage in or are suspected of engaging in prostitution are subject either to special registration or to the possession of a special document or to any exceptional requirements for supervision or notification.

Article 7

Previous convictions pronounced in foreign States for offences referred to in the present Convention shall, to the extent permitted by domestic law, be taken into account for the purpose of:
1. Establishing recidivism;
2. Disqualifying the offender from the exercise of civil rights.

Article 8

The offences referred to in articles 1 and 2 of the present Convention shall be regarded as extraditable offences in any extradition treaty which has been or may hereafter be concluded between any of the Parties to this Convention,

The Parties to the present Convention, which

do not make extradition conditional on the existence of a treaty shall henceforward recognize the offences referred to in articles 1 and 2 of the present Convention as cases for extradition between themselves.

Extradition shall be granted in accordance with the law of the State to which the request is made.

Article 9

In States where the extradition of nationals is not permitted by law, nationals who have returned to their own State after the commission abroad of any of the offences referred to in articles 1 and 2 of the present Convention shall be prosecuted in and punished by the courts of their own State.

This provision shall not apply if, in a similar case between the Parties to the present Convention, the extradition of an alien cannot be granted.

Article 10

The provisions of Article 9 shall not apply when the person charged with the offence has been tried in a foreign State and, if convicted, has served his sentence or had it remitted or reduced in conformity with the laws of that foreign State.

Article 11

Nothing in the present Convention shall be interpreted as determining the attitude of a Party towards the general question of the limits of criminal jurisdiction under international law.

Article 12

The present Convention does not affect the principle that the offences to which it refers shall in each State be defined, prosecuted and punished in conformity with its domestic law.

Article 13

The Parties to the present Convention shall be bound to execute letters of request relating to offences referred to in the Convention in accordance with their domestic law and practice.

The transmission of letters of request shall be effected:

1. By direct communication between the judicial authorities; or

2. By direct communication between the Ministers of justice of the two States, or by direct communication from another competent authority of the State making the request to the Minister of Justice of the State to which the request is made; or

3. Through the diplomatic or consular representative of the State making the request in the State to which the request is made; this representative shall send the letters of request direct to the competent judicial authority or to the authority indicated by the Government of the State to which the request is made, and shall receive direct from such authority the papers constituting the execution of the letters of request.

In cases 1 and 3 a copy of the letters of request shall always be sent to the superior authority of the state to which application is made.

Unless otherwise agreed, the letters of request shall be drawn up in the language of the authority making the request, provided always that the State to which the request is made may require a translation in its own language, certified correct by the authority making the request.

Each Party to the present Convention shall notify to each of the other Parties to the Convention the method or methods of transmission mentioned above which it will recognize for the letters of request of the latter State. Until such notification is made by a State, its existing procedure in regard to letters of request shall remain in force.

Execution of letters of request shall not give rise to a claim for reimbursement of charges or expenses of any nature whatever other than expenses of experts.

Nothing in the present article shall be construed as undertaking on the part of the Parties to the present Convention to adopt in criminal matters any form or methods of proof contrary to their own domestic laws.

Article 14

Each Party to the present Convention shall establish or maintain a service charge with the co-ordination and centralization of the results of the investigation of offences referred to in the present Convention.

Such services should compile all information calculated to facilitate the prevention and punishment of the offences referred to in the present Convention and should be in close contact with the corresponding services in other States.

Article 15

To the extent permitted by domestic law and to the extent to which the authorities responsible for the services referred to in article 14 may judge desirable, they shall famish to the authorities responsible for the corresponding services in other States the following information:

1. Particulars of any offence referred to in the present Convention or any attempt to commit such offence;

2. Particulars of any search for and any prosecution, arrest, conviction, refusal of admission or expulsion of persons guilty of any of the offences referred to in the present Convention, the movements of such persons and any other useful information with regard to them.

The information so furnished shall include descriptions of the offenders, their fingerprints, photographs, methods of operation, police records and records of conviction.

Article 16

The Parties to the present Convention agree to take or to encourage, through their public and private educational, health, social, economic and other related services, measures for the prevention of prostitution and for the rehabilitation and social adjustment of the victim of prostitution and of the offences referred to in the present Convention.

Article 17

The Parties to the present Convention undertake, in connection with immigration and emigration, to adopt or maintain such measures as are required m terms of their obligations under the present Convention, to check the traffic in persons of either sex for the purpose of prostitution.

In particular they undertake:

1. To make such regulations as are necessary for the protection of immigrants or emigrants, and in particular, women and children, both at the place of arrival and departure and while en route;

2. To arrange for appropriate publicity

warning the public of the dangers of the aforesaid traffic;

3. To take appropriate measures to ensure supervision of railway stations, airports, seaports and en route, and of other public places, in order to prevent international traffic in persons for the purpose of prostitution;

4. To take appropriate measures in order that the appropriate authorities be informed of the arrival of persons who appear, prima facie, to be the principals and accomplices in or victims of such traffic.

Article 18

The Parties to the present Convention undertake, in accordance with the conditions laid down by domestic law, to have declarations taken from aliens who are prostitutes, in order to establish their identity and civil status and to discover who has caused them to leave their State. The information obtained shall be communicated to the authorities of the State of origin of the said persons with a view to their eventual repatriation.

Article 19

The Parties to the present Convention undertake, in accordance with the conditions laid down by domestic law and without prejudice to prosecution or other action for violations thereunder and so far as possible:

1. Pending the completion of arrangements for the repatriation of destitute victims of international traffic in persons for the purpose of prostitution, to make suitable provisions for their temporary care and maintenance;

2. To repatriate persons referred to in article

18 who desire to be repatriated or who may be claimed by persons exercising authority over them or whose expulsion is ordered in conformity with the law. Repatriation shall take place only after agreement is reached with the State of destination as to identity and nationality as well as to the place and date of arrival at frontiers. Each Party to the present Convention shall facilitate the passage of such persons through its territory.

Where the persons referred to in the preceding paragraph cannot themselves repay the cost of repatriation and have neither spouse, relatives nor guardian to pay for them, the cost of repatriation as far as the nearest frontier or port of embarkation or airport in the direction of the State of origin shall be borne by the State where they are in residence, and the cost of the remainder of the journey shall be borne by the State of origin.

Article 20

The Parties to the present Convention shall, if they have not already done so, take the necessary measures for the supervision of employment agencies in order to prevent persons seeking employment, in particular women and children, from being exposed to the danger of prostitution.

Article 21

The Parties to the present Convention shall communicate to the Secretary-General of the United Nations such laws and regulations as have already been promulgated in their States, and thereafter annually such laws and regulations as may be promulgated, relating to the subjects of the present Convention, as well as all measures taken by them concerning the application of the Convention. The information received shall be published periodically by the Secretary-General and sent to all Members of the United Nations and to non-member States to which the present Convention is officially communicated in accordance with Article 23.

Article 22

If any dispute shall arise between the Parties to the present Convention relating to its interpretation or application and if such dispute cannot be settled by other means, the dispute shall, at the request of any one of the Parties to the dispute, be referred to the International Court of Justice.

Article 23

The present Convention shall be open for signature on behalf of any Member of the United Nations and also on behalf of any other State to which an invitation has been addressed by the Economic and Social Council.

The present Convention shall be ratified and the instruments of ratification shall be deposited with the Secretary-General of the United Nations.

The States mentioned in the first paragraph which have not signed the Convention may accede to it.

Accession shall be effected by deposit of an instrument of accession with the Secretary-General of the United Nations. For the purpose of the present Convention the word "State" shall include all the colonies and Trust Territories of a State signatory or acceding to the Convention and all territories for which such State is internationally responsible.

Article 24

The present Convention shall come into force on the ninetieth day following the date of deposit of the second instrument of ratification or accession.

For each State ratifying or acceding to the Convention after the deposit of the second instrument of ratification or accession, the Convention shall enter into force ninety days after the deposit by such State of its instrument of ratification or accession.

Article 25

After the expiration of five years from the entry into force of the present Convention, any Party to the Convention may denounce it by a written notification addressed to the Secretary-General of the United Nations

Such denunciation shall take effect for the Party making it one year from the date upon which it is received by the Secretary-General of the United Nations.

Article 26

The Secretary-General of the United Nations shall inform all Members of the United Nations and non-member States referred to in Article 23:

(a) Of signatures, ratifications and accessions received in accordance with Article 23;
(b) Of the date on which the present Convention will come into force in accordance with Article 24;
(c) Of denunciations received in accordance with Article 25.

Article 27

Each Party to the present Convention undertakes to adopt, in accordance with its Constitution, the legislative or other measures necessary to ensure the application of the Convention.

Article 28

The provisions of the present Convention shall supersede in the relations between the Parties thereto the provisions of the international instruments referred to in Sub-paragraphs 1, 2, 3 and 4 of the second paragraph of the Preamble, each of which shall be deemed to be terminated when all the Parties thereto shall have become Parties to the present Convention.

IN FAITH WHEREOF the undersigned, being duly authorized thereto by their respective Governments, have signed the present Convention, opened for signature at Lake Success, New York, on the twenty-first day of March, one thousand nine hundred and fifty, a certified true copy of which shall be transmitted by the Secretary-General to all the Members of the United Nations and to the non-member States referred to in Article 23.

FINAL PROTOCOL

Nothing in the present Convention shall be deemed to prejudice any legislation which ensures, for the enforcement of the provisions for securing the suppression of the traffic in persons and of the exploitation of others for purposes of prostitution, stricter conditions than those provided by the present Convention.

The provisions of Articles 23 to 26 inclusive of the Convention shall apply to the present Protocol.

B. NATIONAL LAWS

Pertinent national laws and implementing rules and regulations preventing the worst forms of child labor already exist in the Philippine legal framework even before the ratification of ILO Convention NO. 182. But the issue on child labor, especially that which involves the worst forms has not been squarely addressed. With the ratification of ILO Convention No. 182 it is now imperative for the Philippines to take immediate and effective measures through development of legislation and programs of action to secure the prohibition and elimination of the worst forms of child labor.

1. Worst Form: All Forms Of Slavery Or Practices

1.1 Slavery

1.1.1 RPC ART. 272

Art. 272. Slavery. - The penalty of *prision mayor* and a fine of not exceeding Ten thousand pesos (₱10,000.00) shall be imposed upon anyone who shall purchase, sell, kidnap or detain a human being for the purpose of enslaving him.

If the crime be committed for the purpose of assigning the offended party to some immoral traffic, the penalty shall be imposed in its maximum period.

1.2 Forced Or Compulsory Labor

1.2.1 RPC ART. 272

Art. 273. Exploitation of Child Labor. - The penalty of *prision correccional* in its minimum and medium periods and a fine not exceeding Five hundred pesos (P500.00) shall be imposed upon anyone who, under the pretext of reimbursing himself of a debt incurred by an ascendant, guardian or person entrusted with the custody of a minor, shall against the latter's will, retain him in his service.

1.3   Debt Bondage

1.3.1 RPC ART. 274

Art. 274.   Services Rendered under Compulsion in Payment of Debt. - The penalty of *arresto mayor* in its maximum period to *prision correccional* in its minimum period shall be imposed upon any person who, in order to require or enforce the payment of a debt, shall compel the debtor to work for him, against his will, as household servant or farm laborer.

1.4   Sale Of Children And Trafficking In Children

1.4.1 RPC ART. 271

The provision seems to address the act of inducing children to leave home with the end view of trafficking them, but it is intended more to discourage disruption of filial relationships and undue interference with the parents' custodial rights over children. Under this provision the minor need not actually abandon his or her home as long as the inducement is actual and committed with the criminal intent to cause damage to the minor. [78]

Art. 271.   Inducing a Minor to Abandon his Home. - The penalty of *prision correccional* and a fine not exceeding Seven hundred pesos (P700.00) shall be imposed upon anyone who shall induce a minor

---

[78]   Amparita Sta. Maria, Mary Jane Zantua, Rea Chiongson, *Internal Trafficking in Children for the Worst Forms of Child Labor: Final Report*, p. 10 citing Revised Penal Code by Luis Reyes, vol. 2 p. 557, citing P. v. Apolinar (CA) 62 OG 9044. (forthcoming 2002)

to abandon the home of his parents or guardians or the persons entrusted with his custody.

If the person committing any of the crimes covered by the two preceding articles shall be the father or the mother of the minor, the penalty shall be *arresto mayor* or a fine not exceeding Three hundred pesos (P300.00), or both.

1.4.2 R.A. 7610

ARTICLE IV
CHILD TRAFFICKING

Sec. 7. Child Trafficking. - Any person who shall engage in trading and dealing with children including, but not limited to, the act of buying and selling of a child for money, or for any other consideration, or barter, shall suffer the penalty of reclusion temporal to reclusion perpetua. The penalty shall be imposed in its maximum period when the victim under twelve (12) years of age.

Sec. 8. Attempt to Commit Child Trafficking. - There is an attempt to commit child trafficking under Section 7 of this Act:

(a)   When a child travels alone to a foreign country without valid reason therefor and without clearance issued by the Department of Social Welfare and Development or written permit or justification from the child's parents or legal guardian;

(b)   When a pregnant mother executes an affidavit of consent for adoption for a consideration;

(c)   When a person, agency, establishment or child-caring institution recruits women or couples to bear a children for the purpose of child trafficking; or;

(d)   When doctor, hospital or clinic official or employee, nurse, midwife, local civil registrar or any other person simulates birth for the purpose of child trafficking; or

(e)   When a person engages in the act of finding children among low-income families, hospitals, clinics, nurseries, day-care centers, or other child-during institutions who can be offered for the purpose of child trafficking.

A penalty lower two (2) degrees than that prescribed for the consummated felony under Section 7 hereof shall be imposed upon the principals of the attempt to commit child trafficking under this Act.

1.4.3 Rules And Regulations On The Trafficking Of Children

RULES AND REGULATIONS ON
THE TRAFFICKING OF CHILDREN

Pursuant to Section 32 of Republic Act No. 7610 entitled   "AN ACT PROVIDING FOR STRONGER DETERRENCE AND SPECIAL PRO-TECTION AGAINST CHILD ABUSE, EXPLOITATION AND DISCRIMINATION, PROVIDING PENALTIES FOR ITS VIOLATION AND FOR OTHER PURPOSES, the following rules and regulations are hereby issued to implement Article IV of said Act concerning "Child Trafficking":

Sec. 1. Definition of Terms - As used in these Rules, unless the context otherwise requires-

a. "Child" shall refer to a Filipino citizen who is below eighteen (18) years of age;
b.   "Trafficking" shall refer to the act of trading or dealing with children, including but not

limited to, the buying and selling of children for money, or for any other consideration, or barter;

c. "Parent" shall refer to the natural parents, legal guardian of a child or one exercising parental authority over the child;

d. "Department" shall refer to the Department of Social Welfare and Development;

e. "Code" shall refer to Presidential Decree No. 603, "The Child and Youth Welfare and Development Code".

Sec. 2. Child Abandoned in an Institution. -- A hospital, clinic or duly licensed child-caring or placement agency shall report to the Department any child in its care whenever the parent has left the child in the said hospital clinic or child-caring or placement agency for seven (7) days without any valid reason and without providing for his care and support.

Sec. 3.   Child Left with a Private Individual.-- If a child is left by   the parent with a private individual for the same period mentioned in Section 2 above without providing for the care and support of the child, the private individual who has custody over the child shall report such fact to the Department.

Sec. 4. Presumption of Abandonment of Child. -- The following shall be presumed as intent on the part of a parent to abandon a child:

a. failure to provide for the care and support of a child for at least six (6) continuous months for no valid reason shall be presumed as intent to abandon the child unless said failure is due to reasons beyond the control of the parent or is due to financial reasons; or

b. failure to report to a law enforcement agency or to the Department that the child is missing within seventy-two (72) hours after his disappearance is discovered.

Sec. 5. Action of Department.-- Upon receipt of the report of the presence of an abandoned child in a hospital, clinic or private individual, the Department shall, if found true, immediately take custody of said child or arrange for the immediate transfer of the child to a duly accredited child-caring or placement agency. Thereafter, the Department shall file a petition for the involuntary commitment of the abandoned child in favor of a duly accredited child placement agency or private individual in accordance with the provisions of the Code. The Department shall also file the appropriate criminal complaint against the parent who abandoned the child.

Sec. 6. Prohibited Act.-- It shall be unlawful for a hospital, clinic, duly accredited child placement agency or person to deliver an abandoned child under its custody to a public institution or private individual without the written consent of the parent or person who entrusted such child to its or his care, or in the absence of the latter, of the Department.

Violation of this provision will subject the guilty party to the penalty of *arresto mayor* and payment of a fine not exceeding five hundred pesos (P500.00). This is without prejudice to the filing of a separate complaint against the guilty party under Article 210 of the Code.

Sec. 7. Criminal Liability for Abandonment of Child. -- A parent who abandons a child who is under seven (7) years of age for six (6) continuous months shall, if found guilty, be punished with *arresto mayor* and payment of a fine not exceeding five hundred pesos (P500.00).

If the child dies as a result of the abandonment, the culprit shall be punished by *prision correccional* in its medium and maximum periods.

If the child is merely exposed to danger by reason of the abandonment, the culprit shall be punished by *prision correccional* in its minimum and medium periods.

Sec. 8. Unaccompanied Foreign Travel of a Child. -- A child shall not be allowed to travel alone to a foreign country without a travel clearance therefor issued by the Department or a written permit issued under oath by both natural or adoptive parents, or the legal guardian or other person having legal custody of the child.

Sec. 9. Department Travel Clearance.-- An application for travel clearance authorizing the unaccompanied foreign travel of a child shall be filed with the Department. The application shall be in the form prescribed by the Department and shall be signed under oath by both natural or adoptive parents of the child, or the guardian or legal custodian of the child.

Sec. 10. Parental Travel Permit.-- The written permission given by the natural or adoptive parents, guardian or legal custodian for the unaccompanied foreign travel of their child shall be in the form prescribed by the Department. It shall be under oath and signed by both natural parents, the adoptive parent/s or the legal guardian or other person having legal custody of the child.

If the child will travel in the company of one of the natural parents or adoptive parents, the permit shall be signed by the parent who will stay behind in the Philippines.

Sec. 11.   Contents of Application for Department Travel Clearance and Parental Travel Permit.-- An application for a department travel clearance and a parental travel permit shall, among others, indicate the exact address of the child at the point of destination, the date of departure, the purpose and duration of the child's travel and the arrangements for the welfare of the child in the country of destination.

Sec. 12. Supporting Documents of Application for Department Travel Clearance and Parental Travel Permit.-- An application for the issuance of a Department travel clearance and a parental travel permit shall be accompanied by certified true copies of the following documents:

a.   the passport or other travel document of the child, including the visa or other appropriate documentation;

b.   the child's birth certificate and marriage certificate of the natural parents or, if the same are not available, other proof of the child's age and filiation, or the adoption decree, guardianship or custody papers of the adoptive parent, guardian or person having legal custody of the child; and

c.   proof that the child will not become a public charge in the country of destination.

Sec. 13.   Department Action on a Parental Travel Permit.-- A copy of the parental travel permit shall be filed with the Department at least seven (7) working days before the scheduled departure of the child.

If the Department, after investigation, finds that the foreign travel is inimical to the interest of the child, it shall request the Bureau of Immigration to place the child in its hold-departure list and shall notify the parent of the child of said action.

Sec. 14. Holding of Departure of Child.-- An unaccompanied child shall not be allowed by the Bureau of Immigration personnel at the port of embarkation to depart for a foreign destination except upon presentation of the Department travel clearance or parental travel permit, as the case may be, duly stamped having been received by the Department.

The authorized representative of the Department of the port of embarkation shall provide the immigration personnel thereat with such assistance as may be necessary.

Sec. 15. Attempt to Commit Child Trafficking.-- The following shall be liable for the offense of attempt to commit child trafficking as defined and penalized under Section 8 of Republic Act No. 7610:

a. The parent or other person who is responsible for the travel arrangements of the unaccompanied child;

b. The pregnant mother who executes an affidavit consenting to the adoption of her unborn child for a consideration;

c. The head of an agency, establishment, child-caring institution or person who recruits women to bear children or couples to procreate;

d. The physician, surgeon, public officer or other person who, in violation of his profession or office, cooperates in the simulation of the birth for the purpose of trafficking;

e. The person, whether natural or juridical, who locates children among low-income families, hospitals, clinics, nurseries, day care centers, or other child-caring institutions for the purpose of offering said children for placement or adoption.

Sec. 16. Presumption of Child Trafficking. -- There shall be presumption of child trafficking if a person, whether natural or juridical, has under his custody two or more children without any legal basis or without being licensed to act as a foster parent or a child placement agency.

Sec. 17. Criminal Liability. -- If any of the offenses described herein is committed by a juridical person, the penalty shall be imposed upon the manager, administrator, representative, director, agent, or employee who committed the violation or who caused, directed, cooperated or participated in said violation.

Sec. 18. Effectivity. -- These Rules shall take effect upon approval by the Secretary of Justice and fifteen (15) days after its publication in two (2) newspapers of general circulation.

Done in the City of Manila this 24th day of January 1994.

FRANKLIN M. DRILON
Secretary of Justice

CONFORME:
CORAZON ALMA G. DE LEON
Secretary of Social Welfare and Development

1.5 Children In Situations Of Armed Conflict

1.5.1 R.A. 7610

ARTICLE X
CHILDREN IN SITUATIONS OF ARMED CONFLICT

Sec. 22.   Children as Zones of Peace. - Children are hereby declared as Zones of Peace. It shall be the responsibility of the State and all other sectors concerned to resolve armed conflicts in order to promote the goal of children as zones of peace. To attain this objective, the following policies shall be observed.

(a)   Children shall not be the object of attack and shall be entitled to special respect. They shall be protected from any form of threat, assault, torture or other cruel, inhumane or degrading treatment;

(b)   Children shall not be recruited to become members of the Armed Forces of the Philippines of its civilian units or other armed groups, nor be allowed to take part in the fighting, or used as guides, couriers, or spies;

(c)   Delivery of basic social services such as education, primary health and emergency relief services shall be kept unhampered;

(d)   The safety and protection of those who provide services including those involved in fact-finding missions from both government and non-government institutions shall be ensured. They shall not be subjected to undue harassment in the performance of their work;

(e)   Public infrastructure such as schools, hospitals and rural health units shall not be utilized for military purposes such as command posts, barracks, detachments, and supply depots; and

(f)   All appropriate steps shall be taken to facilitate the reunion of families temporarily separated due to armed conflict.

Sec. 23.   Evacuation of Children During Armed Conflict. - Children shall be given priority during evacuation as a result of armed conflict. Existing community organizations shall be tapped to look after the safety and well-being of children during evacuation operations. Measures shall be taken to ensure that children evacuated are accompanied by persons responsible for their safety and well-being.

Sec. 24.   Family Life and Temporary Shelter. - Whenever possible, members of the same family shall be housed in the same premises and given separate accommodation from other evacuees and provided with facilities to lead a normal family life. In places of temporary shelter, expectant and nursing mothers and children shall be given additional food in proportion to their physiological needs. Whenever feasible, children shall be given opportunities for physical exercise, sports and outdoor games.

Sec. 25.   Rights of Children Arrested for Reasons Related to Armed Conflict. - Any child who has been arrested for reasons related to armed conflict, either as combatant, courier, guide or spy is entitled to the following units;

(a)   Separate detention from adults except where families are accommodated as family units;
(b)   Immediate free legal assistance;
(c)   Immediate notice of such arrest to the parents or guardians of the child; and
(d)   Release of the child on recognizance within twenty-four (24) hours to the custody of the Department of Social Welfare and Development or

any responsible member of the community as determined by the court.

If after hearing the evidence in the proper proceedings the court should find that the aforesaid child committed the acts charged against him, the court shall determine the imposable penalty, including any civil liability chargeable against him. However, instead of pronouncing judgment of conviction, the court shall suspend all further proceedings and shall commit such child to the custody or care of the Department of Social Welfare and Development or to any training institution operated by the Government, or duly-licensed agencies or any other responsible person, until he has had reached eighteen (18) years of age or, for a shorter period as the court may deem proper, after considering the reports and recommendations of the Department of Social Welfare and Development or the agency or responsible individual under whose care he has been committed.

The aforesaid child shall subject to visitation and supervision Development or any duly-licensed agency such other officer as the court may designate subject to such conditions as it may prescribe.

The aforesaid child whose sentence is suspended can appeal from the order of the court in the same manner as appeals in criminal cases.
The aforesaid child whose sentence is suspended can appeal from the order of the court in the same manner as appeals in criminal cases.

Sec. 26.   Monitoring and Reporting of Children in Situations of Armed Conflict. - The chairman of the barangay affected by the armed conflict shall submit the names of children residing in said barangay to the municipal social welfare and development officer within twenty-four (24) hours from the occurrence of the armed conflict.

1.5.2 Rules And Regulation On Children In Situations Of Armed Conflict

Republika ng Pilipinas
KAGAWARAN NG KATARUNGAN
Department of Justice
Manila
RULES AND REGULATIONS ON
CHILDREN IN SITUATIONS OF ARMED CONFLICT

Pursuant to Section 32 of Republic Act No. 7610 entitled "AN ACT PRO VIDING FOR STRONGER DETERRENCE AND SPECIAL PROTECTION AGAINST CHILD ABUSE, EXPLOITATION AND DISCRIMINATION, PRO VIDING PENALTIES FOR ITS VIOLATION AND FOR OTHER PURPOSES," the following rules and regulations are hereby issued to implement Article X of said Act concerning "Children In Situations Of Armed Conflict";

Sec. 1. Definition of Terms - As used in these Rules, unless the context otherwise requires -

a. "armed conflict" refers to any conflict between government forces and organized groups which involves the actual use of armed force and which disrupts normal social, economic, political and cultural activi ties in a specific geographical area;

b. "government forces" refers to the Armed Forces of the Philippines, the Philippine National Police and other armed groups supporting the go vernment forces

c. "child" refers to one who is below eighteen (18) years of age;

d. "social worker" refers to a social welfare and development officer of a local government unit;

e. "non-government worker" refers to a member of a duly licensed private group or entity that has been accredited by the appropriate government agency concerned to perform primary health and emergency relief ser vices. Ti: term includes doctors, nurses, dentist, trained community health workers and allied professionals such as social workers and volunteer relief workers;

f. "government worker" refers to a public officer or employee who provides health, educational, social and relief services;

g. "service worker" refers to a social worker, a government or non- government worker;

h. "Department" refers to the Department of Social Welfare and Develop ment of the national government or a duly authorized officer thereof; and

i. "Commission" refers to the Commission on Human Rights.

Sec. 2. Policy - Children shall be considered as zones of peace and shall enjoy the protection of the State against dangers arising from an armed conflict.

Sec. 3. Non-Recruitment of Children. - Children shall recruited or employed by government forces to perform or engage in necessary to and in direct connection with an armed conflict either as . guide, courier or in a similar capacity which would result in his being id as an active member of an organized group that is hostile to the government forces.

Sec. 4. Use of Public Infrastructure for Military Puroses - Hospitals, rural health units, school buildings, madaris, day care (barangay halls, places of worship and similar places shall not be utilized by government forces as a command post, detachment, supply depot or similarly facility.

Sec. 5. Delivery of Basic Services by Government - Consistent with the needs of public safety, government forces shall fad assure the delivery by government workers of goods and basic services; education, primary health and emergency relief services, to their field t areas of armed conflict.

Sec. 6. Delivery of Basic Services by Non-Government Workers - Government forces shall allow non-government workers to visitation centers to provide health, educational and social services and to relief assistance to the evacuees thereat.

Sec. 7. Free Passage of Service Workers and Flow of Goods - The government forces shall coordinate with the Peace and Order (POC) concerned and the social worker in ensuring, under normal the immediate and unimpeded flow to and from areas of armed health personnel and patients, medical supplies and equipment, foodstuffs and other basic necessities, and relief goods.

Sec. 8. Limitation of Entry Into Areas of Armed Conflict - The government forces may prevent or limit the entry of service worker the delivery of goods into an area of armed conflict if the same will interfere directly with ongoing combat operations, or will endanger the lives or safe service workers or those delivering the goods.

Any dispute arising from the restriction of the flow of goods and ser shall be resolved by the POC concerned.

If the POC upholds the temporary restriction of the flow of good services, the POC shall expedite the release of the goods or the rendition services upon the termination of combat operations, provided that in shall said temporary suspension be for a period longer than three (3) days provided further, that in no case shall the restriction lead to the starvation of those inside the combat area.

In emergency situations, the government forces shall adopt special m to allow relief goods and needed services to reach children in the comb In such a case, the government forces may, if requested, provide protection to ensure the delivery of said goods and services to the children.

Sec. 9. *Activities Prior to Armed Conflict.* - In case of a threatened or impending outbreak of an armed conflict, a social worker shall

a. identify, in consultation with government forces, the areas where serious combat action is likely to occur and the evacuation areas or centers;

b. prepare a master list of the families in the affected areas, with a separate list of children and a written assessment of their requirements for food, medicine and other basic needs;

c. recommend the activation of the local Disaster Coordinating Council; and

d. conduct disaster preparedness orientation meetings in coordination with government and non-government organizations.

The social worker shall submit a copy of the results of the activities enumerated in paragraphs a and b above to the Department.

Sec. 10. *Evacuation Priority* - Before and upon the outbreak of an armed conflict, children shall he the first to be rescued, evacuated and given assistance.

In the evacuation of children, the social worker shall, in coordination with the government forces and the local Disaster Coordinating Council and non- government organizations, place the children to be evacuated under the care of persons who shall be responsible for their transfer to an evacuation area/center; Provided, that the separation of children from their families shall be avoided and if this is not possible, the social worker shall ensure that at least one parent or relative shall accompany the child in the evacuation area/center.

Sec. 11, Monitoring and Report on Children in Situations of Armed Conflict. - Within twenty-four (24) hours from the occurrence of combat action between the government and hostile forces, the chairman of the affected barangay, or in his absence, any member of the Sangguniang Barangay, shall submit to the social worker a list of the children residing in the barangay. The list shall be used to determine the children who were evacuated and to ascertain their whereabouts.

Sec. 12. - Family Life And Temporary Shelter. - The Department shall establish the minimum standards for evacuation centers.

Whenever possible, members of the same family shall be housed in the same premises in an evacuation center or other temporary shelter; given separate accommodations from other evacuees; and provided with facilities to enable them to lead a normal family life. Children shall be given opportunities for early childhood care and dev alternative learning system, physical exercise, sports and outdoor games. They shall he given immunization and protection from endemic diseases and with nursing mothers, given food in proportion to their phys needs. When necessary, children shall be provided psycho-social intervention.

Sec. 13. Unaccompanied Children. - The social worker shall identify the children who have been separated from their parents or guardians during an evacuation. Said children shall be provided with individual and sustained care in the evacuation center to minimize stress. The name of the unaccompanied child shall be registered by the head of the evacuation center or social worker in a record book to be opened and maintained for said purpose. Whenever practicable, the child shall be photographed and an individual file shall be made containing all available information about him.

Efforts shall be made ensure the early reunion of the unaccompanied child with his parents or guardians.

Sec. 14.Return of Evacuees to Their Homes. - The government forces shall allow the evacuees to return to their homes or to be reunited with their families as soon as tactical considerations permit.

Sec. 15. Rights of Child Under the Custody of Government Forces - A child who is taken into custody by government forces in an area of armed conflict shall be informed of his constitutional rights and treated humanely. He shall not be subjected to torture or to cruet, inhuman or degrading treatment, or used in a military operation in any capacity. The government forces shall ensure the physical safety of the child under its custody; provide him with food and the necessary medical attention or treatment; and remove him from the area of armed conflict and transfer him at the earliest possible time to higher echelons of command/office for proper disposition.

The government forces shall, within twenty-four hours after the child is transferred to a military camp, inform the parents or guardians of the child and the social worker or the Department, of the presence of the child in the said camp.

Sec. 16. Transfer of Child to the Philippine National Police - In case a child is taken into custody by the Armed Forces of the Philippines, the military commander concerned shall immediately transfer custody over said child to the nearest station of the Philippine National Police, prefer ably to the Child and Youth Relations unit thereof. Whenever possible, the parents of the child shall be given previous notice of said transfer.

In the proper case, the affidavits/statements of the persons who have personal knowledge of the child's offense shall be transmitted by the military commander concerned to the Philippine National Police.

Sec. 17. Duty of Philippine National Police. - Immediately after a child is taken into custody of the Philippine National Police in an area of armed conflict or upon receipt of custody of a child from the Armed Forces of the Philippines, the police officer concerned shall -

a. arrest/detain the suspect and notify the parents or guardian of the child and the Commission, the Department or social worker of the detention;

b. refer the case of the child to the nearest public or private agency which provides free legal assistance; and

c. give the child a thorough physical and mental examination as required under Article 10 of Presidential Decree No. 603, as amended.

Sec. 18. Place of Detention of Child - The government forces shall keep the child who is taken into custody in a detention/jail facility that is separate from adults, except where the child and his family are accommodated in a family detention unit.

Whenever practicable, the child shall be provided alternative education while under detention.

Sec. 19. Visitation Rights of the Child. - The family members, relatives, friends, legal counsels of the child under custody shall be granted free access to the detention center where the child is held. Private physicians and other health personnel shall be given the same access in accordance with existing government guidelines on the matter.

Sec. 20. Referral of Case Prosecutor. - If warranted, the Philippine National Police shall forward the records of the investigation of the case of the child under custody to the prosecutor concerned for the conduct of an inquest and/or preliminary investigation to determine whether or not the child should remain under custody and correspondingly charged in court.

Sec. 21. Visitation of Child. - Upon being informed of the detention/ arrest of the child by government forces, the Department or the local representative of the Commission shall immediately visit the child to determine the observance by the government forces of the human rights of the suspect.

As used herein, the term "human rights" refers to the rights of children under the Philippine Constitution, Presidential Decree No. 603, as amended, Republic Act No. 7610, the Universal Declaration of Human Rights adopted by the United Nations General Assembly on 10 December 1948, the Declaration of the Rights of the Child, the United Nations Convention on the Rights of the Child, the International Covenant on Economic, Social and Cultural Rights and the Geneva Conventions Relating to the Protection of Victims of Non-International Conflicts (Protocol II), relevant laws and government issuances.

Sec. 22. Reports Of Violation Of Rights Of Children. - Reports of specific incidents of violations of human rights of children in situations of armed conflict shall be filed with the Department or the Commission or non- governmental organizations duly accredited by the Commission to monitor human rights violations. The Commission shall forward said reports to the general headquarters of the government forces or may file in the same directly with the office of the city/provincial prosecutor for appropriate action.

Sec. 23. Filing of Complaint Information. - If the evidence submitted in the inquest/preliminary investigation engenders a well-founded belief that a crime has been committed and the child is probably guilty thereof, the prosecutor shall file the corresponding complaint/information against the child in court.

Sec. 24. Release of Child on Recognizance. - Within twenty-four (24) hours after the filing of a criminal complaint/information against the child in court, the legal counsel of the child, or in his absence, the representative of the Department or Commission may request the appropriate Court to release the child on recognizance to the representative of the Department or Commission or to any responsible member of the community who shall be responsible for the child's appearance in court. The child who is released on recognizance may be placed with a family, in a government rehabilitation center, or in an accredited welfare agency.

Sec. 25. Suspension of Sentence. - If after hearing, the court finds that the child committed the acts charged against him, the court shall determine the imposable penalty including any civil liability chargeable against him.

However, instead of pronouncing judgment of Conviction, the court shall suspend all further proceeding and shall commit the child to the custody or care of the Department, or to any training institution operated by the Government, or duly licensed agency, or any responsible person, until he has reached eighteen years of age or for a shorter period as the court may deem proper, after considering the reports and recommendation of the Department, or the licensed agency, or responsible individual under whose care the child had been committed.

The child shall be subject to visitation and supervision by the Department or any duly licensed agency or such other officer as the court may designate, subject to such conditions as it may prescribe.

Sec. 26. Appeal. - The child whose sentence is suspended can appeal from the order of the court in the same manner as appeals in criminal cases. He shall be accorded the rights and privileges enjoyed by a Youth Offender under the provisions of Presidential Decree No. 603, as amended.

Sec. 27 Effectivity. - These Rules shall take effect upon approval by the Secretary of Justice and fifteen (15) days after its publication in two (2) newspapers of general circulation.

Done in the City of Manila this 21st day of January 1994.

(Original Signed)
(Sgd.) FRANKLIN M. DRILON
Secretary of Justice

CONFORME:
(Original Signed)
(Sgd.) CORAZON ALMA C. DE LEON
Secretary of Social Welfare and Development

2. Worst Form: Child Prostitution

2.1 R.A. 7610

ARTICLE III
CHILD PROSTITUTION AND OTHER SEXUAL ABUSE

Sec. 5. Child Prostitution and Other Sexual Abuse. - Children, whether male or female, who for money, profit, or any other consideration or due to the coercion or influence of any adult, syndicate or group, indulge in sexual intercourse or lascivious conduct, are deemed to be children exploited in prostitution and other sexual abuse.

The penalty of reclusion temporal in its medium period to reclusion perpetua shall be imposed upon the following:

(a) Those who engage in or promote, facilitate or induce child prostitution which include, but are not limited to, the following:

(1) Acting as a procurer of a child prostitute;
(2) Inducing a person to be a client of a child prostitute by means of written or oral advertisements or other similar means;
(3) Taking advantage of influence or relationship to procure a child as prostitute;
(4) Threatening or using violence towards a child to engage him as a prostitute; or
(5) Giving monetary consideration goods or other pecuniary benefit to a child with intent to engage such child in prostitution.

(b) Those who commit the act of sexual intercourse of lascivious conduct with a child exploited in prostitution or subject to other sexual abuse; Provided, That when the victims is under twelve (12) years of age, the perpetrators shall be prosecuted under Article 335, paragraph 3, for rape and Article 336 of Act No. 3815, as amended, the Revised Penal Code, for rape or lascivious conduct, as the case may be: Provided, That the penalty for lascivious conduct when the victim is under twelve (12) years of age shall reclusion temporal in its medium period; and

(c)   Those who derive profit or advantage therefrom, whether as manager or owner of the establishment where the prostitution takes place, or of the sauna, disco, bar, resort, place of entertainment or establishment serving as a cover or which engages in prostitution in addition to the activity for which the license has been issued to said establishment.

Sec. 6.Attempt To Commit Child Prostitution. - There is an attempt to commit child prostitution under Section 5, paragraph (a) hereof when any person who, not being a relative of a child, is found alone with the said child inside the room or cubicle of a house, an inn, hotel, motel, pension house, apartelle or other similar establishments, vessel, vehicle or any other hidden or secluded area under circumstances which would lead a reasonable person to believe that the child is about to be exploited in prostitution and other sexual abuse.

There is also an attempt to commit child prostitution, under paragraph (b) of Section 5 hereof when any person is receiving services from a child in a sauna parlor or bath, massage clinic, health club and other similar establishments. A penalty lower by two (2) degrees than that prescribed for the consummated felony under Section 5 hereof shall be imposed upon the principals of the attempt to commit the crime of child prostitution under this

Act, or, in the proper case, under the Revised Penal Code.

[See The Anti-Rape Law of 1997 or R.A. 8353 Amending RPC ART. 266 and Crimes Against Chastity RPC ARTS. 336-343 on pages 289-294.]

2.2   RPC ART. 201

Art. 202.   Vagrants and Prostitutes - Penalty. –

The following are *vagrants*:

1. Any person having no apparent means of subsistence, who has the physical ability to work and who neglects to apply himself or herself to some lawful calling;

2. Any person found loitering about public or semi-public buildings or places or tramping or wandering about the country or the streets without visible means of support;

3. Any idle or dissolute person who lodges in houses of ill-fame; ruffians or pimps and those who habitually associate with prostitutes;

4. Any person who, not being included in the provisions of other articles of this Code, shall be found loitering in any inhabited or uninhabited place belonging to another without any lawful or justifiable purpose;

5. Prostitutes.

For the purposes of this article, women who, for money or profit, habitually indulge in sexual intercourse or lascivious conduct, are deemed to be prostitutes.

Any person found guilty of any of the offenses covered by this article shall be punished by *arresto menor* or a fine not exceeding Two hundred pesos (₱

200.00), and in case of recidivism, by *arresto mayor* in its medium period to *prision correccional* in its minimum period or a fine ranging from Two hundred pesos (₱200.00) to Two thousand pesos (₱ 2,000.00), or both, in the discretion of the court.

2.3 Executive Order No. 56

EXECUTIVE ORDER NO. 56
AUTHORIZING THE MINISTRY OF SOCIAL
SERVICES AND DEVELOPMENT TO TAKE
PROTECTIVE CUSTODY OF CHILD PROSTITUTES
AND SEXUALLY EXPLOITED CHILDREN, AND FOR
OTHER PURPOSES

WHEREAS, for those who fall prey to prostitution and other forms of sexual exploitation due to their fragile age, immediate protection must be accorded by the government to arrest their moral decline and lead them back to the path of morality;

WHEREAS, in pursuance of its responsibility over the welfare of the youth, the Ministry of Social Services and Development must be given more powers to implement effectively the government's commitment against child prostitution and exploitation.

NOW, THEREFORE, I, CORAZON C. AQUINO, President of the Philippines, do hereby by order:

Sec. 1. Notwithstanding any provision of law to the contrary, any minor who is apprehended or taken into custody by any peace officer of by the duly authorized officers of the Ministry of Social Services and Development for engaging in prostitution or other illicit conduct punished under existing laws shall, immediately from such apprehension, be delivered by the arresting officer to the Ministry of Social Services and Development or to its duly authorized office or agency within a particular territorial jurisdiction for protective custody.

The Ministry of Social Services and Development shall be responsible for the appearance of the minor under its protective custody in court or any administrative agency whenever required.

For the purpose of this Executive Order, a minor shall refer to any person below sixteen (16) years of age.

Sec. 2. The Ministry of Social Services and Development shall provide suitable programs for the full rehabilitation of the minors under its custody which shall, among others, include the appreciation of proper moral values, psychological or psychiatric treatment, education in the probable physical ailment or disease which they may contract or the dangers of unwanted pregnancy, and appropriate training for work-skills to prepare them for a decent living.

Sec. 3. The custody of persons, other than the apprehended minor, shall be in accordance with the ordinary criminal procedure as prescribed by the Rules of Court and other laws.

Sec. 4. The Ministry of Social Services and Development shall notify the mayors of the municipalities and cities of the business establishments, clubs, or houses, used or allowed to be used for prostitution of minors, and petition for the immediate forfeiture of their business licenses and closure of their business establishments.

Sec. 5. The sum of Three Million Pesos (P3,000,000.00) is hereby appropriated out of any available funds in the National Treasury not otherwise appropriated, to defray the expenses of the Ministry of Social Services and Development in the implementation of this Executive Order. Thereafter, such sums as may be necessary for this purpose shall be included in the annual General Appropriations Act.

Sec. 6. The Ministry of Social Services and Development is hereby authorized to call upon any ministry, bureau, office, agency or instrumentality of the government for assistance in the implementation of this Executive Order.

Sec. 7. The Ministry of Social Services and Development shall, in coordination with the Ministry of Justice, promulgate the necessary rules and regulations to implement this Executive Order.

Sec. 8. All laws, orders, issuances and rules and regulations or parts thereof inconsistent with this Executive Order are hereby repealed or modified accordingly.

Sec. 9. This Executive Order shall take effect immediately.

Done in the City of Manila, this 6th day of November, in the year of Our Lord, nineteen hundred and eighty-six.

CORAZON C. AQUINO
President

JOKER P. ARROYO
Executive Secretary

[See also page 390]

3. Worst Form: Child Pornography

3.1 R.A. 7610

ARTICLE V
OBSCENE PUBLICATIONS AND INDECENT SHOWS

Sec. 9. Obscene Publications and Indecent Shows. - Any person who shall hire, employ, use, persuade, induce or coerce a child to perform in obscene exhibitions and indecent shows, whether live or in video, or model in obscene publications or pornographic materials or to sell or distribute the said materials shall suffer the penalty of prision mayor in its medium Period.

If the child used as a performer, subject or seller/distributor is below twelve (12) years of age, the penalty shall be imposed in its maximum period.

Any ascendant, guardian, or person entrusted in any capacity with the care of a child who shall cause and/or allow such child to be employed or to participate in an obscene play, scene, act, movie or show or in any other acts covered by this section shall suffer the penalty of prision mayor in its medium period.

3.2 RPC ART. 201

Art. 201. Immoral Doctrines, Obscene Publications and Exhibitions, and Indecent Shows. - The penalty of *prision mayor* or a fine ranging from Six thousand (P6,000.00) to Twelve thousand (P12,000.00) pesos, or both such imprisonment and fine, shall be imposed upon:

1. Those who shall publicly expound or proclaim doctrines openly contrary to public morals;

2.(a).   The authors of obscene literature, published with their knowledge in any form; the editors publishing such literature; and the owners/operators of the establishment selling the same;

(b).   Those who, in theaters, fairs, cinematographs or any other place, exhibit indecent or immoral plays, scenes, acts or shows, whether live or in film, which are prescribed by virtue hereof, shall include those which (1) glorify criminals or condone crimes; (2) serve no other purpose but to satisfy the market for violence, lust or pornography; (3) offend any race or religion; (4) tend to abet traffic in and use of prohibited drugs; and (5) are contrary to law, public order, morals, good customs, established policies, lawful orders, decrees and edicts;

3. Those who shall sell, give away or exhibit films, prints, engravings, sculpture or literature which are offensive to morals.

4. Worst Form: Production And Trafficking Of Drugs[79]

4.1   R.A. 6425, As Amended

R.A. 6425
DANGEROUS DRUGS LAW
(As Amended by R.A. 7659,
Death Penalty Law)

x x x

Sec.   4.   Sale, Administration, Delivery, Distribution and Transportation of Prohibited Drugs. -- The penalty of *reclusion perpetua* to death and a fine ranging from five hundred thousand pesos (P500,000.00) to ten million pesos (P10,000,000.00) shall be imposed upon any person who, unless authorized by law, shall sell, administer, deliver, give away to another, distribute, dispatch in transit or transport any prohibited drug, or shall act as broker in any of such transactions.

Notwithstanding the provisions of Section 20 of this Act to the contrary, if the victim of the offense is a minor, or should a prohibited drug involved in any offense under this Section be the proximate cause of the death of a victim thereof, the maximum penalty herein provided shall be imposed.

x x x

Sec. 15.   Sale, Administration, Dispensation, Delivery,   Transportation   and   Distribution   of Regulated Drugs. -- The penalty of *reclusion perpetua* to death and a fine ranging from five hundred thousand pesos (P500,000.00) to ten million pesos

---

[79] *See* Revised Penal Code, Art. 12(2 & 3) and Art. 13(2) on criminal responsibility of a minor and Presidential Decree No. 603 Chapter 3, Arts. 189-204 on Youth Offender.

(P10,000,000.00) shall be imposed upon any person who, unless authorized by law, shall sell, dispense, deliver, transport or distribute any regulated drug.

Notwithstanding the provisions of Section 20 of this Act to the contrary, if the victim of the offense is a minor, or should a regulated drug involved in any offense under this Section be the proximate cause of the death of a victim thereof, the maximum penalty herein provided shall be imposed.

xxx

4.2   R.A. 8364

R. A. 8369
THE FAMILY COURTS OF 1997

xxx

Sec. 5.   Jurisdiction of Family Courts. — The Family Courts shall have exclusive original jurisdiction to hear and decide the following cases:

a) Criminal cases where one or more of the accused is below eighteen (18) years of age but not less than nine (9) years of age, or where one or more of the victims is a minor at the time of the commission of the offense: Provided, That if the minor is found guilty, the court shall promulgate sentence and ascertain any civil liability which the accused may have incurred. The sentence, however, shall be suspended without need of application pursuant to Presidential Decree No. 603, otherwise known as the "Child and Youth Welfare Code; *[Underscoring supplied]*

xxx

4.3   R.A. 7610

ARTICLE VI
OTHER ACTS OF ABUSE

Sec. 10.   Other Acts of Neglect, Abuse, Cruelty or Exploitation and Other Conditions Prejudicial to the Child's Development. –

xxx

(e)   Any person who shall use, coerce, force or intimidate a street child or any other child to;

xxx

(2)   Act as conduit or middlemen in drug trafficking or pushing; or

(3)   Conduct any illegal activities, shall suffer the penalty of prision correccional in its medium period to reclusion perpetua.

xxx

The victim of the acts committed under this section shall be entrusted to the care of the department of Social Welfare and Development.

5. Other Worst Forms

5.1   RPC ART. 278

Art. 278. Exploitation of Minors. - The penalty of *prision correccional* in its minimum and medium periods and   a fine not exceeding Five hundred pesos (₱500.00) shall be imposed upon:

1. Any person who shall cause any boy or girl under sixteen years of age to perform any dangerous feat of balancing physical strength or contortion.

2. Any person who, being an acrobat, gymnast, ropewalker, diver, wild-animal tamer or circus manager or engaged in a similar calling, shall employ in exhibitions of these kinds children under sixteen years of age who are not his children or descendants.

3. Any person engaged in any of the callings enumerated in the next preceding paragraph who shall employ any descendants of his under twelve years of age in such dangerous exhibitions.

4. Any ascendant, guardian, teacher or person entrusted in any capacity with the care of a child under sixteen years of age, who shall deliver such child gratuitously to any person following any of the callings enumerated in paragraph 2 hereof, or to any habitual vagrant or beggar.

If the delivery shall have been made in consideration of any price, compensation, or promise, the penalty shall in every case be imposed in its maximum period.

In either case, the guardian or curator convicted shall also be removed from office as guardian or curator; and in the case of the parents of the child, they may be deprived, temporarily or perpetually, in the discretion of the court, of their parental authority.

5. Any person who shall induce any child under sixteen years of age to abandon the home of its ascendants, guardians, curators or teachers to follow any person engaged in any of the callings mentioned in paragraph 2 hereof, or to accompany any habitual vagrant or beggar.

5.2　R.A. 7610

ARTICLE VI
OTHER ACTS OF ABUSE
Sec. 10.　　Other Acts of Neglect, Abuse, Cruelty or Exploitation and Other Conditions Prejudicial to the Child's Development. –

xxx

(e) Any person who shall use, coerce, force or intimidate a street child or any other child to;

(1)　Beg or use begging as a means of living;

xxx

5.3　Department Order No.4

[See page 61]

IV. TERMS AND CONDITIONS OF EMPLOYMENT

A. INTERNATIONAL CONVENTIONS

Several Conventions adopted by the International Labour Organization deal with the terms and conditions of employment of children. These are: ILO Convention No. 77, Medical Examination of Young Persons (Industry); ILO Convention No. 78, Medical Examination of Young Persons (Non-Industrial Occupations); ILO Convention No. 90, Night Work of Young Persons (Industry); and ILO Convention No. 79, Night Work of Young Persons (Non-Industrial Occupations). Among these Conventions, the country only ratified ILO Conventions No. 77 and No. 90, concerning industry, which are presented below.

1. ILO Convention No. 77

CONVENTION CONCERNING MEDICAL
EXAMINATION FOR FITNESS
FOR EMPLOYMENT IN INDUSTRY
OF CHILDREN AND YOUNG PERSONS
[Ratified by the Philippines in May, 1960]

The General Conference of the International Labour Organisation,

Having been convened at Montreal by the Governing Body of the International Labour Office and having met in its Twenty-ninth Session on 19 September 1946, and

Having decided upon the adoption of certain proposals with regard to medical examination for fitness for employment in industry of children and young persons, which is included in the third item on the agenda of the Session, and

Having determined that these proposals shall take the form of an International Convention, adopts this ninth day of October of the year one thousand nine hundred and forty-six, the following Convention, which may be cited as the Medical Examination of Young Persons (Industry) Convention, 1946:

PART I. GENERAL PROVISIONS

Article 1

1. This Convention applies to children and young persons employed or working in, or in connection with, industrial undertakings, whether public or private.

2. For the purpose of this Convention, the term "industrial undertaking" includes particularly:

(a) mines, quarries, and other works for the extraction of minerals from the earth;

(b) undertakings in which articles are manufactured, altered, cleaned, repaired, ornamented, finished, adapted for sale, broken up or demolished, or in which materials are transformed, including undertakings engaged in shipbuilding or in the generation, transformation or transmission of electricity or motive power of any kind;

(c) undertakings engaged in building and civil engineering work, including constructional, repair, maintenance, alteration and demolition work; and

(d) undertakings engaged in the transport of passengers or goods by road, rail, inland waterway or air, including the handling of goods at docks, quays, wharves, warehouses or airports.

3. The competent authority shall define the line of division, which separates industry from agriculture, commerce and other non-industrial occupations.

Article 2

1. Children and young persons under eighteen years of age shall not be admitted to employment by an industrial undertaking unless they have been found fit for the work in which they are to be employed by a thorough medical examination.

2. The medical examination for fitness for employment shall be carried out by a qualified physician approved by the competent authority and shall be certified either by a medical certificate or by an endorsement on the work permit or in the workbook.

3. The document certifying fitness for employment may be issued:

(a) subject to specified conditions of employment;
(b) for a specified job or for a group of jobs or occupations involving similar health risks which have been classified as a group by the authority responsible for the enforcement of the laws and regulations concerning medical examinations for fitness for employment.

4. National laws or regulations shall specify the authority competent to issue the document certifying fitness for employment and shall define the conditions to be observed in drawing up and issuing the document.

Article 3

1. The fitness of a child or young person for the employment in which he is engaged shall be subject to medical supervision until he has attained the age of eighteen years.

2. The continued employment of a child or young person under eighteen years of age shall be subject to the repetition of medical examinations at intervals of not more than one year.

3. National laws or regulations shall -

(a) make provision for the special circumstances in which a medical re-examination shall be required in addition to the annual examination or at more frequent intervals in order to ensure effective supervision in respect of the risks involved in the occupation and of the state of health of the child or young person as shown by previous examinations; or

(b) empower the competent authority to require medical re-examinations in exceptional cases.

Article 4

1. In occupations, which involve high health risks medical examination and re-examinations for fitness for employment shall be required until at least the age of twenty-one years.

2. National laws or regulations shall either specify, or empower an appropriate authority to specify, the occupations or categories of occupations in which medical examination and re-examinations for fitness for employment shall be required until at least the age of twenty-one years.

Article 5

The medical examination required by the preceding Articles shall not involve the child or young person, or his parents, in any expense.

Article 6

1. Appropriate measures shall be taken by the competent authority for vocational guidance and physical and vocational rehabilitation of children and young persons found by medical examination to be unsuited to certain types of work or to have physical handicaps or limitations.

2. The nature and extent of such measures shall be determined by the competent authority; for this purpose co-operation shall be established between the labour, health, educational and social services concerned, and effective liaison shall be maintained between these services in order to carry out such measures.

3. National laws or regulations may provide for the issue to children and young persons whose fitness for employment is not clearly determined -

(a) of temporary work permits or medical certificates valid for a limited period at the expiration of which the young worker will be required to undergo re-examination;
(b) of permits or certificates requiring special conditions of employment.

Article 7

1. The employer shall be required to file and keep available to labour inspectors either the medical certificate for fitness for employment or the work permit or workbook showing that there are no medical objections to the employment as may be prescribed by national laws or regulations.

2. National laws or regulations shall determine the other methods of supervision to be adopted for ensuring the strict enforcement of this Convention.

Article 8

1. In the case of a Member the territory of which includes large areas where, by reason of the sparseness of the population or the stage of development of the area, the competent authority considers it impracticable to enforce the provisions of this Convention, the authority may exempt such areas from the application of the Convention either generally or with such exceptions in respect of particular undertakings or occupations as it thinks fit.

2. Each Member shall indicate in its first annual report upon the application of this Convention submitted under Article 22 of the Constitution of the International Labour Organisation any areas in respect of which it proposes to have recourse to the provisions of the present Article and no Member shall, after the date of its first annual report, have recourse to the provisions of the present Article except in respect of areas so indicated.

3. Each Member having recourse to the provisions of the present Article shall indicate in subsequent annual reports any areas in respect of which it renounces the right to have recourse to the provisions of the present Article.

Article 9

1. Any Member which, before the date of the adoption of the laws or regulations permitting the ratification of this Convention, had no laws or regulations concerning medical examination for fitness for employment in industry of children and young persons may, by a declaration accompanying its ratification, substitute an age lower than eighteen years, but in no case lower than sixteen years, for the age of eighteen years prescribed in Articles 2 and 3, and an age lower than twenty-one

years, but in no case lower than nineteen years, for the age of twenty-one years prescribed in Article 4.

2. Any Member which has made such a declaration may at any time cancel the declaration by a subsequent declaration.

3. Every Member for which a declaration made in virtue of paragraph 1 of this Article is in force shall indicate each year in its annual report upon the application of this Convention the extent to which any progress has been made with a view to the full application of the provisions of the Convention.

Article 10

Modifications in the application of the Convention to India.

Article 11

Nothing in this Convention shall affect any law, award, custom or agreement between employers and workers, which ensures more favourable conditions than those provided by this Convention.

Article 12

1. This Convention shall be binding only upon those Members of the International Labour Organisation whose ratifications have been registered with the Director-General.

2. It shall come into force twelve months after the date on which the ratifications of two Members have been registered with the Director-General.

3.   Thereafter, this Convention shall come into force for any Member twelve months after the date on which its ratification has been registered.

Article 13

1.   A Member which has ratified this Convention may denounce it after the expiration of ten years from the date on which the Convention first comes into force, by an act communicated to the Director-General of the International Labour Office for registration. Such denunciation shall not take effect until one year after the date on which it is registered.

2.   Each Member which has ratified this Convention and which does not, within the year following the expiration of the period of ten years mentioned in the preceding paragraph, exercise the right of denunciation provided for in this Article, will be bound for another period of ten years and, thereafter, may denounce this Convention at the expiration of each period of ten years under the terms provided for in this Article.

Article 14

1. The Director-General of the International Labour Office shall notify all Members of the International Labour Organisation of the registration of all ratifications and denunciations communicated to him by the Members of the Organisation.

2.   When notifying the Members of the Organisation of the registration of the second ratification communicated to him, the Director-General shall draw the attention of the Members of the Organisation to the date upon which the Convention will come into force.

Article 15

1. The Director-General of the International Labour Office shall communicate to the Secretary-General of the United Nations for registration in accordance with Article 102 of the Charter of the United Nations full particulars of all ratifications and acts of denunciation registered by him in accordance with the provisions of the preceding Articles.

Article 16

At such times as it may consider necessary the Governing Body of the International Labour Office shall present to the General Conference a report on the working of this Convention and shall examine the desirability of placing on the agenda of the Conference the question of its revision in whole or in part.

Article 17

1. Should the Conference adopt a new Convention revising this Convention in whole or in part, then, unless the new Convention otherwise provides:

(a) the ratification by a Member of the new revising Convention shall *ipso jure* involve the immediate denunciation of this Convention, notwithstanding the provisions of Article 13, above, if and when the new revising Convention shall have come into force;

(b) as from the date when the new revising Convention comes into force this Convention shall cease to be open to ratification by the Members.

2. This Convention shall in any case remain in force in its actual form and content for those

Members which have ratified it but have not ratified the revised Convention.

Article 18

The English and French versions of the text of this Convention are equally authoritative.

2.   ILO Convention No. 90

CONVENTION CONCERNING THE NIGHT WORK OF YOUNG PERSONS EMPLOYED IN INDUSTRY (REVISED 1948)
[Ratified by the Philippines in May, 1953]

The General Conference of the International Labour Organisation,

Having been convened at San Francisco by the Governing Body of the International Labour Office, and having met in its Thirty-first Session on 17 June 1948, and

Having decided upon the adoption of certain proposals with regard to the partial revision of the Night Work of Young Persons (Industry) Convention, 1919, adopted by the Conference at its First Session, which is the tenth item on the agenda of the session, and

Considering that these proposals must take the form of an international Convention,

adopts this tenth day of July of the year one thousand nine hundred and forty-eight, the following Convention, which may be cited as the Night Work of Young Persons (Industry) Convention (Revised), 1948:

PART I. GENERAL PROVISIONS

Article 1

1. For the purpose of this Convention, the term "industrial undertaking" includes particularly-

(a) mines, quarries, and other works for the extraction of minerals from the earth;

(b) undertakings in which articles are manufactured, altered, cleaned, repaired, ornamented, finished, adapted for sale, broken up or demolished, or in which materials are transformed, including undertakings engaged in shipbuilding or in the generation, transformation or transmission of electricity or motive power of any kind;

(c) undertakings engaged in building and civil engineering work, including constructional, repair, maintenance, alteration and demolition work;

(d) undertakings engaged in the transport of passengers or goods by road or rail, including the handling of goods at docks, quays, wharves, warehouses or airports.

2. The competent authority shall define the line of division which separates industry from agriculture, commerce and other non-industrial occupations.

3. National laws or regulations may exempt from the application of this Convention employment or work which is not deemed to be harmful, prejudicial, or dangerous to young persons in family undertakings in which only parents and their children or wards are employed.

Article 2

1. For the purpose of this Convention the term "night" signifies a period of at least twelve consecutive hours.

2. In the case of young persons under sixteen years of age, this period shall include the interval between ten o'clock in the evening and six o'clock in the morning.

3. In the case of young persons who have attained the age of sixteen years but are under the age of eighteen years, this period shall include an interval prescribed by the competent authority of at least seven consecutive hours falling between ten o'clock in the evening and seven o'clock in the morning; the competent authority may prescribe different intervals for different areas, industries, undertakings or branches of industries or undertakings, but shall consult the employers' and workers' organisations concerned before prescribing an interval beginning after eleven o'clock in the evening.

Article 3

1. Young persons under eighteen years of age shall not be employed or work during the night in any public or private industrial undertaking or in any branch thereof except as hereinafter provided for.

2. For purposes of apprenticeship or vocational training in specified industries or occupations which are required to be carried on continuously, the competent authority may, after consultation with the employers' and workers' organisations concerned, authorize the employment in night work of young persons who have attained the age of sixteen years but are under the age of eighteen years.

3. Young persons employed in night work in virtue of the preceding paragraph shall be granted a rest period of at least thirteen consecutive hours between two working periods.

4. Where night work in the baking industry is prohibited for all workers, the interval between nine o'clock in the evening and four o'clock in the morning may, for purposes of apprenticeship or vocational training of young persons who have attained the age of sixteen years, be substituted by the competent authority for the interval of at least seven consecutive hours falling between ten o'clock in the evening and seven o'clock in the morning prescribed by the authority in virtue of paragraph 3 of Article 2.

Article 4

1. In countries where the climate renders work by day particularly trying, the night period and barred interval may be shorter than that prescribed in the above Articles if compensatory rest is accorded during the day.

2. The provisions of Articles 2 and 3 shall not apply to the night work of young persons between the ages of sixteen and eighteen years in case of emergencies which could not have been controlled or foreseen, which are not of a periodical character, and which interfere with the normal working of the industrial undertaking.

Article 5

The prohibition of night work may be suspended by the government, for young persons between the ages of sixteen and eighteen years, when in case of serious emergency the public interest demands it.

Article 6

1.   The laws or regulations giving effect to the provisions of this Convention shall -

(a) make appropriate provision for ensuring that they are known to the persons concerned;
(b) define the persons responsible for compliance therewith;
(c) prescribe adequate penalties for any violation thereof;   (d) provide for the maintenance of a system of inspection adequate to ensure effective enforcement; and
(e) require every employer in a public or private industrial undertaking to keep a register, or to keep available official records, showing the names and dates of birth of all persons under eighteen years of age employed by him and such other pertinent information as may be required by the competent authority.

2.   The annual reports submitted by Members under article 22 of the Constitution of the International Labour Organisation shall contain full information concerning such laws and regulations and a general survey of the results of the inspections made in accordance therewith.

PART II. SPECIAL PROVISIONS FOR CERTAIN COUNTRIES

Article 7

1. Any Member which, before the date of the adoption of the laws or regulations permitting the ratification of this Convention, had laws or organizations restricting the night work of young persons in industry which provide for   an age-limit lower than   eighteen years may, by a declaration   accompanying   its   ratification, substitute an age-limit prescribed in paragraph 1 of Article 3.

2.   Any Member which has made such a declaration may at any time cancel that declaration by a subsequent declaration.

3.   Every Member for which a declaration made in virtue of paragraph 1 of this Article is in force shall indicate each year in its annual report upon the application of this Convention the extent to which any progress has been made with a view to the full application of the provisions of the Convention.

Articles 8-10

Modifications in the application of the Convention to India and Pakistan and procedure for their amendment.

PART III. FINAL PROVISIONS

Article 11

Nothing in this Convention shall affect any law, award, custom or agreement between employers and workers, which ensures more favourable conditions than those provided by this Convention.

Article 12

1.   This Convention shall be binding only upon those Members of the International Labour Organisation whose ratifications have been registered with the Director-General.

2.   It shall come into force twelve months after the date on which the ratifications of two Members have been registered with the Director-General.

3.   Thereafter, this Convention shall come into force for any Member twelve months after the date on which its ratification has been registered.

Article 13

1.   A Member which has ratified this Convention may denounce it after the expiration of ten years from the date on which the Convention first comes into force, by an act communicated to the Director-General of the International Labour Office for registration. Such denunciation shall not take effect until one year after the date on which it is registered.

2.   Each Member which has ratified this Convention and which does not, within the year following the expiration of the period of ten years mentioned in the preceding paragraph, exercise the right of denunciation provided for in this Article, will be bound for another period of ten years and, thereafter, may denounce this Convention at the expiration of each period of ten years under the terms provided for in this Article.

Article 14

1. The Director-General of the International Labour Office shall notify all Members of the International Labour Organisation of the registration of all ratifications and denunciations communicated to him by the Members of the Organisation.

2.   When notifying the Members of the Organisation of the registration of the second ratification communicated to him, the Director-General shall draw the attention of the Members of the Organisation to the date upon which the Convention will come into force.

Article 15

1. The Director-General of the International Labour Office shall communicate to the Secretary-General of the United Nations for registration in accordance with Article 102 of the Charter of the United Nations full particulars of all ratifications and acts of denunciation registered by him in accordance with the provisions of the preceding Articles.

Article 16

At such times as it may consider necessary the Governing Body of the International Labour Office shall present to the General Conference a report on the working of this Convention and shall examine the desirability of placing on the agenda of the Conference the question of its revision in whole or in part.

Article 17

1. Should the Conference adopt a new Convention revising this Convention in whole or in part, then, unless the new Convention otherwise provides:

(a) the ratification by a Member of the new revising Convention shall *ipso jure* involve the immediate denunciation of this Convention, notwithstanding the provisions of Article 13, above, if and when the new revising Convention shall have come into force;

(b) as from the date when the new revising Convention comes into force this Convention shall cease to be open to ratification by the Members.

2. This Convention shall in any case remain in force in its actual form and content for those

Members which have ratified it but have not ratified the revised Convention.

Article 18

The English and French versions of the text of this Convention are equally authoritative.

B. NATIONAL LAWS

The laws governing the terms and conditions of employment of child workers are scattered among the different statutes of the country. As already expounded in the introduction of this chapter, early laws which provided for the terms and conditions of employment of child workers have been repealed by the passage of the Labor Code. Nevertheless several provisions of the Labor Code and the Child and Youth Welfare Code remain useful for protecting children in their workplaces. Moreover, after the Labor Code's enactment in 1974, a few administrative regulations were passed in the late 1970s dealing with the hours and conditions of work of children. These are: MOLE Policy Instruction No. 23 Concerning Hours of Work, Night Work and Physical Examination of Children; and the Rules and Regulations on the Employment of Children in the Movie, Television, Radio and Entertainment Industry. These regulations, however, need to be updated considering that almost 20 years have passed since their enactment and the child labor laws have already undergone several changes since then. The rules and regulations of the latest child labor law, which is R.A. 7658 have already been passed to govern the conditions of work of children below 15 years of age in exclusive family undertakings and in the entertainment industry.

The existing laws governing the conditions of work of children, however, are not sufficient to cover all types of work situations of children. To fill-in the gaps in these laws, resort may be had on the laws dealing with the general work force. It should be impressed at this point that Art. 140 of the Labor Code, which deals with "prohibition against child discrimination", prohibits an employer from discriminating against any person in respect to terms and conditions of employment on account of his age. Therefore, in the absence of laws specific to child workers (e.g., wages, rest periods, insurance and social welfare benefits, occupational safety and health, etc.), the laws intended to protect the regular labor force should be equally imposed upon the employers of child workers. Employers should not be allowed to use the ploy of hiring children in order to escape their obligations under the beneficial provisions of the labor laws.

It should be emphasized, though, that the provisions of the Labor Code regarding terms and conditions of employment may only be invoked by a child worker if an employment relationship truly exists between the child and his/her employer. In the case of a child worker, an employer-employee relationship is deemed to exist where the selection and engagement of the child, the payment of his/her wages, the power of dismissal, and the power to control the child's conduct at work are exercised by the alleged employer. Under Philippine jurisprudence, the element of control is the most important element, such that where the employer controls or has reserved the right to control the child worker not only as to the result of the work to be done but also as to the means and methods by which the same is to be accomplished, the employer-employee relationship test is met.

With respect to special groups of child workers (e.g., children in domestic work, children in homework, and children in apprentice work), there is again a dearth of laws specifically covering their work situations. Thus, resort to the provisions of the Labor Code relating to the employment of apprentices, homeworkers and domestic workers, and also of the Civil Code with respect to the latter, may be had.

Presented in the following pages are the terms and conditions of employment applicable to child workers as contained in administrative regulations, the Labor Code and other Philippine laws.

1. Non-Discrimination

LABOR CODE

Art. 140. Prohibition against child discrimination. -- No employer shall discriminate against any person in respect to terms and conditions of employment on account of his age.

2. Employer's Reportorial Duties

CHILD AND YOUTH WELFARE CODE

Art. 108. Duty of Employer to Submit Report.- The employer shall submit to the Department of Labor a report of all children employed by him. A separate report shall be made of all such children who are found to be handicapped after medical examination. The Secretary of Labor shall refer such handicapped children to the proper government or private agencies for vocational guidance, physical and vocational rehabilitation, and placement in employment.

Art. 109. Register of Children. - Every employer in any commercial, industrial or agricultural establishment or enterprise shall keep:

(1) A register of all children employed by him, indicating the dates of their birth;
(2) A separate file for the written consent to their employment given by their parents or guardians;
(3) A separate file for their educational and medical certifications; and
(4) A separate file for special work permits issued by the Secretary of Labor in accordance with existing laws.

3. Hours Of Work, Night Work And Physical Examination Of Children

Republic of the Philippines
MINISTRY OF LABOR AND EMPLOYMENT
MANILA

POLICY INSTRUCTION NO. 23
TO   :   All Concerned
SUBJECT   :   Hours of Work of Children;
Night Work and Physical Examination of Children

Pursuant to the power vested upon the Secretary of Labor by Article 139(b) of the Labor Code as amended and in order to protect the health and welfare of the employed minor, the following regulations are hereby promulgated for the guidance of all concerned:

Sec. 1 - Hours of Work of Children; Night Work -

(a)   No child below sixteen years of age shall be employed or permitted or suffered to work in any applicable industrial undertaking:
(1)   for more than seven hours daily or forty-two hours weekly;
(2)   between six o'clock in the afternoon and six o'clock in the morning of the following day.

(b)   No child who has attained the age of sixteen years but below eighteen years shall be permitted or suffered to work in any industrial undertaking between ten o'clock at night and seven o'clock in the morning of the following day. Children employed at night under the provision of this sub-section shall be granted a rest of at least thirteen consecutive hours between two working periods.

(c)   No children and young persons [below] eighteen years of age shall be admitted to employment in any industrial undertaking unless they have been found fit for the work of which they are to be employed by a duly licensed physician after thorough pre-employment medical examination.

Sec. 2 - The physician engaged by an employer pursuant to this rule shall, in addition to providing medical service to the workers in cases of emergency, perform among others, the following duties:

(a) Conduct pre-employment medical examination free of charge for proper selection and placement of all workers especially minor workers from fifteen years of age to eighteen years of age;

(b) Collaborate closely with the safety and technical personnel of the establishment to assure selection and placement of workers from the standpoint of physical, mental, physiological and psychological suitability, including investigation of accidents where the probable causes are exposure to occupational health hazards;

(c) Conduct free annual physical examination of the workers;

(d) Develop and implement a comprehensive occupational health program for the employees of the establishment. A report shall be submitted annually to the Bureau of Labor Standards describing the program established and implementation thereof.

These regulations shall take effect immediately.

30 May 1977

(Sgd.) BLAS F. OPLE
Secretary

4. Children Below 15 Years

Republic of the Philippines
DEPARTMENT OF LABOR AND EMPLOYMENT
MANILA

DEPARTMENT ORDER NO. 18
Rules and Regulations Implementing
Republic Act No. 7658

By virtue of the provisions of Section 2 of Republic Act No. 7658, An Act Prohibiting the Employment of Children Below Fifteen (15) Years of Age in Public and Private Undertakings, amending Section 12, Article VIII of Republic Act No. 7610, the following Rules and Regulations governing the employment of children are hereby issued:

Sec. 1.General Prohibition.   - Except as otherwise provided in these Rules, children below 15 years of age shall not be employed, permitted or suffered to work, in any public or private establishment in the Philippines.

Sec. 2.Definition of Terms.

   a.   "Employer" - any parent, legal guardian or producer acting as employer who hires or engages the services of any child below 15 years of age.
   b.   "Legal Guardian" - any person duly appointed by a court of competent authority to exercise care and custody of or parental authority over the person of such child/employee.
   c.   "Producer" - any individual or group of individuals engaged in the production of movies, films, motion pictures, shows or advertisements, whether on cinema, theater, radio or television, wherein the services of such child/employee are hired.
   d.   "Members of the family" - those persons having family relations referred to under Article 150 of the Family Code of the Philippines. It

shall include the employer parent's or legal guardian's husband or wife, parents, children, other ascendants or descendants, brothers and sisters whether of full or half blood.

e. "Department" - The Department of Labor and Employment.

Sec. 3. Exceptions and Conditions. - The following shall be the only exceptions to the prohibition on the employment of children below 15 years of age and the conditions for availment of said exceptions:

a. When the child works directly under the sole responsibility of his/her parents or legal guardian who employs members of his/her family only, under the following conditions:

1. the employment does not endanger the child's life, safety, health and morals;

2. the employment does not impair the child's normal development; and,

3. the employer parent or legal guardian provides the child with the primary and/or secondary education prescribed by the Department of Education, Culture and Sports.

b. Where the child's employment or participation in public entertainment or information through cinema, theater, radio or television is essential, provided that:

1. the employment does not involve advertisements or commercials promoting alcoholic beverages, intoxicating drinks, tobacco and its by-products or exhibiting violence;

    2.   there is a written contract approved by the Department of Labor and Employment; and

    3.   the conditions prescribed in Section 3(a) above are met.

Sec. 4. Pre-employment Requirements. - Before an employer engages a child for employment under the exceptions enumerated above, he/she must first secure a work permit from the Regional Office of the Department having jurisdiction over the workplace.

The Regional Office shall require the employer to submit the following documents in support of the application for a work permit:

    a. two (2) pictures of the child, one full body and the other showing the child's face, both of which must be recently taken and recognizable;

    b. the child's Birth Certificate or in its absence, his/her Baptismal Certificate and a joint affidavit of his/her two nearest of kin showing the year he/she was born, and duly authenticated proof of legal guardianship where the employer is the legal guardian;

    c. a certificate of enrollment issued by the school where he/she is currently or last enrolled or a statement from the parent or legal guardian that the child is attending school;

    d. a written undertaking that:

    1. measures shall be instituted by the employer to prevent the child's exploitation and discrimination such as payment of minimum wage, hours of work and other terms and conditions required by law; and

    2. the employer shall ensure the protection, health, safety, morals and normal development of the child;

e. a medical certificate showing that the child is fit for employment;

f. a certification of a continuing program for training and skills acquisition approved and supervised by any competent authority, nearest the place of work, which may be recognized vocational or training school, the regional or local office of the Department of Social Welfare and Development, and the National Manpower and Youth Council; and

g. a written contract of employment concluded by the child's parent or legal guardian with the employer in cases of employment or participation in public entertainment or information through cinema, theater, radio or television. Said contract shall bear the express agreement of the child concerned, if possible, and shall state the nature or full description of the job and the justification that the child's employment or participation is essential.

Sec. 5. Hours of Work. - Subject to consultations with the sectors concerned, the Department shall, by appropriate regulations, issue standards governing the hours of work and time of day that children may be allowed to work.

Sec. 6. Effect on Other Issuances. - The provisions of existing rules and administrative issuances not otherwise repealed, modified or inconsistent with this Order shall continue to have full force and effect.

Sec. 7. Penalties. - Any person who shall violate any provision of Article 12 of R.A. 7610 as amended by R.A. 7658, shall suffer the penalty of a fine of not less than One Thousand Pesos (P1,000) but not more than Ten Thousand Pesos (P10,000) or imprisonment of not less than three (3) months but not more than three (3) years, or both, at the discretion of the court: Provided that in case of repeated violations of the provisions of this Article, the offender's license to operate shall be revoked.

Sec. 8. Effectivity. - These Rules and Regulations shall take effect fifteen (15) days after its publication in a newspaper of general circulation.

Signed this 12th day of May, 1994 in the City of Manila, Philippines.

(Sgd.)MA. NIEVES R. CONFESOR
Secretary

Received by the AS-Records on May 13, 1994 and disseminated on May 13, 1994.

ANNEXES TO R.A. 7658: WORK PERMITS FOR MINORS

REPUBLIC OF THE PHILIPPINES
DEPARTMENT OF LABOR AND EMPLOYMENT
REGIONAL OFFICE NO. _____

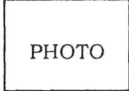

PHOTO

MINOR'S WORK PERMIT

PERMIT NO. _____

ISSUED TO:_____

           (Last Name)   (First Name)   (M.I.)

ADDRESS: _____

DATE OF BIRTH:_____ PLACE OF BIRTH:_____

NATURE OF WORK:
   I. Public entertainment or information, please check appropriate blank.
   / / cinema / / radio   / /   commercials
   / / theater / / television / /   others, specify _____

   II. Others, describe briefly _____

EMPLOYER: _____

ADDRESS: _____

LICENSE ISSUED ON: _____ VALID UNTIL: _____

PLACE OF ISSUANCE:_____

SIGNATURE OF
PARENT/LEGAL GUARDIAN: SIGNATURE OF BEARER:

_____   _____

SIGNATURE OF EMPLOYER:

_____

APPROVED:

_____ By:_____

        Secretary   RegionalDirector
Department of Labor and Employment

CL-DOLE FORM NO. 2

Republic of the Philippines
Department of Labor and Employment
Regional Office No. _____

NAME OF MINOR: _____
                       (First Name)   (Last Name)   (M.I.)
HOME ADDRESS: _____
DATE OF BIRTH: _____PLACE OF BIRTH: _____
AGE: ____ SEX: Male __ Female __ HEIGHT: _____ WEIGHT: _____

CERTIFICATE OF ENROLLMENT

This is to certify that the above-named minor is a registered student of _____ located at _____.
          (Name of School)   (School Address)

It has been verified through our records that she/he:

/ / is presently enrolled as _____ for the school year _____
/ / was last enrolled as _____ for the school year _____
VERIFIED BY: _____   NOTED BY: _____
              (Registrar)   (Principal)

                                        _____
                                        (Parents/Legal Guardian)

WRITTEN UNDERTAKING BY THE EMPLOYER

          I _____
                              (Name of Employer)
with address at _____ certify that as
the employer of the above-named minor, shall institute measures to prevent the
minor's exploitation and discrimination such as payment of minimum wage,
hours of work and other terms and conditions required by law and shall ensure
the protection, health, safety, morals and normal development of the minor
during the course of his/her employment. As to employment or participation in
public entertainment or information, I also certify that the child's employment
will not involve advertisement or commercials promoting alcoholic beverages,
intoxicating drinks, tobacco and its by-product or exhibiting violence.
EMPLOYER'S SIGNATURE:_____ LICENSE/PERMIT NO._____

(continuation of previous form)

MEDICAL CERTIFICATE

I certify that I personally examined the above-named minor and found him/her to be:

/ /   physically and mentally fit for employment
/ /   not physically and mentally fit for employment

Remarks:_____

PHYSICIAN'S NAME: _____

PHYSICIAN'S ADDRESS: _____ TEL. NO.:_____

PHYSICIAN'S SIGNATURE:_____ LICENSE NO.: _____

CERTIFICATE OF A CONTINUING PROGRAM FOR TRAINING AND SKILLS ACQUISITION

This is to certify that the above-named minor was referred to us by

_____ for further training/skills acquisition in
(Name of Employer)

_____ to be conducted by _____
(Specify)

located at _____. The training shall start from
(Complete Address)

_____ to _____
(Day)   (Month)   (Year)   (Day)   (Month)   (Year)

NAME: _____ Designation: _____

Signature_____ Office:_____

CL-DOLE FORM NO. ___

Republic of the Philippines
Department of Labor and Employment
Regional Office No. _____

APPLICATION FORM FOR
WORK PERMIT OF MINORS
(Below 15 Years Old)

To be filled up by the employer:
PERSONAL DATA ON MINOR:

NAME OF MINOR: _____
                    (First Name)   (Last Name)   (M.I.)
HOME ADDRESS:_____TEL. NO._____
DATE OF BIRTH:_____ PLACE OF BIRTH:_____
SEX: Male____ Female____ HEIGHT:_____ WEIGHT:_____

NATURE OF WORK:
1. for public entertainment or information, please check appropriate
blank: / /   / /   / /   / /
       cinema   theater   radio   television
       / /commercials: specify what products will be promoted
       / /others: specify_____

2. for other work activities, please describe briefly
_____

   / / Yes   / / No   Will the child work under the sole respon-
                      sibility of the parents/legal guardian?
   / / Yes   / / No   Are all employees in this work/undertaking
                      members of the employer's family?

DURATION AND EFFECTIVITY OF EMPLOYMENT/
WORK CONTRACT:
   employment to start on _____
                          (day)   (month)   (year)
                     to _____
                          (day)   (month)   (year)
       NAME OF PARENTS:
           FATHER: _____
           MOTHER: _____
           LEGAL GUARDIAN: _____

(continuation of previous form)

DATA ON EMPLOYER:

NAME OF EMPLOYER: _____

ADDRESS: _____ TEL. NO. _____

LICENSE NO._____ PLACE AND DATE ISSUED:_____

I certify that the above information is true and correct.

_____   _____
APPLICANT'S SIGNATURE   EMPLOYER'S SIGNATURE

_____
PARENT'S/LEGAL GUARDIAN'S   Date:_____
SIGNATURE

ACTION TAKEN:

   / / APPROVED

   / / DISAPPROVED
     Remarks: _____

_____
REGIONAL DIRECTOR

5. Children In The Movie, Television, Radio And Entertainment Industry

Republic of the Philippines
Office of the President
COUNCIL FOR THE WELFARE OF CHILDREN

RULES AND REGULATIONS ON THE
EMPLOYMENT OF CHILDREN IN THE MOVIE,
TELEVISION, RADIO AND ENTERTAINMENT
INDUSTRY

PURSUANT to the authority of the Council for the Welfare of Children to promulgate rules and regulations under Article 209 of Presidential Decree No. 603, and to protect every child employed in the movie, television, radio and entertainment industry against exploitation, improper influence, hazards and other conditions or circumstances prejudicial to his physical, mental, emotional, social and moral development, the following Rules and Regulations are hereby promulgated:

Sec. 1. Definition of Terms. - As used in these Rules and Regulations unless specifically provided otherwise:

a)   "CHILD" refers to a child, minor, or youth below twenty-one (21) years of age; except those emancipated in accordance with law and subject to Article 9 of the Code. [Now amended by R.A. 6809 lowering the age of majority from 21 years to 18 years.]

b)   "CODE" refers to Presidential Decree No. 603, otherwise known as the Child and Youth Welfare Code.

c)   "COUNCIL" refers to the Council for the Welfare of Children, Office of the President.

d)   "DIRECTOR" refers to the Director of the Bureau of Women and Minors of the Ministry of Labor.   [Now the Bureau of Women and Young

Workers of the Department of Labor and Employment.]

e) 'EMPLOYMENT" refers to the appearance, performance, or any work done by a child in the movie, television, radio, stage and the entertainment industry, including motion pictures or television programs of whatever length; live, video-taped, or film commercials; still pictures; recordings.

Sec. 2. Applicability to Employment Contracts. - These Rules and Regulations shall be applicable to all employment contracts of a child employed in the entertainment industry.

Sec. 3. Employment of a Child. - The employment of a child shall not be allowed unless said employment is covered by a valid and written contract duly signed by the employer and by the parents or legal guardian of the child, containing the following stipulations:

a) that the parties shall protect the child against exploitation, improper influences, hazards, and other conditions or circumstances prejudicial to his physical, mental, emotional, social, educational, and moral development; and

b) that the employer shall furnish a copy of the contract as well as all amendments thereto to the parents or legal guardian and to the Director within fifteen (15) days from the execution thereof.

Sec. 4. Trust Fund. - It shall be the duty of the parents or legal guardian to set up a trust fund for the child.

Sec. 5. Duties of the Director. - It shall be the duty of the Director to see to it that:

a) these Rules and Regulations have been complied with;

b)   the employment will not be inimical to the child's safety and welfare; and

c)   the child will not be subjected to exploitation thereby.

Sec. 6. Involuntary Commitment of the Child. - The Minister of Social Services and Development [now Secretary of Social Welfare and Development] may, motu propio, or upon the recommendation of the Director, file a verified petition in Court for the involuntary commitment of a child who is physically or emotionally neglected under Title VIII, Chapter I of the Code or whose parent or guardian is found guilty of any of the crimes punishable under Articles 59 and 204 of the Code.

Sec. 7. Penalty. - A parent, guardian, producer, director, or other persons violating or causing the violation of these Rules and Regulations shall upon conviction, suffer the penalties provided in Article 210 of the Code.

Sec. 8. Separability Clause. - The validity of any provision of these Rules and Regulations shall not be affected by the declaration of the invalidity of any other provision or provisions thereof.

Sec. 9. Repealing Clause. - These Rules and Regulations supersede any other rules and regulations on the employment of children in the movie, television, radio, and entertainment industry.

Sec 10. Effectivity Clause. - These Rules and Regulations on the Employment of Children in the Movie, Television, Radio and Entertainment Industry shall take effect upon their publication in a newspaper of general circulation in the Philippines.

(SGD.) HON. CLEMENTE S. GATMAITAN
    Minister, Ministry of Health
    Chairman

(SGD.) HON. JUAN L. MANUEL
    Minister, Ministry of Education and   Culture
    Member

(SGD.) HON. BLAS F. OPLE
    Minister, Ministry of Labor
    Member

(SGD.) HON. CATALINO MACARAIG, JR.
    Deputy Minister, Ministry of Justice
    Member

(SGD.) HON. SYLVIA P. MONTES
    Deputy Minister and Office-In-Charge
    Ministry of Social Services and Development
    Member

(SGD.) HON. REGINA ORDONEZ-BENITEZ
    Presiding Judge, Juvenile & Domestic
        Relations Court
    Member

(SGD.) DR. FE DEL MUNDO
    Medical Director
        Children's Medical Center of the Philippines
    Member

(SGD.) MAYOR ADELINA S. RODRIGUEZ
    President, Council of Welfare Agencies
        of the Philippines
    Member

ATTEST:
(SGD.) ATTY. ESTER DE JESUS
    Executive Director

Published on November 25, 1978, Times Journal, Manila, Philippines

6. Children In Apprentice Work

6.1 Labor Code

Art. 61. Contents of Apprenticeship Agreements. - Apprenticeship agreements, including the main rates of apprentices, shall conform to the rules issued by the Secretary of Labor and Employment. The period of apprenticeship shall not exceed six months. Apprenticeship agreements providing for wage rates below the legal minimum wage, which in no case shall start below 75 per cent of the applicable minimum wage, may be entered into only in accordance with apprenticeship programs duly approved by the Secretary of Labor and Employment. The Department shall develop standard model programs of apprenticeship.

Art. 62. Signing of Apprenticeship Agreement. - Every apprenticeship agreement shall be signed by the employer or his agent, or by an authorized representative of any of the recognized organizations, associations or groups, and by the apprentice.

An apprenticeship agreement with a minor shall be signed in his behalf by his parent or guardian or, if the latter is not available, by an authorized representative of the Department of Labor; and the same shall be binding during its lifetime. [*Underscoring supplied.*]

Every apprenticeship agreement entered into under this "Title" shall be ratified by the appropriate apprenticeship committees, if any, and a copy thereof shall be furnished both the employer and the apprentice.

6.2 Omnibus Rules Implementing The Labor Code

BOOK II
NATIONAL MANPOWER
DEVELOPMENT PROGRAM
RULE VI
APPRENTICESHIP TRAINING

xxx

Sec. 11. Qualifications of Apprentices. - To qualify as an apprentice, an applicant shall:

(a) Be <u>at least fifteen years of age</u>; provided those who are at least fifteen years of age but less than eighteen may be eligible for apprenticeship only in non-hazardous occupations; [*Underscoring supplied.*]
(b) Be physically fit for the occupation in which he desires to be trained;
(c) Possess vocational aptitude and capacity for the particular occupation as established through appropriate tests; and
(d) Possess the ability to comprehend and follow oral and written instructions.

Trade and industry associations may, however, recommend to the Secretary of Labor appropriate educational qualifications for apprentices in certain occupations. Such qualifications, if approved, shall be the educational requirements for apprenticeship in such occupations unless waived by an employer in favor of an applicant who has demonstrated exceptional ability. A certification explaining briefly the ground for such waiver, and signed by the person in charge of the program shall be attached to the apprenticeship agreement of the applicant concerned.

Sec. 12. Aptitude Tests. - An employer who has a recognized apprenticeship program shall provide aptitude tests to apprentice-applicants. However, if the employer does not have adequate facilities, the Department of Labor may provide the service free of charge.

Sec. 13. Physical Fitness. - Total physical fitness need not be required of an apprentice-applicant unless it is essential to the expeditious and effective learning of the occupation. Only physical defects which constitute real impediments to effective performance as determined by the plant apprenticeship committee may disqualify an applicant.

Sec. 14. Free Physical Examination. - Physical examination of apprentice-applicants preparatory to employment shall be provided free of charge by the Department of Health or any government hospital. If this is not feasible, the firm or entity screening the applicant shall extend such services free of charge.

All entities with an apprenticeship program may elect to assume the responsibility for physical examination provided its facilities are adequate and all expenses are borne, exclusively by it.

Sec. 15. Apprenticeable Trades. - The Bureau shall evaluate crafts and operative, technical, nautical, commercial, clerical, technological, supervisory service and managerial activities which may be declared apprenticeable by the Secretary of Labor and shall have exclusive jurisdiction to formulate model national apprenticeship standards therefor.

x x x

Sec. 18. Contents of Agreement. - Every apprenticeship agreement shall include the following:

(a)   The full names and addresses of the contracting parties;

(b) Date of birth of the apprentice;

(c) Name of the trade, occupation or job in which the apprentice will be trained and the dates on which such training will begin and will approximately end;

(d) The approximate number of hours of on-the-job training as well as of supplementary theoretical instructions which the apprentice shall undergo during his training;

(e) A schedule of the work processes of the trade/occupation in which the apprentice shall be trained and the approximate time to be spent on the job in each process;

(f) The graduated scale of wages to be paid the apprentice;

(g)   The   probationary   period   of   the apprentice   during   which   either   party   may summarily terminate their agreement; and

(h) A clause that if the employer is unable to fulfill his training obligation, he may transfer the agreement, with the consent of the apprentice, to any other employer who is willing to assume such obligation.

Sec. 19.   Apprenticeship Period.   -   The period of appren- ticeship shall not exceed six (6) months.

Sec. 20. Hours of Work. - Hours of work of the apprentice shall not exceed the maximum number of hours of work prescribed by law, if any, for a worker of his age and sex.   Time spent in related theoretical instructions shall be considered as hours of work and shall be reckoned jointly with on-the-job training time in computing in the agreement the appropriate periods for giving wage increases to the apprentice.

An apprentice not otherwise barred by law from working eight hours a day may be requested by his employer to work overtime and paid accordingly, provided there are no available regular workers to do the job, and the overtime work thus rendered is duly credited toward his training time.

x x x

Sec. 29.   Wages. - The wage rate of the apprentice shall start at seventy-five (75) per cent of the statutory minimum wage for the first six (6) months;   thereafter, he shall be paid the full minimum wage, including the full cost-of-living allowance.

x x x

Sec.   40.   Apprenticeship   without compensation. - The Secretary of Labor through the Apprenticeship Division may authorize the hiring of apprentices without compensation, whose training on the job is required by the school curriculum as a prerequisite for graduation or for taking a government board examination.

7. Children In Domestic Work

Employers of children in domestic work are mandated by law to give the latter an opportunity for elementary education.   This requirement, found in Art. 1691 of the Civil Code, in Art. 110 of P.D. 603 and in the Omnibus Rules Implementing the Labor Code, is the only proviso contained in the country's laws which deal specifically with children in domestic service.

The other terms and conditions of employment of children in domestic work are governed by the general laws on domestic work which are contained in the Labor Code and Civil Code as follows:

7.1 Labor Code

Art. 143. Minimum Wage. - (a) Househelpers shall be paid the following minimum wage rates:

(1) Eight hundred pesos (P800.00) a month for househelpers in Manila, Quezon, Pasay and Caloocan cities and the municipalities of Makati, San Juan, Mandaluyong, Muntinlupa, Navotas, Malabon, Paranaque, Las Pinas, Pasig and Marikina in Rizal Province;
(2) Six hundred fifty pesos (P650.00) a month for those in other chartered cities and first-class municipalities; and
(3) Five hundred fifty pesos (P550.00) a month for those in other municipalities.

Provided, That the employers shall review the employment contracts of their househelpers every three (3) years with the end in view of improving the terms and conditions thereof.

Provided, further, That those househelpers who are receiving at least One thousand pesos (P1,000.00) shall be covered by the Social Security System (SSS) and be entitled to all the benefits provided thereunder. [As Amended by R.A. 7655]

Art. 144. Minimum Cash Wage. - The minimum wage rates prescribed under this Chapter shall be the basic cash wages which shall be paid to the househelpers in addition to lodging, food and medical attendance.

Art. 145. Assignment to Non-household Work- No househelper shall be assigned to work in a commercial, industrial or agricultural enterprise at a wage or salary rate lower than that provided for agricultural or non-agricultural workers as prescribed herein.

Art. 146. Opportunity for Education. - <u>If the
househelper is under the age of eighteen (18) years,
the employer shall give him or her an opportunity
for at least elementary education.</u> The cost of such
education shall be part of the househelper's
compensation, unless there is a stipulation to the
contrary. [*Underscoring supplied.*]

Art. 147. Treatment of Househelpers. - The
employer shall treat the househelper in a just and
humane manner. In no case shall physical
violence be used upon the househelper.

*Art. 148. Board, Lodging and Medical
Attendance.* - The employer shall furnish the
househelper free of charge suitable and sanitary
living quarters as well as adequate food and
medical attendance.

*Art. 149. Indemnity for Unjust Termination of
Services.* - If the period of household service is
fixed, neither the employer nor the househelper
may terminate the contract before the expiration of
the term, except for a just cause. If the househelper is unjustly dismissed, he or she shall be
paid the compensation already earned plus that for
fifteen (15) days by way of indemnity.

If the househelper leaves without justifiable
cause, he or she shall forfeit any unpaid salary due
him or her not exceeding fifteen (15) days.

Art. 150. Service of Termination Notice. - If
the duration of the household service is not
determined either in stipulation or by the nature of
the service, the employer or the househelper may
give notice to put an end to the relationship five (5)
days before the intended termination of the service.

Art. 151. Employment Certification. - Upon
the severance of the household service relation, the
employer shall give the househelper a written
statement of the nature and duration of the service

and his or her efficiency and conduct as househelper.

Art. 152. Employment Records. -- The employer may keep such records as he may deem necessary to reflect the actual terms and conditions of employment of his househelper, which the latter shall authenticate by signature or thumbmark upon request of the employer.

7.2 Omnibus Rules Implementing The Labor Code

BOOK III, RULE XIII
EMPLOYMENT OF HOUSEHELPERS

Sec. 1. General Statement on Coverage. -

x x x

(b) The term "househelper" as used herein is synonymous to the term "domestic servant" and shall refer to any person, whether male or female, who renders services in and about the employer's home and which services are usually necessary or desirable for the maintenance and enjoyment thereof, and ministers exclusively to the personal comfort and enjoyment of the employer's family.

x x x

Sec. 3. Children of Househelpers. - The children and relatives of a househelper who live under the employer's roof and who share the accommodations provided for the househelpers by the employer shall not be deemed as househelpers if they are not otherwise engaged as such and are not required to perform any substantial household work.

x x x

Sec. 9. *Time and Manner of Payment.* - Wages shall be paid directly to the househelper to whom they are due at least once a month. No deductions therefrom shall be made by the employer unless authorized by the househelper himself or by existing laws.

x x x

Sec. 11. *Opportunity for Education.* - If the househelper is under the age of eighteen years the employer shall give him or her an opportunity for at least elementary education. The cost of such education shall be part of the househelper's compensation, unless there is a stipulation to the contrary. [*Underscoring supplied.*]

7.3   The New Civil Code

Art. 1689. Household service shall always be reasonably compensated. Any stipulation that household service is without compensation shall be void. Such compensation shall be in addition to the househelper's lodging, food, and medical attendance.

Art. 1690. The head of the family shall furnish, free of charge, to the househelper, suitable and sanitary quarters as well as adequate food and medical attendance.

Art. 1691. If the househelper is under the age of eighteen years, the head of the family shall give an opportunity to the househelper for at least elementary education. The cost of such education shall be a part of the househelper's compensation, unless there is a stipulation to the contrary. [*Underscoring supplied.*]

Art. 1692. No contract for household service shall last for more than two years. However, such contract may be renewed from year to year.

Art. 1693. The househelper's clothes shall be subject to stipulation. However, any contract for household service shall be void if, thereby, the househelper cannot afford to acquire suitable clothing.

Art. 1694. The head of the family shall treat the househelper in a just and humane manner. In no case shall physical violence be used upon the househelper.

Art. 1695. Househelpers shall not be required to work more than ten hours a day. Every househelper shall be allowed four days' vacation each month, with pay.

x x x

Art. 1697. If the period for household service is fixed neither the head of the family nor the househelper may terminate the contract before the expiration of the term, except for a just cause. If the househelper is unjustly dismissed, he shall be paid the compensation already earned plus that for fifteen days by way of indemnity. If the househelper leaves without justifiable reason, he shall forfeit any salary due him and unpaid for not exceeding fifteen (15) days.

Art. 1698. If the duration of the household service is not determined either by stipulation or by the nature of the service, the head of the family or the househelper may give notice to put an end to the service relation according to the following rules:

(1) If the compensation is paid by the day, notice may be given on any day that the service shall end at the close of the following day;

(2) If the compensation is paid by the week, notice may be given, at the latest, on the first business day of the week, that the service shall be terminated at the end of the seventh day from the beginning of the week;

(3) If the compensation is paid by the month, notice may be given, at the latest, on the fifth day of the month, that the service shall cease at the end of the month.

Art. 1699. Upon the extinguishment of the service relation, the househelper may demand from the head of the family a written statement on the nature and duration of the service and the efficiency and conduct of the househelper.

8. Children In Homework

There are no laws which govern the terms and conditions of children in the homework industry. The general laws on homework under Department Order No. 5 which became Rule XIV, Book III of the Omnibus Rules Implementing the Labor Code are, therefore, applicable to children in this industry.

DEPARTMENT ORDER NO. 5
RULE XIV OF THE RULES IMPLEMENTING BOOK
III OF THE LABOR CODE
ON EMPLOYMENT OF HOMEWORKERS

x x x

Sec. 2. Definitions. - As used in this Rule, the following terms shall have the meaning indicated hereunder:

(a) "Industrial Homework" is a system of production under which work for an employer or contractor is carried out by a homeworker at his/her home. Materials may or may not be furnished by the employer or contractor.

It differs from regular factory production principally in that, it is a decentralized form of production where there is ordinarily very little supervision on regulation of methods of work.

x x x

Sec. 3. Self-Organization. - Homeworkers shall have the right to form, join or assist organizations of their own choosing, in accordance with law.

x x x

Sec. 6. Payment for Homework. -- Immediately upon receipt of the finished goods or articles, the employer shall pay the homeworker of the contractor or subcontractor, as the case may be, for the work performed less the corresponding homeworker's share of SSS, MEDICARE, and ECC premium contributions which shall be remitted by the contractor/subcontractor or employer to the SSS with the employer's share. However, where payment is made to a contractor, the homeworkers shall likewise be paid immediately after the goods or articles have been collected from the workers.

x x x

Sec. 8. Deductions. - No employer, contractor shall make any deduction from the homeworkers' earnings for the value of materials which have been lost, destroyed, soiled or otherwise damaged unless the following conditions are met:

(a) the homeworker concerned is clearly shown to be responsible for the loss or damage;
(b) the homeworker is given reasonable opportunity to show cause why deductions should not be made;

(c) the amount of such deduction is fair and reasonable and shall not exceed the actual damage; and

(d) the deduction is made at such rate that the amount does not exceed 20% of the homeworker's earnings in a week.

Sec. 9. Conditions for Payment of Work. -

(a) The employer may require the homeworker to redo once the work, which has been improperly executed without having to pay the stipulated rate again.

(b) An employer, contractor, or subcontractor need not pay the homeworker for any work, which has been done on goods and articles which have been returned for reasons attributable to the fault of the homeworker.

x x x

Sec. 11. Duties of Employer, Contractor and Subcontractor. - Whenever an employer shall contract with another for the performance of the employer's work, it shall be the duty of such employer to provide in such contract that the employees or homeworkers of the contractor and the latter's subcontractor shall be paid in accordance with the provisions of this Rule. In the event that such contractor or sub-contractor fails to pay the wages or earnings of his employees or homeworkers as specified in this Rule, such employer shall be jointly and severally liable with the contractor or subcontractor to the workers of the latter, to the extent that such work is performed under such contract, in the same manner as if the employees or homeworkers were directly engaged by the employer. The employer, contractor or subcontractor shall assist the homeworkers in the maintenance of basic safe and healthful working conditions at the homeworkers' place of work.

Sec. 12. Employment of Minors as Homeworkers. - The provisions governing the employment of minors under this Code as well as the provisions on working children under the Child and Youth Welfare Code shall govern the employment of minors as homeworkers. [*Underscoring supplied.*]

Section 13. Prohibitions for Homework. - No homework shall be performed on the following: (1) explosives, fireworks and articles of like character; (2) drugs and poisons; and (3) other articles, the processing of which requires exposure to toxic substances.

9. Children In Subcontracting and Labor-only Contracting

Contractors or subcontractors often hire child workers to perform a specific job consigned by a principal employer. Articles 106 to 109 of the Labor Code and Department Order No. 18-02 provide protection for these child workers insofar as the wages due them are concerned. They may recover not only from the contractor or subcontractor who hired them but the principal employer as well. Where there is labor-only contracting, however, the principal employer's liability extends not only to unpaid wages but also to such other liabilities that may be incurred as if the principal employer had directly hired the child workers.

Art. 106. Contractor or Sub-contractor. — Whenever an employer enters into a contract with another person for the performance of the former's work, the employees of the contractor and of the latter's sub-contractor, if any, shall be paid in accordance with the provisions of this Code.

In the event that the contractor or sub-contractor fails to pay the wages of his employees in accordance with this Code, the employer shall be jointly and severally liable with his contractor or sub-contractor to such employees to the extent of the work performed under the contract, in the same manner and extent that he is liable to employees directly employed by him.

The Secretary of Labor and Employment may, by appropriate regulations, restrict or prohibit the contracting out of labor to protect the rights of workers established under this Code. In so prohibiting or restricting, he may make appropriate distinctions between labor-only contracting and job contracting as well as differentiations within these types of contracting, and determine who among the parties involved shall be considered the employer for purposes of this Code, to prevent any violation or circumvention of any provision of this Code.

There is "labor-only" contracting where the person supplying workers to an employer does not have substantial capital or investment in the form of tools, equipment, machineries, work premises, among others, and the workers recruited and placed by such person are performing activities which are directly related to the principal business of such employer. In such cases, the person or intermediary shall be considered merely as an agent of the employer who shall be responsible to the workers in the same manner and extent as if the latter were directly employed by him.

Art. 107.   Indirect   Employer.   — The provisions of the immediately preceding Article shall likewise apply to any person, partnership, association or corporation which, not being an employer, contracts with an independent contractor for the performance of any work, task, job or project.

Art. 108. *Posting of Bond.* — An employer or indirect employer may require the contractor or sub-contractor to furnish a bond equal to the cost of labor under contract, on condition that the bond will answer for the wages due the employees should the contractor or sub-contractor, as the case may be, fail to pay the same.

Art. 109. *Solidary Liability.* — The provisions of existing laws to the contrary notwithstanding, every employer or indirect employer shall be held responsible with his contractor or subcontractor for any violation of any provision of this Code. For purposes of determining the extent of their civil liability under this Chapter, they shall be considered as direct employers.

9.1 Department Order No. 18-02

Republic of the Philippines
DEPARTMENT OF LABOR AND EMPLOYMENT
lntramuros, Manila

DEPARTMENT ORDER NO. 18-02
Series of 2002

RULES IMPLEMENTING ARTICLES 106 TO 109
OF THE LABOR CODE, AS AMENDED

By virtue of the power vested in the Secretary of Labor and Employment under Articles 5 (Rule-making) and 106 (Contractor or Subcontractor) of the Labor Code of the Philippines as amended, the following regulations governing contracting and subcontracting arrangements are hereby issued:

Sec. 1. Guiding Principles. — Contracting and subcontracting arrangements are expressly allowed by law and are subject to regulation for the promotion of employment and the observance of the rights of workers to just and humane conditions of work, security or tenure, self-organization, and collective bargaining. Labor-only contracting as defined herein shall be prohibited.

Sec. 2. Coverage. — These Rules shall apply to all parties of contracting and subcontracting arrangements where employer-employee relationship exists. Placement activities through private recruitment and placement agencies as governed by Articles 25 to 39 of the Labor Code are not covered by these Rules.

Sec. 3. Trilateral Relationship Arrangements. - In legitimate contracting, there exists a trilateral relationship under which there is a contract for a specific job, work or service between the principal and the contractor or subcontractor, and a contract of employment between the contractor or subcontractor and its workers. Hence, there are three parties involved in these arrangements, the principal which decides to farm out a job or service to a contractor or subcontractor, the contractor or subcontractor which has the capacity to independently undertake the performance of the job, work or service, and the contractual workers engaged by the contractor or subcontractor to accomplish the job work or service.

Sec. 4. Definition of Basic Terms. — The following terms as used in these Rules, shall mean:

(a) "Contracting" or "subcontracting" refers to an arrangement whereby a principal agrees to put out or farm out with a contractor or subcontractor the performance or completion of a specific job, work or service within a definite or predetermined period, regardless of whether such job, work or service is to be performed or completed within or outside the premises of the principal.

(b)   "Contractor or subcontractor" refers to any person or entity engaged in a legitimate contracting or subcontracting arrangement.

(c)   "Contractual employee" includes one employed by a contractor or subcontractor to perform or complete a job, work or service pursuant to an arrangement between the latter and a principal.

(d)   "Principal" refers to any employer who puts out or farms out a job, service or work to a contractor or subcontractor.

Sec.   5.   Prohibition   Against   Labor-only Contracting.- Labor-only   contracting   is   hereby declared prohibited. For this purpose, labor-only contracting shall refer to an arrangement where the contractor or subcontractor merely recruits, supplies or places workers to perform a job, work or service for a principal, and any of the following elements are present:

    i)   The contractor or subcontractor does not have substantial capital or investment which relates to the job, work or service to be performed and the employees recruited, supplied or placed by such contractor   or   subcontractor   are performing activities which arc directly related to the main business of the principal; or

    ii)   the contractor does not exercise the right to control over the performance of the work of the contractual employee.

The foregoing provisions shall be without prejudice to the application of Article 248 (C) of the Labor Code, as amended.

"Substantial capital or investment" refers to capital stocks and subscribed capitalization in the case of corporations, tools, equipment, implements, machineries and work premises, actually and directly used by the contractor or subcontractor in the performance or completion of the job, work or service contracted out.

The 'right to control" shall refer to the right reserved to the person for whom the services of the contractual workers are performed, to determine not only the end to be achieved, but also the manner and means to be used in reaching that end.

Sec. 6. Prohibitions. - Notwithstanding Section 5 of these Rules, the following are hereby declared prohibited for being contrary to law or public policy:

(a) Contracting out of a job, work or service when not done in good faith and not justified by the exigencies of the business and the same results in the termination of regular employees and reduction of work hours or reduction or splitting of the bargaining unit:

(b) Contracting out of work with a "cabo" as defined in Section 1 (ii), Rule I, Book V of these Rules. "Cabo" refers to a person or group of persons or to a labor group which, in the guise of a labor organization, supplies workers to an employer, with or without any monetary or other consideration whether in the capacity of an agent of the employer or as an ostensible independent contractor;

(c) Taking undue advantage of the economic situation or lack of bargaining strength of the contractual employee, or undermining his security of tenure or basic rights, or circumventing the provisions of regular employment, in any of the following instances:

    i) In addition to his assigned functions, requiring the contractual employee to perform functions which are currently being performed by the regular employees of the principal or of the contractor or subcontractor;

ii) Requiring him to sign, as a precondition to employment or continued employment, an antedated resignation letter; a blank payroll; a waiver of labor standards including minimum wages and social or welfare benefits; or a quitclaim releasing the principal. contractor or subcontractor from any liability as to payment future claims; and

iii) Requiring him to sign a contract fixing the period of employment to a term shorter than the term of the contract between the principal and the contractor or subcontractor, unless the latter contract is divisible into phases for which substantially different skills are required and this is made known to the employee at the time of engagement;

(d) Contracting out of a job, work or service through an in-house agency which refers to a contractor, or subcontractor engaged in the supply of labor which is owned, managed or controlled by the principal and which operates solely tot the principal;

(e) Contracting out of a lob, work or service directly related to the business or operation of the principal by reason of a strike or lockout whether actual or imminent;

(f) Contracting out of a job, work or service being performed by union members when such will interfere with, restrain or coerce employees in the exercise of their rights to self-organization as provided in Art. 248 (c) of the Labor Code, as amended.

Sec. 7 Existence of an Employer-Employee Relationship. - The contractor or subcontractor shall be considered the employer of the contractual employee for purposes of enforcing the provisions of the Labor Code and other social legislation. The principal, however, shall be solidarily liable with the contractor in the event of any violation of any provision of the Labor Code, including time failure to pay wages.

The principal shall be deemed the employer of the contractual employee in any or the following cases, as declared by a competent authority:

(a) where theme is labor-only contracting; or
(b) where the contracting arrangement falls within the prohibitions provided in Section 6 (Prohibitions) hereof.

Sec. 8. Rights of Contractual Employees.- Consistent with Section 7 of these Rules, the contractual employee shall be entitled to all the rights and privileges due a regular employee as provided for in the Labor Code, as amended, to include the following:

(a)   Safe and healthful working conditions;
(b)   Labor standards such as service incentive leave, rest days, overtime pay, holiday pay. 13th month pay and separation pay;
(c)   Social security and welfare benefits;
(d)   Self-organization, collective bargaining and peaceful concerted action; and
(e)   Security of tenure.

Sec. 9. Contract Between Contractor or Subcontractor and Contractual Employee.- Notwithstanding oral or written stipulations to the contrary, the contract between the contractor or subcontractor and the contractual employee, which shall be in writing, shall include the following terms and conditions:

(a)   The specific description of the job, work or service to be performed by the contractual employee;

(b) The place of work and terms and conditions of employment, including a statement of the wage rate applicable to the individual contractual employee; and

[c] The term or duration of employment, which shall be coextensive with the contract of the principal and subcontractor, or with the specific phase for which the contractual employee is engaged, as the case may be.

The contractor or subcontractor shall inform the contractual employee of the foregoing terms and conditions on or before the first day of his employment.

Sec. 10 Effect of Termination of Contractual Employment. - In cases of termination of employment prior to the expiration of the contract between the principal and the contractor or subcontractor, the right of the contractual employee to separation pay or other related benefits shall he governed by the applicable laws and jurisprudence on termination of employment.

Where the termination results from the expiration of the contract between the principal and the contractor or subcontractor, or from the completion of the phase of the job, work or service for which the contractual employee is engaged, the latter shall not be entitled to separation pay. However, this shall be without prejudice to completion bonuses or other emoluments, including retirement pay as may be provided by law or in the contract between the principal and the contractor or subcontractor.

Sec. 11. Registration of Contractors or Subcontractors.- Consistent with the authority of the Secretary of Labor and Employment to restrict or prohibit the contracting out of labor through appropriate regulations, a registration system to govern contracting arrangements and to be implemented by the Regional Offices is hereby established.

The registration of contractors and subcontractors shall be necessary for purposes of establishing an effective labor market information and monitoring.

Failure to register shall give rise to the presumption that the contractor is engaged in labor-only contracting.

Sec. 12. Requirements for Registration.- A contractor or subcontractor, shall be listed in the registry of contractors and subcontractors upon completion of an application form to be provided by the DOLE. The applicant contractor or subcontractor shall provide in the application form the following information:

    (a)   The name and business address of the applicant and the area or areas where it seeks to operate;

    (b)   The names and addresses of officers, if the applicant is a corporation, partnership, cooperative or union;

    (c)   The nature of the applicant's business and the industry or industries where the applicant seeks to operate;

    (d)   The number of regular workers: the list of clients, if any; the number of personnel assigned to each client, if any and the services provided to the client;

    (e)   The description of the phases of the contract and the number of employees covered in each phase, where appropriate; and

    (f)   A copy of audited financial statements if the applicant is a corporation, partnership, cooperative or a union, or copy of the latest ITR if the applicant is a sole proprietorship.

The application shall be supported by:

(a)   A certified copy of a certificate of registration of firm or business name from the Securities and Exchange Commission (SEC), Department of Trade and Industry (DTI), Cooperative Development Authority (CDA), or from the DOLE if the applicant is a union; and

(b)   A certified copy of the license or business permit issued by the local government unit or units where the contractor or subcontractor operates.

The application shall be verified and shall include an undertaking that the contractor or subcontractor shall abide by all applicable labor laws and regulations.

Sec. 13. Filing and Processing of Applications. - The application and its supporting documents shall be filed in triplicate iii the Regional Offices where the applicant principally operates. No application for registration shall be accepted unless all the foregoing requirements are complied with. The contractor or subcontractor shall be deemed registered upon payment of a registration fee of P100.00 to the Regional Office.

Where all the supporting documents have been submitted, the Regional Office shall deny or approve the application within seven (7) working days after its filing.

Upon registration, the 'Regional Office shall return one set of the duly-stamped application docwncnts to the applicant, retain one set for its file, and transmit the remaining set to the Bureau of Local Employment. The Bureau shall devise the necessary, forms for the expeditious processing of all applications for registration.

Sec. 14. Duty to Produce Copy of Contract Between the Principal and the Contractor or Subcontractor.- The principal or the contractor or subcontractor shall be under an obligation to produce a copy of the contract between the principal and the contractor in the ordinary course of inspection. The contractor shall likewise be under an obligation to produce a copy of the contract of employment of the contractual worker when directed to do so by The Regional Director or his authorized representative.

A copy of the contract between the contractual employee and the contractor or subcontractor shall be furnished the certified bargaining agent, if there is any.

Sec. 13. Annual Reporting of Registered Contractors.- The contractor or subcontractor shall submit in triplicate its annual report using a prescribed form to the appropriate Regional Office not later than the 15th of January of the following year. mc report shall include:

(a) A list of contracts entered with the principal during the subject reporting period;
(b)   The number of workers covered by each contract with the principal;
(c) A. sworn undertaking that the benefits from the Social Security System (SSS), the Home Development Mutual Fund (HDMF), Phil-Health, Employees Compensation Commission (ECC), and remittances to the Bureau of internal Revenue (BIR) due its contractual employees have been made during the subject reporting period.

The Regional Office shall return one set of the duly-stamped report to the contractor or subcontractor, retain one set for its file, and transmit the remaining set to the Bureau of Local Employment within five (5) days from receipt thereof.

Sec. 16. Delisting of Contractors or Subcontractors. - Subject to due process, the Regional Director shall cancel the registration of contractors or subcontractors based on any of the following grounds:

(a) Non-submission of contracts between the. principal and the contractor or subcontractor when required to do so;

(b) Non-submission of annual report;

(c) Findings through arbitration that the contractor or subcontractor has engaged in labor-only contracting and the prohibited activities as provided in Section 6 (Prohibitions) hereof; and

(d) Non-compliance with labor standards and working conditions.

Sec. 17. Renewal of Registration of Contractors or Subcontractors. - All registered contractors or subcontractors may apply for renewal of registration every three years. For this purpose, the Tripartite Industrial Peace Council (TIPC) as created under Executive Order No. 49, shall servo as the oversight committee to verify and monitor the following:

(a) Engaging in allowable contracting activities; and

(b) Compliance with administrative reporting requirements.

Sec. 18. Enforcement of Labor Standards and Working Conditions. - Consistent with Article 128 (Visitorial and Enforcement Power) of the Labor Code, as amended, the Regional Director through his duly authorized representatives, including labor regulation officers shall have the authority to conduct routine inspection of establishments engaged in contracting or subcontracting and shall have access to employer's records and premises at any time of the day or night whenever work is being undertaken therein, and the right to copy therefrom, to question any employee and investigate any fact, condition or matter which may be necessary to determine violations or which may aid in the enforcement of the Labor Code and of any labor law, wage order, or rules and regulations issued pursuant thereto.

The findings of the duly authorized representative shall be referred to the Regional Director for appropriate, action as provided for in Article 128, arid shall be furnished the collective bargaining agent, if any.

Based on the visitorial and enforcement power of' the Secretary of Labor and Employment in Article 128 (a), (b), (c) and (d), the Regional Director shall issue compliance orders to give effect to the labor standards provisions of the Labor Code, other labor legislation and these guidelines.

Sec. 19. Solidary Liability.- The principal shall be deemed as the direct employer of the contractual employees and therefore, solidarily liable with the contractor or subcontractor for whatever monetary claims the contractual employees may have against the former in the case of violations as provided for in Sections 5 (Labor-Only contracting), 6 (Prohibitions), 8 (Rights of Contractual Employees) and 16 (Delisting) of these Rules. In addition, the principal shall also be solidarily liable in case the contract between the principal and contractor or subcontractor is preterminated for reasons not attributable to the fault of the contractor or subcontractor.

Sec. 20. Supersession - All rules and regulations issued by the Secretary of Labor and Employment inconsistent with the provisions of this Rule are hereby superseded. Contracting or subcontracting arrangements in the construction industry, under the licensing coverage of the PCAB and shall not include shipbuilding and ship repairing works, however, shall continue to be governed by Department Order No. 19, series of 1993.

Sec. 21. Effectivity - This Order shall be effective fifteen (15) days after completion of its publication in two (2) newspapers of general circulation.

Manila, Philippines, 21 February 2002.

(SGD.) PATRICIA STO. TOMAS
Secretary of Labor

10. Workers In General

10.1 Working Hours And Rest Periods

The provisions on "Working Conditions and Rest Periods" of the Labor Code which are presented below, will not apply to "field personnel, members of the family of the employer who are dependent on him for support, domestic helpers, persons in the personal service of another, and workers who are paid by results", among others.[80]

LABOR CODE

Art. 83. Normal Hours of Work. -- The normal hours of work of any employee shall not exceed eight (8) hours a day.[81]

x x x

---

[80] Pursuant to the Labor Code, Art. 82.
[81] Note that if the employee is less than 16 years of age, MOLE Policy Order No. 23 provides a stricter requirement of 7 hours daily.

Art. 85. Meal Periods. -- Subject to such regulations as the Secretary of Labor may prescribe, it shall be the duty of every employer to give his employees not less than sixty (60) minutes time-off for their regular meals.

x x x

Art. 91. Right to Weekly Rest Day. - (a) It shall be the duty of every employer, whether operating for profit or not, to provide each of his employees a rest period of not less than twenty-four (24) consecutive hours after every six (6) consecutive normal work days.

x x x

Art. 95. Right to Service Incentive Leave. –
(a) Every employee who has rendered at least one year of service shall be entitled to a yearly service incentive leave of five days with pay.

(b) This provision shall not apply to those who are already enjoying the benefit herein provided, those enjoying vacation leave with pay of at least five days and those employed in establishments regularly employing less than ten employees or in establishments exempted from granting this benefit by the Secretary of Labor after considering the viability or financial condition of such establishment.

10.2. Wages

By virtue of the Labor Code's prohibition against child discrimination with respect to terms and conditions of employment, the minimum wage laws should be extended to children. The provisions of the Labor Code on wages and of P.D. 851 on 13th-month pay should equally apply to child workers.

10.2.1 Labor Code

Articles 86 to 94 which are presented below shall not apply to "field personnel, members of the family of the employer who are dependent on him for support, domestic helpers, persons in the personal service of another, and workers who are paid by results".[82] On the other hand,. Articles 102 to 118 shall not apply to domestic helpers, homeworkers engaged in needlework or cottage industries, and workers in duly registered cooperatives.[83]

> *Art. 86. Night Shift Differential.* -- Every employee shall be paid a night shift differential of not less than ten per cent (10%) of his regular wage for each hour of work performed between ten o'clock in the evening and six o'clock in the morning.[84]

> *Art. 87. Overtime Work.* -- Work may be performed beyond eight (8) hours a day provided that the employee is paid for the overtime work, an additional compensation equivalent to his regular wage plus at least twenty-five (25%) percent thereof. Work performed beyond eight hours on a holiday or rest day shall be paid an additional compensation equivalent to the rate of the first eight hours on a holiday or rest day plus at least thirty (30%) percent hereof.
>
> x x x

> *Art. 90. Computation of Additional Compensation.* - For purposes of computing overtime and other additional remuneration as required by this Chapter the "regular wage" of an employee shall include the cash wage only, without

---

[82] Pursuant to the Labor Code, Art. 82.
[83] Pursuant to the Labor Code, Art. 98.
[84] Note that MOLE Policy Order No. 23 and ILO Convention No. 90 prohibit the night work of young persons. Nevertheless, the child who is forced to work at night may avail of this additional wage benefit called night shift differential.

deduction on account of facilities provided by the employer.

x x x

Art. 93. Compensation for Rest Day, Sunday or Holiday Work. –

(a) Where an employee is made or permitted to work on his scheduled rest day, he shall be paid an additional compensation of at least thirty (30%) percent of his regular wage. An employee shall be entitled to such additional compensation for work performed on Sunday only when it is his established rest day.

(b) When the nature of the work of the employee is such that he has no regular workdays and no regular rest days can be scheduled, he shall be paid an additional compensation of at least thirty (30%) percent of his regular wage for work performed on Sundays and holidays.

(c) Work performed on any special holiday shall be paid an additional compensation of at least thirty (30%) percent of the regular wage of the employee. Where such holiday work falls on the employees scheduled rest day, he shall be entitled to an additional compensation of at least fifty (50%) percent of his regular wage.

(d) Where the collective bargaining agreement or other applicable employment contract stipulates the payment of a higher premium pay than that prescribed under this Article, the employer shall pay such higher rate.

Art. 94. Right to Holiday Pay. –

(a) Every worker shall be paid his regular daily wage during regular holidays, except in retail and service establishments regularly employing less than ten (10) workers;

(b) The employer may require an employee to work on any holiday but such employee shall be paid a compensation equivalent to twice his regular rate;

x x x

Art. 102. Forms of Payment. -- No employer shall pay the wages of an employee by means of promissory notes, vouchers, coupons, tokens, tickets, chits or any object other than legal tender, even when expressly requested by the employee.

Payment of wages by check or money order shall be allowed when such manner of payment is customary on the date of effectivity of this Code, or is necessary because of special circumstances as specified in appropriate regulations to be issued by the Secretary of Labor or as stipulated in a collective bargaining agreement.

Art. 103. Time of Payment. -- Wages shall be paid at least once every two (2) weeks or twice a month at intervals not exceeding sixteen (16) days. If on account of force majeure or circumstances beyond the employer's control, payment of wages on or within the time herein provided cannot be made, the employer shall pay the wages immediately after such force majeure or circumstances have ceased. No employer shall make payment with less frequency than once a month.

The payment of wages of employees engaged to perform a task which cannot be completed in two (2) weeks shall be subject to the following conditions, in the absence of a collective bargaining agreement or arbitration award:

(1) That payments are made at intervals not exceeding sixteen (16) days, in proportion to the amount of work completed;

(2) That final settlement is made upon completion of the work.

Art. 104. Place of Payment. -- Payment of wages shall be made at or near the place of undertaking, except as otherwise provided by such regulations as the Secretary of Labor may prescribe under conditions to ensure greater protection of wages.

Art. 105. Direct Payment of Wages. -- Wages shall be paid directly to the workers to whom they are due.

x x x.

Art. 111. Attorney's Fees. –

(a) In cases of unlawful withholding of wages the culpable party may be assessed attorney's fees equivalent to ten percent of the amount of wages recovered.

x x x

Art. 112. Non-Interference in Disposal of Wages. -- No employer shall limit or otherwise interfere with the freedom of any employee to dispose of his wages. He shall not in any manner force, compel, or oblige his employees to purchase merchandise, commodities or other property from the employer or from any other person, or otherwise make use of any store or services of such employer or any other person.

Art. 113. Wage Deduction. -- No employer, in his own behalf or in behalf of any person, shall make any deduction from the wages of his employees, except:

(a) In cases where the worker is insured with his consent by the employer, and the deduction is to recompense the employer for the amount paid by him as premium on the insurance;
(b) For union dues, in cases where the right of the worker or his union to check-off has been recognized by the employer or authorized in writing by the individual worker concerned; and

(c) In cases where the employer is authorized by law or regulations issued by the Secretary of Labor.

Art. 114. Deposits for Loss or Damage. -- No employer shall require his worker to make deposits from which deductions shall be made for the reimbursement of loss or of damage to tools, materials, or equipment supplied by the employer, except when the employer is engaged in such trades, occupations or business where the practice of making deductions or requiring deposits is a recognized one, or is necessary or desirable as determined by the Secretary of Labor in appropriate rules and regulations.

Art. 115. Limitations. -- No deduction from the deposits of an employee for the actual amount of the loss or damage shall be made unless the employee has been heard thereon, and his responsibility has been clearly shown.

Art. 116. Withholding of Wages and Kickbacks Prohibited. -- It shall be unlawful for any person, directly or indirectly, to withhold any amount from the wages of a worker or induce him to give up any part of his wages by force, stealth, intimidation, threat or by any other means whatsoever without the worker's consent.

Art. 117. Deduction to Ensure Employment. -- It shall be unlawful to make any deduction from the wages of any employee for the benefit of the employer or his representative or intermediary as consideration of a promise of employment or retention in employment.

Art. 118. Retaliatory Measures. -- It shall be unlawful for an employer to refuse to pay or reduce the wages and benefits, discharge or in any manner discriminate against any employee who has filed any complaint or instituted any proceeding under this Title or has testified or is about to testify in such proceedings.

Art. 119. False Reporting. -- It shall be unlawful for any person to make any statement, report, or record filed or kept pursuant to the provisions of this Code knowing such statement, report or record to be false in any material respect.

10.2.2 13th-Month Pay

The law on 13th-month pay covers only the rank-and-file employees. However, it does not cover household helpers and those paid on purely commission or task basis. Employees paid on piece rate basis are included in the coverage of the 13th-month pay law.[85]

PRESIDENTIAL DECREE NO. 851
13TH-MONTH PAY LAW
[AS AMENDED BY
MEMORANDUM ORDER NO. 28]

Sec. 1 All employers are hereby required to pay all their rank-and-file employees a 13th month pay not later than December 24 of every year.

10.3 Occupational Safety And Health

10.3.1 Labor Code

Art. 156. First Aid Treatment. -- Every employer shall keep in his establishment such first-aid medicines and equipment as the nature and conditions of work may require, in accordance with such regulations as the Department of Labor shall prescribe.

---

[85]　P.D. 851, Sec. 3.

The employer shall take steps for the training of a sufficient number of employees in first-aid treatment.

Art. 157. Emergency Medical and Dental Services. -- It shall be the duty of every employer to furnish his employees in any locality with free medical and dental attendance and facilities consisting of:

(a) The services of a full-time registered nurse when the number of employees exceeds fifty (50) but not more than two hundred (200) except when the employer does not maintain hazardous workplaces, in which case the services of a graduate first-aider shall be provided for the protection of the workers, where no registered nurse is available....;

(b) The services of a full-time registered nurse, a part-time physician and dentist, and an emergency clinic, when the number of employees exceeds two hundred (200) but not more than three hundred (300); and,

(c) The services of a full-time physician, dentist and a full-time registered nurse as well as a dental clinic, and an infirmary or emergency hospital with one bed capacity for every one hundred (100) employees when the number of employees exceeds three hundred (300).

In cases of hazardous workplaces, no employer shall engage the services of a physician or dentist who cannot stay in the premises of the establishment for at least two (2) hours, in the case of those engaged on part-time basis, and not less than eight (8) hours in the case of those employed on full-time basis. Where the undertaking is non-hazardous in nature, the physician and dentist may be engaged on retained basis, subject to such regulations as the Secretary of Labor may prescribe to insure immediate availability of medical and dental treatment and attendance in case of emergency.

x x x

Art. 161.   Assistance of Employer. -- It shall be the duty of any employer to provide all the necessary assistance to ensure the adequate and immediate medical and dental attendance and treatment to an injured or sick employee in case of emergency.

10.3.2 Omnibus Rules Implementing The Labor Code

RULE II
OCCUPATIONAL HEALTH AND SAFETY

Sec. 2.   General Occupational Health and Safety Standards. -- Every employer covered by this Rule shall keep and maintain his workplace free from work hazards that are causing or likely to cause physical harm to the workers or damage to property.

x x x

Sec. 5.   Training of Personnel in Safety and Health. -- Every employer shall take steps to train a sufficient number of his supervisors or technical personnel in occupational safety and health.

10.4   Social Security Benefits

The U.N. Convention on the Rights of the Child guarantees the right of the child to social security. Social security laws give employees the needed security and stability in terms of their basic financial needs in case they sustain any physical disability or infirmity while in the actual performance of their work. Aside from the Labor Code, existing laws on social security include the Social Security Law (R.A. 1161) and the Medical Care Act.

10.4.1. R.A. 1161, Social Security Law

The Social Security Law provides to covered employees and their families protection against the hazards of disability, sickness, old age, and death, with a view to promoting their well-being in the spirit of social justice. The law imposes upon employers and employees the obligation to become members of and make contributions to the Social Security System (SSS).

Employed children are understood to be covered by the system since the law states that:

> *Sec. 9. Compulsory Coverage.* -- (a) Coverage in the SSS shall be compulsory upon all employees not over sixty years of age and their employers....

Several types of employment, however, are excluded from the coverage of the law, such as: agricultural labor when performed by a worker who is not paid any regular daily wage or base pay and who does not work for at least six continuous months in a year; employment purely casual and not for purpose of the business of the employer; service performed by a child in the employ of his parents; etc..[86]

Under the Social Security Law, both the employer and the employee have the obligation to contribute to the System a certain amount every month based on the monthly salary of the employee. The obligation to remit both the employer's and employees' contributions to the SSS, however, is imposed only upon the employer.

---

[86] R.A. 1161, Sec. 8 (j).

Sec. 18. Employee's Contributions. --

(a)   Beginning as of the last day of the calendar month when an employee's compulsory coverage takes effect and every month thereafter during his employment, the employer shall deduct and withhold from such employee's monthly salary....

(b) Every employer shall issue a receipt for all contributions deducted from the employee's compensation or shall indicate such deductions on the employee's pay envelopes.

Sec. 19. Employer's Contributions. --

(a) Beginning as of the last day of the month when an employee's compulsory coverage takes effect and every month thereafter during his employment, his employer shall pay, with respect to such covered employee, the employer's contribution in accordance with the schedule indicated....   Notwithstanding any contract to the contrary, an employer shall not deduct, directly or indirectly, from the compensation of his employees covered by the SSS or otherwise recover from them the employer's contributions with respect to such employees.

10.4.2 Employees' Compensation And State Insurance Fund

Under the employees' compensation program, a fund known as the State Insurance Fund is established through premium payments exacted from employers and from which employees and their dependents in the event of work-connected disability or death, may promptly secure adequate income benefit, and medical or related benefits. The employees' compensation law applies to all employers, public or private; and to all employees, public or private, including casual, emergency, temporary or substitute employment. Thus, children who are employed in establishments are also entitled to such insurance coverage by virtue of the Labor Code's mandate that:

> Art. 168. *Compulsory Coverage.* --- Coverage in the State Insurance Fund shall be compulsory upon all employers and their employees not over sixty (60) years of age....

Private employers are required to remit to the Social Security System a monthly contribution as follows:
> Art. 183. *Employers Contributions.* --

> (a) Under such regulations as the System may prescribe, beginning as of the last day of the month when an employee's compulsory coverage takes effect and every month thereafter during his employment, his employer shall prepare to remit to the System a contribution equivalent to one percent of his monthly salary credit.

> x x x

> (c) Contributions under this Title shall be paid in their entirety by the employer and any contract or device for the deduction of any portion thereof from the wages or salaries of the employees shall be null and void.

10.4.3 Medicare Act / Health Insurance Act

R.A. 7875 or the National Health Insurance Act of 1995 created a National Health Insurance Fund under the administration of the newly-established Philippine Health Insurance Corporation, from which members may secure essential goods, health and other social services at affordable cost. Although this law repealed the Revised Philippine Medicare Act, the obligation of both employers and employees under the Medicare Act to contribute to the existing Health Insurance Fund of the SSS, still subsists. Moreover, until such time that the new National Health Insurance Program of the Philippine Health Insurance Corporation is firmly established, the SSS shall continue to operate its former Medicare Program and collect medicare contributions from members.

Under the former Medicare Act, all employers who are compulsorily covered under the Social Security Law are required to perform the following obligations:

PRESIDENTIAL DECREE 1519
REVISED PHILIPPINE MEDICARE ACT
[Superseded by the National Health Insurance Act of 1995]

Sec. 19. Collection of Contributions to the Health Insurance Fund. - The employer shall deduct from his employee's monthly compensation the employee's contribution. The employee's contribution and the employer's counterpart thereof shall be remitted by the employer directly to the...SSS... in the same manner as other SSS...contributions, and shall be subject to the same penalties for late payment. The employer's counterpart contribution shall not in any manner be recovered from the employee. Failure of the employer to remit to the...SSS the corresponding employee's and employer's contributions shall not be a reason for depriving the employee of the benefits of this Decree.

10.5   Security Of Tenure

Children who have attained the status of regular employment are entitled to security of tenure. Attached to this right is the right to file a case for illegal dismissal, when appropriate, and to ask for damages and/or reinstatement. The right to security of tenure, however, is only available to legally employed children such as those between 15 to 18 years who are employed in non-hazardous undertakings, or children in the public entertainment or information industry as allowed by R.A. 7658. Illegally employed children do not have the right to security of tenure since they are not supposed to be employed in the first place. To allow them to go back to their employment will be tantamount to breaking the law.

> *Art. 279. Security of Tenure.* -- In cases of regular employment, the employer shall not terminate the services of an employee except for a just cause or when authorized by this Title. An employee who is unjustly dismissed from work shall be entitled to reinstatement without loss of seniority rights and other privileges and to his full backwages, inclusive of allowances, and to his other benefits or their monetary equivalent computed from the time his compensation was withheld from him up to the time of his actual reinstatement.

V. RIGHTS AND PRIVILEGES OF WORKING CHILDREN

A child worker is protected both insofar as his/her status as a child and as a worker is concerned.

As a child, he/she is entitled to all the rights of the child contained in the Child and Youth Welfare Code (Art. 3) and in the U.N. Convention on the Rights of the Child (CRC). These rights encompass social rights, economic rights, cultural rights, and civil and political rights. Under the CRC, which the Philippines ratified in July 1990, the child is entitled to a broad range of rights which may be grouped into survival rights (e.g., right to life, right to the highest standard of health and medical care available, right to adequate standard of living, right to parental care and support, right to social security, etc.), protection rights (e.g., right to a name, nationality and identity; right to protection from discrimination, abuse, neglect and exploitation; etc.), development rights (e.g., right to information, education, leisure, recreation and cultural activities, etc.), and participation rights (e.g., right to opinion; right to freedom of expression; right to freedom of thought, conscience and religion; right to freedom of association; right to privacy; etc.).

As a worker, the child is entitled to the basic rights of all workers such as the right to just and favorable conditions of work, the right to social security, the right to form or join labor unions, and the right to a just and living wage. Although not all these rights have been framed into specific laws for child workers, a child who enters the labor force automatically becomes entitled to these rights in addition to his/her rights as a child.

There are several laws, however, which take into consideration the needs of the child worker both as a child and as a laborer. Presented in this section are the laws which provide special rights and privileges to child workers.

A. THE SAMAHAN

CHILD AND YOUTH WELFARE CODE
TITLE VI
CHILD AND YOUTH WELFARE
AND THE SAMAHAN
CHAPTER 1
DUTIES IN GENERAL OF THE SAMAHAN

Art. 104. "Samahan" Defined. - As used in this Code, the term "Samahan" shall refer to the aggregate of persons working in commercial, industrial, and agricultural establishments or enterprises, whether belonging to labor or management.

Art. 105. Organization. - The barangay, municipal and city councils, whenever necessary, shall provide by ordinance for the formation and organization of a Samahan in their respective communities. Membership in the Samahan shall be on voluntary basis from among responsible persons from the various sectors of the community mentioned in the preceding article.

Art. 106. Duties of the Samahan. - The Samahan shall:

(1) Prevent the employment of children in any kind of occupation or calling which is harmful to their normal growth and development;

(2) Forestall their exploitation by insuring that their rates of pay, hours of work and other conditions of employment are in accordance not only with law but also with equity;

(3) Give adequate protection from all hazards to their safety, health, and morals, and secure to them their basic right to an education;

(4) Help out-of-school youth to learn and earn at the same time by helping them look for

opportunities to engage in economic self-sufficient projects;

(5) Coordinate with vocational and handicraft classes in all schools and agencies in the barangay, municipality or city to arrange for possible marketing of the products or articles made by the students; and

(6) Provide work experience, training and employment in those areas where the restoration and conservation of our natural resources is deemed necessary.

x x x

Art. 110. Education of Children Employed as Domestics. - If a domestic is under sixteen years of age, the head of the family shall give him an opportunity to complete at least elementary education as required under Article 71. The cost of such education shall be a part of the domestic's compensation unless there is a stipulation to the contrary.

CHAPTER 3
LABOR-MANAGEMENT PROJECT

Art. 111. Right to Self-Organization. - Working children shall have the same freedom as adults to join the collective bargaining union of their own choosing in accordance with existing law.

Neither management nor any collective bargaining union shall threaten or coerce working children to join, continue or withdraw as members of such union.

Art. 112. Conditions of Employment. - There shall be close collaboration between labor and management in the observance of the conditions of employment required by law for working children.

Art. 113. Educational Assistance Program. - The management may allow time off without loss or reduction of wages for working children with special talents to enable them to pursue formal studies in technical schools on scholarship financed by management or by the collective bargaining union or unions.

Art. 114.   Welfare Programs. - Labor and management shall, in cooperation with the Women and Minors Bureau of the Department of Labor, undertake projects and in-service training programs for working children which shall improve their conditions of employment, improve their capabilities and physical fitness, increase their efficiency, secure opportunities for their promotion, prepare them for more responsible positions, and provide for their social, educational and cultural advancement.

Art. 115.   Research Projects. - Labor and management shall cooperate with any government or private research project on matters affecting the welfare of working children.

CHAPTER 4
COLLABORATION BETWEEN THE HOME AND THE SAMAHAN

Art. 116.   Collaboration Between the Home and the Samahan. - The home shall assist the Samahan in the promotion of the welfare of working children and for this purpose shall:

(1) Instill in the hearts and minds of working children the value of dignity of labor;

(2) Stress the importance of the virtues of honesty, diligence and perseverance in the discharge of their duties;

(3) Counsel them on the provident use of the fruits of their labor for the enrichment of their lives and the improvement of their economic security; and

(4) Protect their general well-being against exploitation by management or unions as well as against conditions of their work prejudicial to their health, education, or morals.

B. NON-FORMAL EDUCATION

R.A. 7610
THE CHILD PROTECTION LAW
ARTICLE VIII
WORKING CHILDREN

Sec. 13. Non-formal Education for Working Children. - The Department of Education Culture and Sports shall promulgate a course design under its non-formal education program aimed at promoting the intellectual, moral and vocational efficiency of working children who have not undergone or finished elementary or secondary education. Such course design shall integrate the learning process deemed most effective under given circumstances.

C. SUMMER EMPLOYMENT

1. Republic Act No. 7323

AN ACT TO HELP POOR BUT DESERVING STUDENTS PURSUE THEIR EDUCATION BY ENCOURAGING THEIR EMPLOYMENT DURING SUMMER AND/OR CHRISTMAS VACATIONS, THROUGH INCENTIVES GRANTED TO EMPLOYERS, ALLOWING THEM TO PAY ONLY SIX PER CENTUM OF THEIR SALARIES OR WAGES AND THE FORTY PER CENTUM THROUGH EDUCATION VOUCHERS TO BE PAID BY THE GOVERNMENT, PROHIBITING AND PENALIZING THE FILING OF FRAUDULENT OR FICTITIOUS CLAIMS AND FOR OTHER PURPOSES

Be it enacted by the Senate and the House of Representatives of the Philippines in Congress assembled:

Sec. 1. Any provision of law to the contrary notwithstanding, any person or entity employing at least fifty (50) persons may during the summer and/or Christmas vacations employ poor but deserving students fifteen (15) years of age but not more than twenty-five (25) years old, paying them a salary or wage not lower than the minimum wage provided by law and other applicable labor rules and regulations.

For purposes of this Act, poor but deserving students refer to those whose parents' combined incomes, together with their income, if any, do not exceed Thirty six thousand pesos (P36,000) per annum. Employment should be at the Labor Exchange Center of the Department of Labor and Employment (DOLE).

Sec. 2. Sixty per centum (60%) of said salary or wage shall be paid by the employer in cash and forty per centum (40%) by the Government in the form of a voucher which shall be applicable in the payment for his tuition fees and books in any educational institution for secondary, tertiary, vocational or technological education. The amount of the education voucher shall be paid by the Government to the educational institution concerned within thirty (30) days from its presentation to the officer or agency designated by the Secretary of Finance.

The voucher shall not be transferable except when the payee thereof dies or for a justifiable cause stops in his duties in which case it can be transferred to his brothers or sisters. If there be none, the amount thereof shall be paid his heirs or to the payee himself, as the case may be.

Sec. 3. The Secretary of Labor and Employment, the Secretary of Education, Culture and Sports and the Secretary of Finance shall issue the corresponding rules and regulations to carry out the purposes of this Act.

The Secretary of Labor and Employment shall be the Project Director of this program.

Sec. 4. Any person or entity who shall make any fraudulent or fictitious claim under this Act, regardless of whether payment has been made, shall upon conviction be punished with imprisonment of not less than six (6) months and not more than one (1) year and a fine of not less than Ten thousand pesos (P10,000), without prejudice to the prosecution and punishment for any other offense punishable under the Revised Penal Code or any other penal statute.

In case of partnerships or corporations, the managing partner, general manager, or chief executive officer, as the case may be, shall be criminally liable.

Sec. 5. The amount necessary to carry out the purposes of this Act is hereby authorized to be appropriated in the General Appropriations Act for 1992 and the subsequent annual general appropriations acts.

Sec. 6. This Act shall take effect after its publication in the Official Gazette or in at least two (2) national newspapers of general circulation.

Approved, March 30, 1992.

2. Implementing Rules Of R.A. 7323

RULES AND REGULATIONS
IMPLEMENTING REPUBLIC ACT 7323 (SPES)

Pursuant to the authority granted to the Secretary of Labor and Employment, Secretary of Education, Culture and Sports and Secretary of Finance under Section 3 of Republic Act No. 7323, the following rules and regulations are hereby promulgated and issued for the guidance of all concerned.

RULE I: Preliminary Provisions

Sec. 1. Title. - This issuance shall be known as the Rules and Regulations Implementing R.A. No. 7323 entitled "An Act to Help Poor But Deserving Students Pursue Their Education by Encouraging Their Employment During Summer and/or Christmas Vacations, Through Incentives Granted to Employers, Allowing Them to Pay Only Sixty Per Centum of Their Salaries or Wages and the Forty Per Centum Through Education Vouchers to be Paid by the Government, Prohibiting and Penalizing the Filing of Fraudulent or Fictitious Claims, and For Other Purposes".

Sec. 2. Construction. - These Rules and Regulations shall be liberally construed to carry out the objectives of R.A. 7323.

Sec. 3. Definition of Terms. - As used in these Rules and Regulations:

(a) "Act" refers to Republic Act No. 7323.
(b) "DOLE" refers to the Department of Labor and Employment.
(c) "DECS" refers to the Department of Education, Culture and Sports.
(d) "DOF" refers to the Department of Finance.

(e) "Program" refers to the scheme of assisting poor but deserving students find employment during summer and/or Christmas vacations.

(f) "Entity" refers to any person, natural or juridical, employing at least 50 workers as defined herein.

(g) "Student" refers to any person at least 15 years of age but not more than 25 years old who is either enrolled in any institution for secondary, tertiary, vocational or technological institution or intending to be enrolled in any of these schools.

(h) "Labor Exchange Center" refers to any employment service unit of the DOLE or other units under its technical supervision which are involved in the facilitation of employment.

RULE II: Coverage

Sec. 1. These rules shall apply to:

(a) Poor but deserving students who are at least 15 years of age but not more than twenty-five years old who are enrolled or intending to enroll in any educational institution for secondary, tertiary, vocational or technological education; and

(b) Participating persons or entities who have employed at least 50 workers at any given time during the past twelve (12) months. For this purpose, employed workers refer to all regular, seasonal, temporary, casual and workers of contracted out services of persons or entities. Participating entities shall include private establishments, national and local government units, government-owned or controlled corporations, labor unions and other similar organizations and associations, among others.

RULE III: Eligibility and Requirements for Employment

Sec. 1.   Qualifications. - Any student may apply for employment under the Program provided he/she meets the following qualifications:

(a) At least 15 years of age but not more than 25 years old;

(b) Enrolled during the school year/term or enrolled during the school year/term immediately preceding the summer vacation or who has dropped out of school and who intends to continue his/her education; and

(c) The combined net income after tax of parents, including his/her income, if any, does not exceed Thirty-six thousand (₱36,000.00) pesos per annum.

(d) At least garnered an average passing grade during the school year/term referred to above.

Sec. 2.   Student Dependents of Displaced or Would-be-Displaced   Workers. - Any student dependent or drop out, dependent of workers who are displaced or about to be displaced due to business closures or work stoppages arising from economic or non-economic reasons, may also qualify under this Program provided he/she meets the qualifications required in subsections (a), (b) and (d) of the preceding section.

Sec. 3.   Requirements for Employment. - In support of his/her qualifications, the following documents shall be required from the student:

(a) Copy of birth or baptismal certificate or joint certification of at least two persons who can attest to the date of birth of the student-applicant;

(b) Certification by the School Registrar as to (1) his/her last enrollment, and (2) his/her passing average grade; and

(c) Certified true copy of the latest income tax return (ITR) of his/her parents or certification from the Barangay Chairman in the locality where his/her family or certification from employer/union president as the employment status of his/her parents.

RULE IV: Program Implementation

Sec. 1.   Program Administration. - The administration of this Program shall be lodged in the DOLE and its implementing units in the regions.

Sec. 2.   Role of DECS. - The DECS shall coordinate with DOLE in the promotion of this Program among students and administrators of all secondary, tertiary, vocational or technological institutions.   The DECS shall ensure that the vouchers presented by students and its application will be honored by all concerned schools and monitored accordingly.

Sec. 3.   Role of DOF. - The DOF shall designate an officer or agency to administer the financial requirements of this Program.   The Financial Management Service Division at the DOLE Regional Offices are hereby deputized for this purpose.

Sec 4. Where to Apply for Employment. - Any qualified student may apply for employment assistance under this Program in any employment service unit of the DOLE Regional Offices. For this purpose, the DOLE Regional Offices shall mobilize the NMYC Training/Placement Centers, Public Employment Service Offices (PESOs) and the Community Employment Centers (CECs) of local government units which are under its technical supervision to assist in the employment needs of students in the provincial and city/municipal levels. The Secretary of Labor and Employment or the DOLE Regional Directors may deputize unions, non-government organizations and employers groups for the purpose of processing SPES participants who shall coordinate such activities to the former.

Sec. 5. Availment Procedure. - The student shall apply in person to the nearest labor exchange center of DOLE, NMYC Training/Placement Centers, PESOs/CECs operated by local government units, or other duly deputized entities mobilized for this purpose. The student shall submit himself/herself to a preliminary interview and screening to determine his/her qualifications. The student's qualifications are then matched with the requirements of vacancies of participating persons or entities. If the student is qualified to a vacancy, he/she is referred for consideration by the Employer. The Employer will either accept or deny his/her application. In case his/her application is denied, the student may return to the public employment office for referral to other vacancies of participating entities where he/she may qualify.

RULE V: Payment of Salary

Sec 1. Procedure in the Payment of Salary or Wage of Employed Students. - At least sixty percent (60%) of the student-employee's salary which shall not be less than sixty percent (60%) of the applicable minimum wage shall be paid in cash by the Employer. The remaining forty percent (40%) of his/her salary shall be paid by the DOLE in the form of education voucher based on information to be provided by the Employer. The education voucher shall be presented by the student - employee to the educational institution where he/she is enrolled or where he/she intends to enroll to cover expenses for his/her tuition fees and books. In case the amount of the education voucher exceeds the amount presented by the educational institution for payment, the DOLE shall refund the balance amount in cash.

RULE VI: Terms and Conditions in the Employment of Students

Sec. 1. Contract of Employment. - The employment of students under this Program shall be covered by an Employment Contract between the Employer and the student-employee.

Sec. 2.   Duties and Responsibilities of Employer. - In addition to other applicable labor rules and regulations, the Employer shall exercise the following duties and responsibilities towards the student-employee;

(a) To pay in cash at least sixty per centum (60%) of his/her salary;

(b) To ensure that the student-employee will not be exposed to hazardous undertakings nor to allow the student-employee to work in nightclubs, cocktail lounges, beerhouses, massage clinics, and bars of similar establishments;

(c) To ensure that the student-employee below 18 years old shall not be required to work beyond 8 hours a day nor should it exceed 48 hours a week or render work during rest days;

(d) To submit periodic reports to DOLE or its subsidiary units to include among others the following: number of students hired, date of hiring and termination of employment, the wage rate and the total cash wage or salary paid to the student-employee, number of hours worked and other pertinent information; and

(e) To ensure that the employment of women and young workers shall be in accordance with the Labor Code and its Implementing Rules.

Sec. 3. Duties and Responsibilities of Student-Employee. - The student-employee shall have the following duties and responsibilities.

(a) To perform tasks and activities assigned by the Emplo-yer;

(b) To strictly adhere to the rules and regulations imposed by the Employer; and

(c) To use the education voucher for the purposes intended in the Act.

Sec. 4. Duties and Responsibilities of DOLE. - It shall be the duty and responsibility of DOLE to ensure:

(a) The payment of forty per centum (40%) of the salary of the student-employee in the form of a voucher which shall be applicable for the payment of his/her tuition fees and books; and

(b) The payment of the amount of the education voucher to the educational institution concerned within thirty (30) days from its presentation to the Regional Office of DOLE; Provided, that the Regional Office of DOLE under whose jurisdiction the school of enrollment of the student-employee is located should pay the education voucher.

RULE VII: Non-Transferability of Education Voucher.

The education voucher shall not be transferable except in the following cases:

(a) Death of the payee; or

(b) When the student stops in his studies due to prolonged illness, incapacity, economic necessity and similar causes. In this case, the voucher can be transferred to his brothers or sisters. If the payee has no brother or sister, the amount of the voucher shall be paid his lawful heirs or to the payee himself, as the case may be.

RULE VIII: Entitlement to Other Benefits and Incentives

Sec. 1. Other Benefits and Incentives. - The student-employee shall be entitled to other monetary benefits and incentives provided under existing laws specifically SSS and Medicare contributions.

RULE IX: Special Provision

Sec. 1.   Effect on Regular Employee. - Nothing in these rules shall be construed to justify an Employer in terminating the services of regular employees to accommodate the student-employee or diminish the benefits of regular employee upon the effectivity of these rules.

RULE X: Penal Provisions

Sec. 1.   Filing of Fraudulent or Fictitious Claim. - Any person or entity who shall make any fraudulent or fictitious claim under this Act, regardless of whether payment has been made, shall upon conviction be punished with imprisonment of not less than six (6) months and not more than one (1) year and a fine of not less than Ten thousand pesos (P10,000.00) without prejudice to their prosecution and punishment for any other offense punishable under the Revised Penal Code or any other penal statute.

In case of partnership or corporations, the managing partner, general manager, or chief executive officer, as the case may be shall be criminally liable.

RULE XI: Effectivity.

These rules and regulations shall take effect immediately.

Signed this 5th day of March 1993 in Manila.

VI. REMEDIES AGAINST ABUSE, EXPLOITATION AND DISCRIMINATION

The remedies available to child workers for the violation of their rights are contained in different laws. Employers or recruiters of children who work in the formal sector may be held liable under the penalty provisions of the Labor Code, the Social Security Law, the Minimum Wage Law and R.A. 7658, for their failure to observe the requirements on terms and conditions of employment. In addition, they may also be held liable under the provisions of the Revised Penal Code and R.A. 7610 for any inhumane treatment, abuse or exploitation suffered by the child workers. Damages may also be claimed under the Civil Code, against the employers.

On the other hand, child workers in the informal sector, such as those engaged in the street trade or in the flesh trade, may invoke the Revised Penal Code, R.A. 7610, the Dangerous Drugs Law, and several ordinances against persons who exploit and abuse them in the course of their work. Moreover, parents of child workers may be held criminally liable under the Child and Youth Welfare Code for abandonment, neglect or exploitation of their children.

Presented below are the details of the remedies mentioned above according to the type of violation committed.

A. ILLEGAL RECRUITMENT

1. Prosecute Under Art. 39 Of The Labor Code

BOOK I - PRE-EMPLOYMENT
TITLE I - RECRUITMENT AND PLACEMENT OF WORKERS

Art. 34. Prohibited Practices. -- It shall be unlawful for any individual, entity, licensee, or holder of authority:

(a) To charge or accept, directly or indirectly, any amount greater than that specified in the schedule of allowable fees prescribed by the Secretary of Labor, or to make a worker pay any amount greater than that actually received by him as a loan or advance;

(b) To furnish or publish any false notice or information or document in relation to recruitment or employment;

x x x

f) To engage in the recruitment or placement of workers in jobs harmful to public health or morality or to the dignity of the Republic of the Philippines. [*Underscoring supplied.*]

x x x

Art. 38. Illegal Recruitment. -

(a) Any recruitment activities, including the prohibited practices enumerated under Article 34 of the Code, to be undertaken by non-licensees or non-holders of authority shall be deemed illegal and punishable under Article 39 of this Code. The Secretary of Labor and Employment or any law enforcement officer may initiate complaints under this Article.

(b) Illegal recruitment when committed by a syndicate or in large scale shall be considered an offense involving economic sabotage and shall be penalized in accordance with Article 39 hereof.

Illegal recruitment is deemed committed by a syndicate if carried out by a group of three (3) or more persons conspiring and/or confederating with one another in carrying out any unlawful or illegal transaction, enterprise or scheme defined under the first paragraph hereof. Illegal recruitment is deemed committed in large scale if committed against three (3) or more persons individually or as a group.

(c) The Secretary of Labor and Employment or his duly authorized representatives shall have the power to cause the arrest and detention of such non-licensee or non-holder of authority if after investigation it is determined that his activities constitute a danger to national security and public order or will lead to further exploitation of job-seekers. The Secretary shall order the search of the office or premises and seizure of documents, paraphernalia, properties and other implements used in illegal recruitment activities and the closure of companies, establishments and entities found to be engaged in the recruitment of workers for overseas employment, without having been licensed or authorized to do so.

[*Note that the Supreme Court issued a ruling on March 14, 1990, in the case of Salazar vs. Achacoso (G.R. No. 81510), stating that "the Secretary of Labor, not being a judge, may no longer issue search or arrest warrants". Hence, the authorities must go through the judicial process to obtain such. The Secretary, however, still has the power to order the closure of illegal recruitment establishments, the same being administrative and regulatory in nature.*]

Art. 39. Penalties. -

(a) The penalty of life imprisonment and a fine of One Hundred Thousand Pesos (P100,000) shall be imposed if illegal recruitment constitutes economic sabotage as defined herein.

(b) Any licensee or holder of authority found violating or causing another to violate any provision of this Title or its implementing rules and regulations shall, upon conviction thereof, suffer the penalty of imprisonment of not less than two (2) years nor more than five (5) years or a fine of not less than Ten Thousand Pesos (P10,000) nor more than Fifty Thousand Pesos (P50,000), or both such imprisonment and fine, at the discretion of the court;

(c) Any person who is neither a licensee nor a holder of authority under this Title found violating any provision thereof or its implementing rules and regulations shall, upon conviction thereof, suffer the penalty of imprisonment of not less than four (4) years nor more than (8) eight years or a fine of not less than Twenty Thousand Pesos (P20,000) nor more than One Hundred Thousand Pesos (P100,000), or both such imprisonment and fine, at the discretion of the court;

(d) If the offender is a corporation, partnership, association or entity, the penalty shall be imposed upon the officer or officers of the corporation, partnership, association or entity responsible for violation; and if such officer is an alien, he shall, in addition to the penalties herein prescribed, be deported without further proceedings;

(e) In every case, conviction shall cause and carry the automatic revocation of license or authority and all the permits and privileges granted to such person or entity under this Title, and the forfeiture of the cash and surety bonds.

2. Order Suspension/Cancellation Of License Or Closure Of Establishment

Art. 35. Suspension and/or Cancellation of License or Authority -- The Secretary of Labor shall have the power to suspend or cancel any license to recruit employees for overseas employment, for violation of rules and regulations issued by the Secretary of Labor and Employment, ...or for violation of the provisions of this and other applicable laws, General Orders and Letters of Instructions.

Art. 36. Regulatory Power. - The Secretary of Labor shall have the power to restrict and regulate the recruitment and placement activities of all agencies within the coverage of this Title and is hereby authorized to issue orders, promulgate rules and regulations to carry out the objectives and implement the provisions of this Title.

3. Prosecute Under R.A. No. 8042 Or The Migrant Workers And Overseas Filipinos Act Of 1995

Republic Act No. 8042 otherwise known as the 'Migrant Workers and Overseas Filipinos Act of 1995' amended Article 38 of the Labor Code on Illegal Recruitment by considering as illegal recruiter even a licensee or holder of authority who commits the acts prohibited under Article 34 of the Labor Code. If the victim of illegal recruitment under R.A. No. 8042 is a minor the maximum penalty under the law shall be imposed.

Sec. 3.   Definitions. - For purposes of this Act:

(a) "Migrant worker" refers to a person who is to be engaged, is engaged or has been engaged in a remunerated activity in a State of which he or she is not a legal resident; to be used interchangeably with overseas Filipino worker.

x x x

Sec. 6. Definition. - For purposes of this Act, illegal recruitment shall mean any act of canvassing, enlisting, contracting, transporting, utilizing, hiring, or procuring workers and includes referring, contract services, promising or advertising for employment abroad, whether for profit or not, when undertaken by a non-licensee or non-holder of authority contemplated under Article 13(f) of Presidential Decree No. 442, as amended, otherwise known as the Labor Code of the Philippines: Provided, That any such non-licensee or non-holder who, in any manner, offers or promises for a fee employment abroad to two or more persons shall be deemed so engaged. It shall likewise include the following acts, whether committed by any person, whether a non-licensee, non-holder, licensee or holder of authority:

(a) To charge or accept directly or indirectly any amount greater than that specified in the schedule of allowable fees prescribed by the Secretary of Labor and Employment, or to make a worker pay any amount greater than that actually received by him as a loan or advance;

(b) To o furnish or publish any false notice or information or document in relation to recruitment or employment;

(c) To give any false notice, testimony, information or document or commit any act of misrepresentation for the purpose of securing a license or authority under the Labor Code;

(d) To induce or attempt to induce a worker already employed to quit his employment in order to offer him another unless the transfer is designed to liberate a worker from oppressive terms and conditions of employment;

(e)   To influence or attempt to influence any person or entity not to employ any worker who has not applied for employment through his agency;

(f)   To engage in the recruitment or placement of workers in jobs harmful to public health or morality or to the dignity of the Republic of the Philippines;

(g)   To obstruct or attempt to obstruct inspection by the Secretary of Labor and Employment or by his duly authorized representative;

(h)   To fail to submit reports on the status of employment, placement vacancies, remittance of foreign exchange earnings, separation from jobs, departures and such other matters or information as may be required by the Secretary of Labor and Employment;

(i)   To substitute or alter to the prejudice of the worker, employment contracts approved and verified by the Department of Labor and Employment from the time of actual signing thereof by the parties up to and including the period of the expiration of the same without the approval of the Department of Labor and Employment;

(j)   For an officer or agent of a recruitment or placement agency to become an officer or member of the Board of any corporation engaged in travel agency or to be engaged directly or indirectly in the management of a travel agency;

(k)   To withhold or deny travel documents from applicant workers before departure for monetary or financial considerations other than those authorized under the Labor Code and its implementing rules and regulations;

(l)   Failure to actually deploy without valid reason as determined by the Department of Labor and Employment ; and

(m)   Failure to reimburse expenses incurred by the worker in connection with his documentation and processing for purposes of deployment, in cases where the deployment does not actually take place without the worker's fault. Illegal recruitment when committed by a syndicate or in large scale shall be considered an offense involving economic sabotage.

Illegal recruitment is deemed committed by a syndicate if carried out by a group of three (3) or more persons conspiring or confederating with one another. It is deemed committed in large scale if committed against three (3) or more persons individually or as a group.

The persons criminally liable for the above offenses are the principals, accomplices and accessories. In case of juridical persons, the officers having control, management or direction of their business shall be liable.

Sec. 7. Penalties –
    (a)   Any person found guilty of illegal recruitment shall suffer the penalty of imprisonment of not less than six (6) years and one (1) day but not more than twelve (12) years and a fine of not less than Two hundred thousand pesos (P200,000.00) nor more than Five hundred thousand pesos (P500,000.00).
    (b)   The penalty of life imprisonment and a fine of not less than Five hundred thousand pesos (P500,000.00) nor more than One million pesos (P1,000,000.00) shall be imposed if illegal recruitment constitutes economic sabotage as defined herein.
    Provided, however, That the maximum penalty shall be imposed if the person illegally recruited is less than eighteen (18) years of age or committed by a non-licensee or non-holder of authority.

B.   VIOLATION OF LABOR CODE PROVISIONS

1. Order Stoppage Of Work Or Suspension Of Operations

Art. 128.   Visitorial and Enforcement Power. -

x x x

(b) [The] Secretary of Labor and Employment or his duly authorized representatives shall have the power to order and administer, after due notice and hearing, compliance with the labor standards provisions of this Code and other labor legislation based on the findings of labor regulation officers or industrial safety engineers made in the course of inspection, and to issue writs of execution to the appropriate authority for the enforcement of their orders, except in cases where the employer contests the findings of the labor regulation officer and raises issues which cannot be resolved without considering evidentiary matters that are not verifiable in the normal course of inspection.

(c).   The Secretary of Labor may likewise order stoppage of work or suspension of operations of any unit or department of an establishment when non-compliance with the law or implementing rules and regulations poses grave and imminent danger to the health and safety of workers in the workplace.   Within twenty-four hours, a hearing shall be conducted to determine whether an order for the stoppage of work or suspension of operations shall be lifted or not.   In case the violation is attributable to the fault of the employer, he shall pay the employees concerned their salaries or wages during the period of such stoppage of work or suspension of operation.

(d) It shall be unlawful for any person or entity to obstruct, impede, delay or otherwise render ineffective the orders of the Secretary of Labor or his duly authorized representatives issued pursuant to the authority granted under this Article, and no inferior court or entity shall issue temporary or permanent injunction or restraining order or otherwise assume jurisdiction over any case involving the enforcement orders issued in accordance with this Article.

(e) Any government employee found guilty of violation of, or abuse of authority, under this Article shall, after appropriate administrative investigation, be subject to summary dismissal from the service.

2. Prosecute Under Art. 288 Of The Labor Code

Art. 288. Penalties. -- Except as otherwise provided in this Code, or unless the acts complained of hinges on a question of interpretation or implementation of ambiguous provisions of an existing collective bargaining agreement, any violation of the provisions of this Code declared to be unlawful or penal in nature shall be punished with a fine of not less than One Thousand Pesos (₱1,000.00) nor more than Ten Thousand Pesos (₱10,000.00), or imprisonment of not less than three months nor more than three years, or both such fine and imprisonment at the discretion of the court. [*Underscoring supplied.*]

In addition to such penalty, any alien found guilty shall be summarily deported upon completion of service of sentence.

Any provision of law to the contrary notwithstanding, any criminal offense punished in this Code shall be under the concurrent jurisdiction of the Municipal or City Courts and the Courts of First Instance [Now Regional Trial Courts].

Art. 289. Who are Liable when Committed by Other than Natural Person. -- If the offense is committed by a corporation, trust, firm, partnership, association or any other entity, the penalty shall be imposed upon the guilty officer or officers of such corporation, trust, firm, partnership, association or entity.

Art. 290. Offenses. -- Offenses penalized under this Code and the rules and regulations issued pursuant thereto shall prescribe in three (3) years.

C. NON-PAYMENT OF PRESCRIBED WAGES

1. File Money Claims With DOLE Regional Director Or The Labor Arbiter

2. Prosecute For Violation Of R.A. 6640, New Minimum Wage Law; R.A. 6726, Wage Rationalization Act; Or R.A. 7655, An Act Increasing The Minimum Wage Of Househelpers

R.A. 6640

Sec. 10. Any person, corporation, trust, firm, partnership, association or entity violating this Act shall be punished by a fine not exceeding Twenty five thousand pesos (P25,000.000) and/or imprisonment for not less than one (1) year nor more than two (2) years....

xxx

R.A. 6726

Sec. 12. Any person, corporation, trust firm, partnership, association or entity which refuses or

fails to pay any of the prescribed increases or
adjustments in the wage rates made in accordance
with this Act shall be punished by a fine not
exceeding Twenty five thousand pesos (P25,000.00)
and/or imprisonment of not less than one (1) year
nor more than two (2) years....

xxx

R.A. 7655

Sec. 2. Any violation of any provision of this
Act shall be punished with an imprisonment of not
more than three (3) months or a fine of not more
than Two thousand pesos (P2,000.00), or both, at
the discretion of the court. [See Art. 143 of the Labor
Code on Employment of Househelpers, as amended
by R.A. 7655, page 98 herein.]

D. VIOLATION OF LAWS ON SOCIAL SECURITY: NON- PAYMENT OF CLAIMS; NON-REMITTANCE OF CONTRIBUTIONS

1. File Money Claims With The Social Security System

2. Prosecute For Violation Of R.A. 1161, Social Security Law

Sec. 28.

x x x

(e) Whoever fails or refuses to comply with the
provisions of this Act or with the rules and
regulations promulgated by the Commission, shall
be punished by a fine of not less than Five hundred
pesos (P500.00) nor more than Five thousand pesos
(P5,000.00), or imprisonment for not less than six
(6) months nor more than one (1) year, or both, at
the discretion of the court: Provided, That where the

violation consists in failure or refusal to register employees...or to deduct contributions from employee's compensation and remit the same to the SSS, the penalty shall be a fine of not less than Five hundred pesos (P500.00) nor more than Five thousand pesos (P5,000.00) and imprisonment for not less than six (6) months nor more than one (1) year.

x x x

(h) Any employer who, after deducting the monthly contributions or loan amortizations from his employee's compensation, fails to remit the said deductions to the SSS within thirty days from the date they became due shall be presumed to have misappropriated such contributions or loan amortizations and shall suffer the penalties provided in Article Three Hundred Fifteen of the Revised Penal Code [Estafa].

3. Prosecute For Violation Of R.A. 7875, National Health Insurance Act Of 1995

Sec. 44. Penal Provisions. -
x x x
Where the violations consist of failure or refusal to deduct contributions from the employee's compensation or to remit the same to the Corporation, the penalty shall be a fine of not less than Five hundred pesos (P500) but not more than One thousand pesos (P1,000) multiplied by the total number of employees employed by the firm and imprisonment of not less than six (6) months but not more than one (1) year....

Any employer or any officer authorized to collect contributions under this Act who, after collecting or deducting the monthly contributions from his employee's compensation, fails to remit the said contributions to the Corporation within thirty (30) days from the date they become due shall be presumed to have misappropriated such contributions and shall suffer the penalties provided for in Article 315 of the Revised Penal Code.

Any employer who shall deduct directly or indirectly from the compensation of the covered employees or otherwise recover from them his own contribution on behalf of such employees shall be punished by a fine not exceeding One thousand pesos (P1,000) multiplied by the total number of employees employed by the firm, or imprisonment not exceeding one (1) year, or both fine and imprisonment, at the discretion of the Court.

4. Prosecute For Violation Of R.A. 7655 If Employer Of Househelper

Sec. 2. Any violation of any provision of this Act shall be punished with an imprisonment of not more than three (3) months or a fine of not more than Two thousand pesos (P2,000.00), or both, at the discretion of the court.

[See Art. 143 of the Labor Code on Employment of Househelpers, as amended by R.A. 7655, page 217 herein.]

E.   INHUMANE TREATMENT

1. Sue For Damages Under The Civil Code

Art. 19. Every person must, in the exercise of his rights and in the performance of his duties, act with justice, give everyone his due, and observe honesty and good faith.

Art. 20. Every person who, contrary to law, wilfully or negligently causes damage to another, shall indemnify the latter for the same.

Art. 21. Any person who wilfully causes loss or injury to another in a manner that is contrary to morals, good customs or public policy shall compensate the latter for the damages.

x x x

Art. 2176. Whoever by act or omission causes damage to another, there being fault or negligence, is obliged to pay for the damage done.

2. Prosecute For Violation Of The Revised Penal Code, R.A. 7610 Or The Child Protection Code, And Other Criminal Laws

F. CRIMES AGAINST CHILDREN UNDER THE REVISED PENAL CODE, AS AMENDED

Crimes under the Revised Penal Code are penalized with distinct penalties depending on the gravity of the offense. The table below serves as a guide in determining the imposable penalties of different crimes. The prescriptive period of the offenses, or the time within which the cases must be filed before the appropriate authorities, are also indicated in the table.

Penalty Prescribed	Duration of Penalty	Prescriptive Period
Death	Death	20 years
Reclusion Perpetua	20 years & 1 day to 40 years	20 years
Reclusion Temporal	12 years & 1 day 20 years	20 years
Prision Mayor	6 years & 1 day to 12 years	15 years
Prision Correccional	6 months & 1 day to 6 years	10 years
Arresto Mayor	1 month & 1 day to 6 months	5 years
Arresto Menor	1 day to 30 days	2 months

The following are the crimes against children contained in the RPC with their corresponding penalties:

1. Offenses Against Decency And Good Customs

Art. 200. Grave Scandal. - The penalties of *arresto mayor* and public censure shall be imposed upon any person who shall offend against decency or good customs by any highly scandalous conduct not expressly falling within any other article of this Code.

Art. 201. Immoral Doctrines, Obscene Publications and Exhibitions, and Indecent Shows. - The penalty of *prision mayor* or a fine ranging from Six thousand (P6,000.00) to Twelve thousand (P12,000.00) pesos, or both such imprisonment and fine, shall be imposed upon:

1. Those who shall publicly expound or proclaim doctrines openly contrary to public morals;

2.(a). The authors of obscene literature, published with their knowledge in any form; the editors publishing such literature; and the owners/operators of the establishment selling the same;

(b). Those who, in theaters, fairs, cinematographs or any other place, exhibit indecent or immoral plays, scenes, acts or shows, whether live or in film, which are prescribed by virtue hereof, shall include those which (1) glorify criminals or condone crimes; (2) serve no other purpose but to satisfy the market for violence, lust or pornography; (3) offend any race or religion; (4) tend to abet traffic in and use of prohibited drugs; and (5) are contrary to law, public order, morals, good customs, traffic in and use of prohibited drugs; and (5) are contrary to law, public order, morals, good customs, established policies, lawful orders, decrees and edicts;

3. Those who shall sell, give away or exhibit films, prints, engravings, sculpture or literature which are offensive to morals.

Art. 202. Vagrants and Prostitutes - Penalty. - The following are *vagrants*:

1. Any person having no apparent means of subsistence, who has the physical ability to work and who neglects to apply himself or herself to some lawful calling;

2. Any person found loitering about public or semi-public buildings or places or tramping or wandering about the country or the streets without visible means of support;

3. Any idle or dissolute person who lodges in houses of ill-fame; ruffians or pimps and those who habitually associate with prostitutes;

4. Any person who, not being included in the provisions of other articles of this Code, shall be found loitering in any inhabited or uninhabited place belonging to another without any lawful or justifiable purpose;

5. Prostitutes.

For the purposes of this article, women who, for money or profit, habitually indulge in sexual intercourse or lascivious conduct, are deemed to be prostitutes.

Any person found guilty of any of the offenses covered by this article shall be punished by *arresto menor* or a fine not exceeding Two hundred pesos (₱ 200.00), and in case of recidivism, by *arresto mayor* in its medium period to *prision correccional* in its

minimum period or a fine ranging from Two
hundred pesos (₱200.00) to Two thousand pesos (₱
2,000.00), or both, in the discretion of the court.

2. Physical Injuries

Art. 262.   Mutilation. - The penalty of
reclusion temporal to *reclusion perpetua* shall be
imposed upon any person who shall intentionally
mutilate another by depriving him, either totally or
partially, of some essential organ of reproduction.

Any other intentional mutilation shall be
punished by prision mayor, in its medium and
maximum periods.

Art. 263.   Serious Physical Injuries. - Any
person who shall wound, beat, or assault another,
shall be guilty of the crime of serious physical
injuries and shall suffer:

1.   The penalty of *prision mayor,* if in
consequence of the physical injuries inflicted, the
injured person shall become insane, imbecile,
impotent, or blind;

2.   The penalty of *prision correccional* in its
medium and maximum periods, if in consequence of
the physical injuries inflicted, the person injured
shall have lost the use of speech or the power to
hear or to smell, or shall have lost an eye, a hand, a
foot, an arm, or a leg or shall have lost the use of
any such member, or shall have become
incapacitated for the work in which he was therefore
habitually engaged;

3.   The penalty of *prision correccional* in its
minimum and medium periods, if in consequence of
the physical injuries inflicted the person injured
shall have become deformed, or shall have lost any
other part of his body, or shall have lost the use
thereof, or shall have been ill or incapacitated for
the performance of the work in which he was

habitually engaged for a period of more than ninety days;

    4. The penalty of *arresto mayor* in its maximum period to *prision correccional* in its minimum period, if the physical injuries inflicted shall have caused the illness or incapacity for labor of the injured person for more than thirty days.

If the offense shall have been committed against any of the persons enumerated in Article 246, or with attendance of any of the circumstances mentioned in Article 248, the case covered by subdivision number 1 of this article shall be punished by reclusion temporal in its medium and maximum periods; the case covered by subdivision number 2 by *prision correccional* in its maximum period to *prision mayor* in its minimum period; the case covered by subdivision number 3 by *prision correccional* in its medium and maximum periods; and the case covered by subdivision number 4 by *prision correccional* in its minimum and medium periods.

The provisions of the preceding paragraph shall not be applicable to a parent who shall inflict physical injuries upon his child by excessive chastisement.

Art. 265. Less Serious Physical Injuries. - Any person who shall inflict upon another physical injuries not described in the preceding articles, but which shall incapacitate the offended party for labor for ten days or more, or shall require medical attendance for the same period, shall be guilty of less serious physical injuries and shall suffer the penalty of *arresto mayor.*

Whenever less serious physical injuries shall have been inflicted with the manifest intent to insult or offend the injured person, or under circumstances adding ignominy to the offense, in addition to the penalty of *arresto mayor,* a fine not exceeding Five hundred pesos (P500.00) shall be imposed.

Any less serious physical injuries inflicted upon the offender's parents, ascendants, guardians, curators, teachers, or persons of rank, or persons in authority, shall be punished by *prision correccional* in its minimum and medium periods, provided that, in the case of persons in authority, the deed does not constitute the crime of assault upon such person.

Art. 266.   Slight Physical Injuries and Maltreatment. - The crime of slight physical injuries shall be punished:

1. By *arresto menor* when the offender has inflicted physical injuries which shall incapacitate the offended party for labor from one to nine days, or shall require medical attendance during the same period.
2. By *arresto menor* or a fine not exceeding Two hundred pesos (P200.00) and censure when the offender has caused physical injuries which do not prevent the offended party from engaging in his habitual work nor require medical attendance.
3. By *arresto menor* in its minimum period or a fine not exceeding Fifty Pesos (P50.00) when the offender shall ill-treat another by deed without causing any injury.

3. Rape

REPUBLIC ACT NO. 8353
AN ACT EXPANDING THE DEFINITION OF THE
CRIME OF RAPE, RECLASSIFYING THE SAME AS A
CRIME AGAINST PERSONS, AMENDING FOR THE
PURPOSE ACT NO. 3815, AS AMENDED,
OTHERWISE KNOWN AS THE REVISED PENAL
CODE AND FOR OTHER PURPOSES

Sec. 1. Short Title. — This Act shall be known as "The Anti-Rape Law of 1997."

Sec 2. Rape as a Crime Against Persons. — The crime of rape shall hereafter be classified as a Crime Against Persons under Title Eight of Act No. 3815, as amended, otherwise known as the Revised Penal Code. Accordingly, there shall be incorporated into Title Eight of the same Code a new chapter to be known as Chapter Three on Rape, to read as follows:

Chapter Three
Rape

Art. 266-A.   Rape; When And How Committed- Rape is Committed —

1) By a man who shall have carnal knowledge of a woman under any of the following circumstances:

a) Through force, threat, or intimidation;
b) When the offended party is deprived of reason or otherwise unconscious;
c) By means of fraudulent machination or grave abuse of authority; and
d) When the offended party is under twelve (12) years of age or is demented, even though none of the circumstances mentioned above be present.

2) By any person who, under any of the circumstances mentioned in paragraph 1 hereof, shall commit an act of sexual assault by inserting his penis into another person's mouth or anal orifice, or any instrument or object, into the genital or anal orifice of another person.

Art. 266-B. Penalties. - Rape under paragraph 1 of the next preceding article shall be punished by reclusion perpetua.

Whenever the rape is committed with the use of a deadly weapon or by two or more persons, the penalty shall be reclusion perpetua to death.

When by reason or on the occasion of the rape, the victim has become insane, the penalty shall be reclusion perpetua to death.

When the rape is attempted and a homicide is committed by reason or on the occasion thereof, the penalty shall be reclusion perpetua to death.

When by reason or on the occasion of the rape, homicide is committed, the penalty shall be death.

The death penalty shall also be imposed if the crime of rape is committed with any of the following aggravating or qualifying circumstances:

1) When the victim is under eighteen (18) years of age and the offender is a parent, ascendant, step-parent, guardian, relative by consanguinity or affinity within the third civil degree, or the common-law spouse of the parent of the victim;

2) When the victim is under the custody of the police or military authorities or any law enforcement or penal institution:

3) When the rape is committed in full view of the spouse, parent, any of the children or other relatives within the third civil degree of consanguinity;

4) When the victim is a religious engaged in legitimate religious vocation or calling and is personally known to be such by the offender before or at the time of the commission of the crime;

5) When the victim is a child below seven (7) years old;

6) When the offender knows that he is afflicted with Human Immuno-Deficiency Virus (HIV/Acquired Immune Deficiency Syndrome (AIDS) or any other sexually transmissible disease and the virus or disease is transmitted to the victim;

7) When committed by any member of the Armed Forces of the Philippines or para-military units thereof or the Philippine National Police or any law enforcement agency or penal institution, when the offender took advantage of his position to facilitate the commission of the crime;

8) When by reason or on the occasion of the rape, the victim has suffered permanent physical mutilation or disability;

9) When the offender knew of the pregnancy of the offended party at the time of the commission of the crime; and

10) When the offender knew of the mental disability emotional disorder and/or physical handicap of the offended party at the time of the commission of the crime.

Rape under paragraph 2 of the next preceding article shall be punished by prision mayor.

Whenever the rape is committed with the use of a deadly weapon or by two or more persons, the penalty shall be prision mayor to reclusion temporal.

When by reason or on the occasion of the rape, the victim has become insane, the penalty shall be reclusion temporal.

When the rape is attempted and a homicide is committed by reason or on the occasion thereof, the penalty shall be reclusion temporal to reclusion perpetua.

When by reason or on the occasion of the rape, homicide is committed, the penalty shall be reclusion perpetua.

Reclusion temporal shall also be imposed if the rape is committed with any of the ten aggravating or qualifying circumstances mentioned in this article.

Art. 266-C. Effect of Pardon. — The subsequent valid marriage between the offender and the offended party shall extinguish the criminal action or the penalty imposed.

In case it is the legal husband who is the offender, the subsequent forgiveness by the wife as the offended party shall extinguish the criminal action or the penalty: Provided, That the crime shall not be extinguished or the penalty shall not be abated if the marriage is void ab initio.

Art. 266-D. Presumptions. — Any physical overt act manifesting resistance against the act of rape in any degree from the offended party, or where the offended party is so situated as to render her/him incapable of giving valid consent, may be accepted as evidence in the prosecution of the acts punished under Article 266-A."

Sec 3. Separability Clause. — If any part, section, or provision of this Act is declared invalid or unconstitutional, the other parts thereof not affected thereby shall remain valid.

Sec. 4. Repealing Clause. — Article 335 of Act No. 3815, as amended, and all laws, acts, presidential decrees, executive orders, administrative orders, rules and regulations inconsistent with or contrary to the provisions of this Act are deemed amended, modified or repealed accordingly.

Sec. 5. *Effectivity.* — This Act shall take effect fifteen (15) days after completion of its publication in two (2) newspapers of general circulation.

Approved: September 30, 1997

4. Crimes Against Chastity

Art 336. Acts of Lasciviousness. -- Any person who shall commit any act of lasciviousness upon other persons of either sex, under any of the circumstances mentioned in the preceding article, shall be punished by *prision correccional.*

Art. 337. Qualified Seduction. -- The seduction of a virgin over twelve years and under eighteen years of age, committed by any person in public authority, priest, home-servant, domestic, guardian, teacher, or any person who, in any capacity, shall be entrusted with the education or custody of the woman seduced, shall be punished by *prision correccional* in its minimum and medium periods.

The penalty next higher in degree shall be imposed upon any person who shall seduce his sister or descendant, whether or not she be a virgin or over eighteen years of age.

Under the provisions of this Chapter, seduction is committed when the offender has carnal knowledge of any of the persons and under the circumstances described herein.

Art. 338. Simple Seduction. -- The seduction of a woman who is single or a widow of good reputation, over twelve but under eighteen years of age, committed by means of deceit, shall be punished by *arresto mayor.*

Art. 339. Acts of Lasciviousness with the Consent of the Offended Party. -- The penalty of *arresto mayor* shall be imposed to punish any other acts of lasciviousness committed by the same persons and the same circumstances as those provided in Articles 337 and 338.

Art. 340. Corruption of Minors. - Any person who shall promote or facilitate the prostitution or corruption of persons underage to satisfy the lust of another, shall be punished by *prision mayor,* and if the culprit is a public officer or employee, including those in government owned or controlled corporations, he shall also suffer the penalty of temporary absolute disqualification.

Art. 341. White Slave Trade. - The penalty of *prision correccional* in its medium and maximum periods shall be imposed upon any person who, in any manner, or under any pretext, shall engage in the business or shall profit by prostitution or shall enlist the services of any other person for the purpose of prostitution.

Art. 342. Forcible Abduction. -- The abduction of any woman against her will and with lewd designs shall be punished by *reclusion temporal.*

The same penalty shall be imposed in every case, if the female abducted be under twelve years of age.

Art 343. Consented Abduction. -- The abduction of a virgin over twelve and under eighteen years of age, carried out with her consent and with lewd designs, shall be punished by the penalty of *prision correccional* in its minimum and medium periods.

5. Crimes Against Liberty And Security

Art. 267.   Kidnapping and Serious Illegal Detention. - Any private individual who shall kidnap or detain another, or in any other manner deprive him of his liberty, shall suffer the penalty of *reclusion perpetua* to death:

1. If the kidnapping or detention shall have lasted more than three days.
2. If it shall have been committed simulating public authority.
3. If any serious physical injuries shall have been inflicted upon the person kidnapped or detained; or if threats to kill him shall have been made.
4. If the person kidnapped or detained shall be a minor except when the accused is any of the parents, female or a public officer.

The penalty shall be death where the kidnapping or detention was committed for the purpose of extorting ransom from the victim or any other person, even if none of the circumstances above mentioned were present in the commission of the offense. [*As amended by R.A. 7659 or the DEATH PENALTY LAW.*]

Art. 268.   Slight Illegal Detention. - The penalty of reclusion temporal shall be imposed upon any private individual who shall commit the crimes described in the next preceding article without the attendance of any of the circumstances enumerated therein.

The same penalty shall be incurred by anyone who shall furnish the place for the perpetration of the crime.

If the offender shall voluntarily release the person so kidnapped or detained within three days from the commencement of the detention, without having attained the purpose intended, and before the institution of criminal proceedings against him, the penalty shall be *prision mayor* in its minimum periods and a fine not exceeding Seven hundred pesos (P700.00).

x x x

Art. 270.   Kidnapping and Failure to Return a Minor. - The penalty of *reclusion perpetua* shall be imposed upon any person who, being entrusted with the custody of a minor person, shall deliberately fail to restore the latter to his parents or guardians.

Art. 271.   Inducing a Minor to Abandon his Home. - The penalty of *prision correccional* and a fine not exceeding Seven hundred pesos (P700.00) shall be imposed upon anyone who shall induce a minor to abandon the home of his parents or guardians or the persons entrusted with his custody.

If the person committing any of the crimes covered by the two preceding articles shall be the father or the mother of the minor, the penalty shall be *arresto mayor* or a fine not exceeding Three hundred pesos (P300.00), or both.

Art. 272.   Slavery. - The penalty of *prision mayor* and a fine of not exceeding Ten thousand pesos (P10,000.00) shall be imposed upon anyone who shall purchase, sell, kidnap or detain a human being for the purpose of enslaving him.

If the crime be committed for the purpose of assigning the offended party to some immoral traffic, the penalty shall be imposed in its maximum period.

Art. 273. Exploitation of Child Labor. - The penalty of *prision correccional* in its minimum and medium periods and a fine not exceeding Five hundred pesos (P500.00) shall be imposed upon anyone who, under the pretext of reimbursing himself of a debt incurred by an ascendant, guardian or person entrusted with the custody of a minor, shall against the latter's will, retain him in his service. [*Underscoring supplied.*]

Art. 274. Services Rendered under Compulsion in Payment of Debt. - The penalty of *arresto mayor* in its maximum period to *prision correccional* in its minimum period shall be imposed upon any person who, in order to require or enforce the payment of a debt, shall compel the debtor to work for him, against his will, as household servant or farm laborer.

x x x

Art. 276. Abandoning a Minor. - The penalty of *arresto mayor* and a fine not exceeding Five hundred pesos (P500.00) shall be imposed upon anyone who shall abandon a child under seven years of age, the custody of which is incumbent upon him.

When the death of the minor shall result from such abandonment, the culprit shall be punished by *prision correccional* in its medium and maximum periods; but if the life of the minor shall have been in danger only, the penalty shall be *prision correccional* in its minimum and medium periods.

The provisions contained in the two preceding paragraphs shall not prevent the imposition of the penalty provided for the act committed, when the same shall constitute a more serious offense.

Art. 277. Abandonment of Minor by Person Entrusted with his Custody; Indifference of Parents.- The penalty of *arresto mayor* and a fine not exceeding Five hundred pesos (P500.00) shall be imposed upon anyone who, having charge of the rearing or education of a minor, shall deliver said minor to a public institution or other persons, without the consent of the one who entrusted such child to his care or in the absence of the latter, without the consent of the proper authorities.

The same penalty shall be imposed upon the parents who shall neglect their children by not giving them the education which their station in life require and financial conditions permit.

ART. 278. Exploitation of Minors. - The penalty of *prision correccional* in its minimum and medium periods and a fine not exceeding Five hundred pesos (₱500.00) shall be imposed upon:

1. Any person who shall cause any boy or girl under sixteen years of age to perform any dangerous feat of balancing physical strength or contortion.

2. Any person who, being an acrobat, gymnast, ropewalker, diver, wild-animal tamer or circus manager or engaged in a similar calling, shall employ in exhibitions of these kinds children under sixteen years of age who are not his children or descendants.

3. Any person engaged in any of the callings enumerated in the next preceding paragraph who shall employ any descendants of his under twelve years of age in such dangerous exhibitions.

4. Any ascendant, guardian, teacher or person entrusted in any capacity with the care of a

child under sixteen years of age, who shall deliver such child gratuitously to any person following any of the callings enumerated in paragraph 2 hereof, or to any habitual vagrant or beggar.

If the delivery shall have been made in consideration of any price, compensation, or promise, the penalty shall in every case be imposed in its maximum period.

In either case, the guardian or curator convicted shall also be removed from office as guardian or curator; and in the case of the parents of the child, they may be deprived, temporarily or perpetually, in the discretion of the court, of their parental authority.

5. Any person who shall induce any child under sixteen years of age to abandon the home of its ascendants, guardians, curators or teachers to follow any person engaged in any of the callings mentioned in paragraph 2 hereof, or to accompany any habitual vagrant or beggar. [*Underscoring supplied.*]

6. Threats And Coercions

Art. 282. Grave Threats. - Any person who shall threaten another with the infliction upon the person, honor or property of the latter or of his family of any wrong amounting to a crime, shall suffer:

1. The penalty next lower in degree than that prescribed by law for the crime he threatened to commit, if the offender shall have made the threat demanding money or imposing any other condition, even though not unlawful, and said offender shall have attained his purpose. If the offender shall not have attained his purpose, the penalty lower by two degrees shall be imposed.

If the threat be made in writing or through a middleman, the penalty shall be imposed in its maximum period.

2. The penalty of *arresto mayor* and a fine not exceeding Five hundred pesos (P500.00), if the threat shall not have been made subject to a condition.

Art. 283. Light Threats. - A threat to commit a wrong not constituting a crime, made in the manner expressed in subdivision 1 of the next preceding article, shall be punished by *arresto mayor.*

x x x

Art. 285. Other Light Threats. - The penalty of *arresto menor* in its minimum period or a fine not exceeding Two hundred pesos (P200.00) shall be imposed upon:

1. Any person who, without being included in the provisions of the next preceding article, shall threaten another with a weapon, or draw such weapon in a quarrel, unless it be lawful self-defense.
2. Any person who, in the heat of anger, shall orally threaten another with some harm not constituting a crime, and who by subsequent acts show that he did not persist in the idea involved in his threat, provided that the circumstances of the offense shall not bring it within the provisions of Article 282 of this Code.
3. Any person who shall orally threaten to do another any harm not constituting a felony.

Art. 286. Grave Coercions. - The penalty of *arresto mayor* and a fine not exceeding Five hundred pesos (P500.00) shall be imposed upon any person who, without authority of law, shall, by means of violence, prevent another from doing something not prohibited by law, or compel him to do something against his will, whether it be right or wrong.

If the coercion be committed for the purpose of compelling another to perform any religious act or to prevent him from so doing, the penalty next higher in degree shall be imposed.

Art. 287. Light Coercions. - Any person who, by means of violence, shall seize anything belonging to his debtor for the purpose of applying the same to the payment of the debt, shall suffer the penalty of *arresto mayor* in its minimum period and a fine equivalent to the value of the thing, but in no case less than Seventy five pesos (P75.00).

Any other coercions or unjust vexations shall be punished by *arresto menor* or a fine ranging from Five pesos (P5.00) to Two hundred pesos (P200.00), or both.

Art. 288. Other Similar Coercions. - (Compulsory purchase of merchandise and payment of wages by means of tokens.) - The penalty of *arresto mayor* or a fine ranging from Two hundred (P200.00) to Five hundred pesos (P500.00), or both, shall be imposed upon any person, agent or officer of any association or corporation who shall force or compel, directly or indirectly, or shall knowingly permit any laborer or employee employed by him or by such firm or corporation to be forced or compelled, to purchase merchandise or commodities of any kind.

The same penalties shall be imposed upon any person who shall pay the wages due a laborer or employee employed by him, by means of tokens or objects other than the legal tender currency of the laborer or employee.

7. Swindling And Other Deceits

Art. 317. Swindling a Minor. - Any person who taking advantage of the inexperience or emotions or feelings of a minor, to his detriment, shall induce him to assume any obligation or to give any release or execute a transfer of any property right in consideration of some loan of money, credit or other personal property, whether the loan clearly appears in the document or is shown in any other form, shall suffer the penalty of *arresto mayor* and a fine of a sum ranging from 10 to 50 percent of the value of the obligation contracted by the minor.

Art. 318. Other Deceits. - The penalty of *arresto mayor* and a fine of not less than the amount of the damage caused and not more than twice such amount shall be imposed upon any person who shall defraud or damage another by any other deceit not mentioned in the preceding articles of this chapter.

x x x

G. LIABILITIES AND RESPONSIBILITIES OF PARENTS

1. Child And Youth Welfare Code (P.D. 603)

TITLE II, CHAPTER IV
LIABILITIES OF PARENTS

Art. 58. Torts. - Parents and guardians are responsible for the damage caused by the child under their parental authority in accordance with the Civil Code.

Art. 59. Crimes. - Criminal liability shall attach to any parent who:

1. conceals or abandons the child with intent to make such child lose his civil status.

2. abandons the child under such circumstances as to deprive him of the love, care and protection he needs.

3. sells or abandons the child to another person for valuable consideration.

4. neglects the child by not giving him the education which the family's station in life and financial conditions permit.

5. fails or refuses, without justifiable grounds, to enroll the child as required by Article 72.

6. causes, abates, or permits the truancy of the child from the school where he is enrolled. "Truancy" as here used means absence without cause for more than twenty school days, not necessarily consecutive.

It shall be the duty of the teacher in charge to report to the parents the absences of the child the moment these exceed five school days.

7. improperly exploits the child by using him, directly or indirectly, such as for purposes of begging and other acts which are inimical to his interest and welfare.

8. inflicts cruel and unusual punishment upon the child or deliberately subjects him to indignities and other excessive chastisement that embarrass or humiliate him.

9. causes or encourages the child to lead an immoral or dissolute life.

10. permits the child to possess, handle or carry a deadly weapon, regardless of its ownership.

11. allows or requires the child to drive without a license or with license which the parent knows to have been illegally procured. If the motor vehicle driven by the child belongs to the parent, it shall be presumed that he permitted or ordered the child to drive.

"Parents" as here used shall include the guardian and the head of the institution or foster home which has custody of the child. [*Underscoring supplied.*]

Art. 60. Penalty. - The act mentioned in the preceding article shall be punishable with imprisonment from two to six months or a fine not exceeding five hundred pesos, or both, at the discretion of the Court, unless a higher penalty is provided for in the Revised Penal Code or special laws, without prejudice to actions for the involuntary commitment of the child under Title VIII of this Code.

[*Note: Article 60 of P.D. 603 has already been amended by R.A. 7610 or the Child Protection Law. Under Section 10, Article VI (Other Acts of Abuse) of R.A. 7610, Article 59 of P.D. 603 is now punishable by a higher penalty of prision mayor in its medium period.*]

2. Family Code

TITLE IX
PARENTAL AUTHORITY

Art. 225. The father or, in his absence or incapacity, the mother, shall be the legal guardian of the property of the unemancipated child without the necessity of a court appointment.

Where the value of the property or the annual income of the child exceeds P50,000.00, the parent concerned shall be required to furnish a bond in such amount as the court may determine, but not less than ten per centum (10%) of the value of the property or annual income, to guarantee the performance of the obligations prescribed for general guardians.

A verified petition for approval of the bond shall be filed in the proper court of the place where the child resides, or, if the child resides in a foreign country, in the proper court of the place where the property or any part thereof is situated.

x x x

Art. 226. The property of the unemancipated child, earned or acquired with his work or industry or by onerous or gratuitous title, shall belong to the child in ownership and shall be devoted exclusively to the latter's support and education, unless the title or transfer provides otherwise.

The right of the parents over the fruits and income of the child's property shall be limited primarily to the child's support and secondarily to the collective daily needs of the family.

x x x

Art. 230. Parental authority is suspended upon conviction of the parent or the person exercising the same of a crime which carries with it the penalty of civil interdiction. The authority is automatically reinstated upon service of the penalty or upon pardon or amnesty of the offender.

Art. 231. The court in an action filed for the purpose or in a related case may also suspend parental authority if the parent or the person exercising the same:

(1) Treats the child with excessive harshness or cruelty;
(2) Gives the child corrupting orders, counsel or example;
(3) Compels the child to beg; or
(4) Subjects the child or allows him to be subjected to acts of lasciviousness.

If the degree of seriousness so warrants, or the welfare of the child so demands, the court shall deprive the guilty party of parental authority or adopt such other measures as may be proper under the circumstances.

The suspension or deprivation may be revoked and the parental authority revived in a case filed for the purpose or in the same proceeding, if the court finds that the cause therefor has ceased and will not be repeated.

Art. 232. If the person exercising parental authority has subjected the child or allowed him to be subjected to sexual abuse, such person shall be permanently deprived by the court of such authority.

H. CHILD ABUSE, EXPLOITATION, AND DISCRIMINATION

R.A. 7610
AN ACT PROVIDING FOR STRONGER
DETERRENCE AND SPECIAL PROTECTION
AGAINST CHILD ABUSE, EXPLOITATION AND
DISCRIMINATION,
PROVIDING PENALTIES FOR ITS VIOLATION,
AND FOR OTHER PURPOSES

APPROVED, JUNE 17, 1992
Be it enacted by the Senate and House of Representatives of the Philippines in Congress assembled:

ARTICLE I
TITLE, POLICY, PRINCIPLES AND
DEFINITION OF TERMS

Sec. 1. Title. - This Act shall be known as the "Special Protection of Children Against Child Abuse, Exploitation and Discrimination Act."

Sec. 2. Declaration of State Policy and Principles. - It is hereby declared to be the policy of the State to provide special protection to children from all forms of abuse, neglect, cruelty, exploitation and discrimination, and other conditions prejudicial to their development; provide sanctions for their commission and carry out a program for prevention and deterrence of and crisis intervention in situations of child abuse, exploitation and discrimination. The State shall intervene on behalf of the child when the parent, guardian, teacher or person having care or custody of the child fails or is unable to protect the child against abuse, exploitation and discrimination or when such acts against the child are committed by the said parent, guardian, teacher or person having care and custody of the same.

It shall be the policy of the State to protect and rehabilitate children gravely threatened or endangered by circumstances which affect or will affect their survival and normal development and over which they have no control.

The best interests of children shall be the paramount consideration in all actions concerning the child, whether undertaken by public or private social welfare institutions, courts of law, administrative authorities, and legislative bodies, consistent with the principle of first Call for Children as enunciated in the United Nations Convention of the Rights of the Child. Every effort shall be exerted to promote the welfare of children and enhance their opportunities for a useful and happy life.

Sec. 3. Definition of Terms. -

a. "Children" refers to persons below eighteen (18) years of age or those over but are unable to fully take care of themselves or protect themselves from abuse, neglect, cruelty, exploitation or discrimination because of a physical or mental disability or condition;

b. "Child Abuse" refers to the maltreatment, whether habitual or not, of the child which includes any of the following:

> 1. psychological and physical abuse, neglect, cruelty, sexual abuse and emotional maltreatment;
> 2. any act by deeds or words which debases, degrades or demeans the intrinsic worth and dignity of a child as a human being;
> 3. unreasonable deprivation of his basic needs for survival, such as food and shelter; or
> 4. failure to immediately give medical treatment to an injured child resulting in serious impairment of his growth and development or in his permanent incapacity or death.

c. "Circumstances which gravely threaten or endanger the survival and normal development of children" include, but are not limited to, the following:

1. being in a community where there is armed conflict or being affected by armed conflict-related activities;

2. working under conditions hazardous to life, safety and morals which unduly interfere with their normal development;

3. living in or fending for themselves in the streets of urban or rural areas without the care of parents or a guardian or any adult supervision needed for their welfare;

4. being a member of an indigenous cultural community and/or living under conditions of extreme poverty or in an area which is undeveloped and/or lacks or has inadequate access to basic services needed for a good quality of life;

5. being a victim of a man-made or natural disaster or calamity; or

6. circumstances analogous to those abovestated which endanger the life, safety or normal development of children.

d. "Comprehensive program against child abuse, exploitation and discrimination" refers to the coordinated program of services and facilities to protect children against:

1. child prostitution and other sexual abuse;

2. child trafficking;

3. obscene publication and indecent shows;

4. other acts of abuse; and

5. circumstances which threaten or endanger the survival and normal development of children.

ARTICLE II
PROGRAM ON CHILD ABUSE, EXPLOITATION
AND DISCRIMINATION

Sec. 4.   Formulation of the Program. - There shall be a comprehensive program to be formulated by the Department of Justice and the Department of Social Welfare and Development in coordination with other government agencies and private sector concerned, within one (1) year from the effectivity of this Act, to protect children against child prostitution and other sexual abuse; child trafficking; obscene publication and indecent shows; other acts of abuse; and circumstances which endanger child survival and normal development.

ARTICLE III
CHILD PROSTITUTION AND OTHER SEXUAL
ABUSE

Sec. 5.   Child Prostitution and Other Sexual Abuse. - Children, whether male or female, who for money, profit, or any other consideration or due to the coercion or influence of any adult, syndicate or group, indulge in sexual intercourse or lascivious conduct, are deemed to be children exploited in prostitution and other sexual abuse.

The penalty of *reclusion temporal* in its medium period to *reclusion perpetua* shall be imposed upon the following:

a. *Those who engage in or promote, facilitate or induce child prostitution* which include, but are not limited to, the following:
    1. acting as a procurer of a child prostitute;
    2. inducing a person to be client of a child prostitute by means of written or oral advertisement or other similar means;

3.taking advantage of influence or relationship to procure a child as a prostitute;

4. threatening or using violence towards a child to engage him as a prostitute; or

5. giving monetary consideration, goods or other pecuniary benefit to a child with the intent to engage such child in prostitution.

b. *Those who commit the act of sexual intercourse or lascivious conduct with a child exploited in prostitution or subjected to other sexual abuse*: Provided, That when the victim is under twelve (12) years of age, the perpetrators shall be prosecuted under Article 335, paragraph 3, for rape and Article 336 of Act No. 3815, as amended, the Revised Penal Code, for rape or lascivious conduct, as the case may be: Provided, That the penalty for lasciviousness conduct when the victim is under twelve (12) years of age shall be reclusion temporal in its medium period; and

c. *Those who derive profit or advantage* therefrom, whether as manager or owner of the establishment where the prostitution takes place, or of the sauna, disco, bar, resort, place of entertainment or establishment serving as a cover or which engages in prostitution in addition to the activity for which the license has been issued to said establishment.

Sec. 6. Attempt to Commit Child Prostitution.- There is an attempt to commit child prostitution under Section 5, paragraph (1) hereof when any person who, not being a relative of a child, is found alone with the said child inside the room or cubicle of a house, an inn, hotel, motel, pension house, apartelle or other similar establishments, vessel, vehicle or any other hidden or secluded area under circumstances which would lead a reasonable person to believe that the child is about to be exploited in prostitution and other sexual abuse.

There is also an attempt to commit child prostitution, under paragraph (b) of Section 5 hereof when any person is receiving services from a child in a sauna parlor or bath, massage clinic, health club and other similar establishments. A penalty lower by two (2) degrees than that prescribed for the consummated felony under Section 5 hereof shall be imposed upon the principals of the attempt to commit the crime of child prostitution under this Act, or, in the proper case, under the Revised Penal Code.

ARTICLE IV
CHILD TRAFFICKING

Sec. 7. Child Trafficking. - Any person who shall engage in trading and dealing with children including, but not limited to, the act of buying and selling of a child for money, or for any other consideration, or barter, shall suffer the penalty of *reclusion temporal* to *reclusion perpetua.* The penalty shall be imposed in its maximum period when the victim is under twelve (12) years of age.

Sec. 8. Attempt to Commit Child Trafficking. - There is an attempt to commit child trafficking under Section 7 of this Act:

a. when a child travels alone to a foreign country without valid reason therefor and without clearance issued by the Department of Social Welfare and Development or written permit or justification from the child's parents or legal guardian;
b. when a pregnant mother executes an affidavit of consent for adoption for a consideration;

c. when a person, agency, establishment or child-caring institution recruits women or couples to bear children for the purpose of child trafficking;

d. when a doctor, hospital or clinic official or employee, nurse, midwife, local civil registrar or any other person simulates birth for the purpose of child trafficking; or

e. when a person engages in the act of finding children among low-income families, hospitals, clinics, nurseries, day-care centers, or other child-caring institutions who can be offered for the purpose of child trafficking.

A penalty lower by two (2) degrees than that prescribed for the consummated felony under Section 7 hereof shall be imposed upon the principals of the attempt to commit child trafficking under this Act.

ARTICLE V
OBSCENE PUBLICATIONS AND INDECENT SHOWS

Sec. 9. Obscene Publications and Indecent Shows. - Any person who shall hire, employ, use, persuade, induce or coerce a child to perform in obscene exhibitions and indecent shows, whether live or in video, pose, or model in obscene publications or pornographic materials, or to sell or distribute the said materials, shall suffer the penalty of *prision mayor* in its medium period.

If the child used as a performer, subject or seller/distributor is below twelve (12) years of age, the penalty shall be imposed in its maximum period.

Any ascendant, guardian, or person entrusted in any capacity with the care of a child who shall cause and/or allow such child to be employed or to participate in an obscene play, scene, act, movie or show or in any other acts covered by this section shall suffer the penalty of *prision mayor* in its medium period.

ARTICLE VI
OTHER ACTS OF ABUSE

Sec. 10.   Other Acts of Neglect, Abuse, Cruelty or Exploitation and Other Conditions Prejudicial to the Child's Development. -

a.   *Any person who shall commit any other acts of child abuse, cruelty or exploitation* or be responsible for other conditions prejudicial to the child's development including those covered by Article 59 of Presidential Decree No. 603, as amended, but not covered by the Revised Penal Code, as amended, shall suffer the penalty of *prision mayor* in its minimum period.

b.   *Any person who shall keep or have in his company a minor,* twelve (12) years or under or who is ten (10) years or more his junior in any public or private place, hotel, motel, beer joint, discotheque, cabaret, pension house, sauna or massage parlor, beach and/or other tourist resort or similar places shall suffer the penalty of *prision mayor* in its maximum period and a fine of not less than Fifty thousand pesos (P50,000.00):   Provided, That this provision shall not apply to any person who is related within the fourth degree of consanguinity or affinity or any bond recognized by law, local custom and tradition, or acts in the performance of a social, moral or legal duty.

c.   *Any person who shall induce, deliver or offer a minor to anyone prohibited by this Act* to keep or have in his company a minor as provided in the preceding paragraph shall suffer the penalty of *prision mayor* in its medium period and a fine of not less than Forty thousand pesos (₱40,000.00):

Provided, however, That should the perpetrator be an ascendant, stepparent or guardian of the minor, the penalty to be imposed shall be *prision mayor* in its maximum period, a fine of not less than Fifty thousand pesos (₱50,000.00), and the loss of parental authority over the minor.

d.   *Any person, owner, manager or one entrusted with the operation of any public or private place of accommodation,* whether for occupancy, food, drink or otherwise, including residential places, who allows any person to take along with him to such place or places any minor herein described shall be imposed a penalty of *prision mayor* in its medium period and a fine of not less than Fifty thousand pesos (₱50,000.00), and the loss of the license to operate such a place or establishment.

e. *Any person who shall use, coerce, force or intimidate a streetchild or any other child to:*
    1.   beg or use begging as a means of living;
    2. act as conduit or middlemen in drug trafficking or pushing; or
    3. conduct any illegal activities, shall suffer the penalty of *prision correccional* in its medium period to *reclusion perpetua.*

For purposes of this Act, the penalty for the commission of acts punishable under Articles 248, 249, 262, paragraph 2, and 263, paragraph 1 of Act No. 3815, as amended, the Revised Penal Code, for the crimes of murder, homicide, other intentional mutilation, and serious physical injuries, respectively, shall be *reclusion perpetua* when the victim is under twelve (12) years of age. The penalty for the commission of acts punishable under Articles 337, 339, 340 and 341 of Act No. 3815, as amended, the Revised Penal Code, for the crimes of qualified seduction, acts of lasciviousness with the consent of the offended party, corruption of minors, and white slave trade, respectively, shall be one (1) degree higher than that imposed by law when the victim is under twelve (12) years of age.

The victim of the acts committed under this section shall be entrusted to the care of the Department of Social Welfare and Development.

ARTICLE VII
SANCTIONS FOR ESTABLISHMENTS OR
ENTERPRISES

Sec. 11. Sanctions for Establishments or Enterprises which Promote, Facilitate, or Conduct Activities Constituting Child Prostitution and Other Sexual Abuse, Child Trafficking, Obscene Publications and Indecent Shows, and Other Acts of Abuse. - All establishments and enterprises which promote or facilitate child prostitution and other sexual abuse, child trafficking, obscene publications and indecent shows, and other acts of abuse shall be immediately closed and their authority or license to operate cancelled, without prejudice to the owner or manager thereof being prosecuted under this Act and/or the Revised Penal Code, as amended, or special laws. A sign with the words "off limits" shall be conspicuously displayed outside the establishments or enterprises by the Department of Social Welfare and Development for such period which shall not be less than one (1) year, as the Department may determine. The unauthorized removal of such sign shall be punishable by *prision correccional.*

An establishment shall be deemed to promote or facilitate child prostitution and other sexual abuse, child trafficking, obscene publications and indecent shows, and other acts of abuse if the acts constituting the same occur in the premises of said establishment under this Act or in violation of the Revised Penal Code, as amended. An enterprise such as sauna, travel agency, or recruitment agency which: promotes the aforementioned acts as part of a tour for foreign tourists; exhibits children in a lewd or indecent show; provides child masseurs for adults of the same or opposite sex and said services include any lascivious conduct with the customer; or solicits children for activities constituting the aforementioned acts shall be deemed to have committed the acts penalized herein.

ARTICLE VIII
WORKING CHILDREN

Sec. 12. Employment of Children. - Children below fifteen (15) years of age may be employed; Provided, That the following minimum requirements are present:

a. The employer shall secure for the child a work permit from the Department of Labor and Employment;

b. The employer shall ensure the protection, health, safety, and morals of the child;

c. The employer shall institute measures to prevent exploitation or discrimination taking into account the system and level of remuneration, and the duration and arrangement of working time; and

d. The employer shall formulate and implement a continuous program for training and skill acquisition of the child.

The Department of Labor and Employment shall promulgate rules and regulations necessary for the effective implementation of this section.

[Note: This Section 12 has been REPEALED by R.A. 7658, pages 56-58.]

Sec. 13. Non-formal Education for Working Children. - The Department of Education, Culture and Sports shall promulgate a course design under its non-formal education program aimed at promoting the intellectual, moral and vocational efficiency of working children who have not undergone or finished elementary or secondary education. Such course design shall integrate the learning process deemed most effective under given circumstances.

Sec. 14. Prohibition on the Employment of Children in Certain Advertisement. - No person shall employ child models in all commercials or advertisement promoting alcoholic beverages, intoxicating drinks, tobacco, and its by-product, and violence.

Sec. 15. Duty of Employer. - Every employer shall comply with the duties provided for in Articles 108 and 109 of Presidential Decree No. 603.

Sec. 16. Penalties. - Any person who shall violate any provision of this Article shall suffer the penalty of fine of not less than One thousand pesos (₱1,000.00) but not more than Ten thousand pesos (₱10,000.00) or imprisonment of not less than three (3) months but not more than three (3) years, or both at the discretion of the court: Provided, That, in case of repeated violations of the provision of this Article, the offender's license to operate shall be revoked.

ARTICLE IX
CHILDREN OF INDIGENOUS CULTURAL
COMMUNITIES
x x x

ARTICLE X
CHILDREN IN SITUATIONS OF ARMED CONFLICT
x x x

ARTICLE XI
REMEDIAL PROCEDURES

Sec. 27. Who May File a Complaint. - Complaints on cases of unlawful acts committed against children as enumerated herein may be filed by the following:

a. Offended party;
b. Parents or guardians;
c. Ascendant or collateral relative within the third degree of consanguinity;
d. Officer, social worker or representative of a licensed child-caring institution;
e. Officer or social worker of the Department of Social Welfare and Development;
f. Barangay chairman; or
g. At least three (3) concerned, responsible citizens where the violations occurred.

Sec. 28. Protective Custody of the Child. - The offended party shall be immediately placed under the protective custody of the Department of Social Welfare and Development pursuant to Executive Order No. 56, series of 1986. In the regular performance of this function, the officer of the Department of Social Welfare and Development shall be free from any administrative, civil or criminal liability. Custody proceedings shall be in accordance with the provisions of Presidential Decree No. 603.

Sec. 29. Confidentiality. - At the instance of the offended party, his name may be withheld from the public until the court acquires jurisdiction over the case. It shall be unlawful for any editor, publisher, and reporter or columnist in case of printed materials, announcer or producer in case of television and radio broadcasting, producer and director of the film in case of the movie industry, to cause any sensationalized publicity of any case of violation of this Act which results in the moral degradation and suffering of the offended party.

Sec. 30. Special Court Proceedings. - Cases involving violations of this Act shall be heard in the chambers of the judge of the Regional Trial Court duly designated as Juvenile and Domestic Relations Court.

Any provision of existing law to the contrary notwithstanding and with the exception of habeas corpus, election cases, and cases involving detention prisoners and persons covered by Republic Act No. 4908, all courts shall give preference to the hearing or disposition of cases involving violations of this Act.

ARTICLE XII
COMMON PENAL PROVISIONS

Sec. 31. Common Penal Provisions.-

a. The penalty provided under this Act shall be imposed in its maximum period if the offender has been previously convicted under this Act;

b. When the offender is a corporation, partnership or association, the officer or employee thereof who is responsible for the violation of this Act shall suffer the penalty imposed in its maximum period;

c. The penalty provided herein shall be imposed in its maximum period when the perpetrator is an ascendant, parent, guardian, stepparent or collateral relative within the second degree of consanguinity or affinity, or a manager or owner of an establishment which has no license to operate or its license has expired or has been revoked;

d. When the offender is a foreigner, he shall be deported immediately after service of sentence and forever barred from entry to the country.

e. The penalty provided for in this Act shall be imposed in its maximum period if the offender is a public officer or employee: Provided, however, That if the penalty imposed is *reclusion perpetua* or *reclusion temporal*, then the penalty of perpetual or temporary absolute disqualification shall also be imposed: Provided, finally, That if the penalty imposed is *prision correccional* or *arresto mayor*, the penalty of suspension shall also be imposed; and

f. A fine to be determined by the court shall be imposed and administered as a cash fund by the Department of Social Welfare and Development and disbursed for the rehabilitation of each child victim, or any immediate member of his family if the latter is the perpetrator of the offense.

ARTICLE XIII
FINAL PROVISIONS

Sec. 32. Rules and Regulations. - Unless otherwise provided in this Act, the Department of Justice in coordination with the Department of Social Welfare and Development, shall promulgate rules and regulations for the effective implementation of this Act.

Such rules and regulations shall take effect upon their publication in two (2) national newspapers of general circulation.

Sec. 33. Appropriations. - The amount necessary to carry out the provisions of this Act is hereby authorized to be appropriated in the General Appropriations Act of the year following its enactment into law and thereafter.

Sec. 34. Separability Clause. - If any provision of this Act is declared invalid or unconstitutional, the remaining provisions not affected thereby shall continue in full force and effect.

Sec. 35. Repealing Clause. - All laws, decrees, or rules inconsistent with the provisions of this Act are hereby repealed or modified accordingly.

Sec. 36. Effectivity Clause. - This Act shall take effect upon completion of its publication in at least two (2) national newspapers of general circulation.

Approved:

(sgd.)NEPTALI A.GONZALES
President of the Senate

(sgd.) RAMON V. MITRA
Speaker of the House of
Representatives

This Act which is a consolidation of House Bill Nos. 6946, 29431, 35354 and Senate Bill No. 1209 was finally passed by the House of Representatives and the Senate on February 7, 1992.

(sgd.) ANACLETO D. BADOY, JR.
Secretary of the Senate

(sgd.) CAMILO L. SABIO
Secretary General
House of Representatives

Approved: June 17, 1992
(SGD.) CORAZON C. AQUINO
President of the Philippines I.

I. CHILD TRAFFICKING

[See pages 140-148]

J. DRUG ABUSE

R.A. 6425
DANGEROUS DRUGS LAW
(As Amended by R.A. 7659,
Death Penalty Law)

x x x

Sec. 4.   Sale, Administration, Delivery, Distribution and Transportation of Prohibited Drugs. -- The penalty of *reclusion perpetua* to death and a fine ranging from five hundred thousand pesos (P500,000.00) to ten million pesos (P10,000,000.00) shall be imposed upon any person who, unless authorized by law, shall sell, administer, deliver, give away to another, distribute, dispatch in transit or transport any prohibited drug, or shall act as broker in any of such transactions.

Notwithstanding the provisions of Section 20 of this Act to the contrary, <u>if the victim of the offense is a minor,</u> or should a prohibited drug involved in any offense under this Section be the proximate cause of the death of a victim thereof, the maximum penalty herein provided shall be imposed. [*Underscoring supplied.*]

Sec. 5. Maintenance of a Den, Dive or Resort for Prohibited Drug Users. -- The penalty of *reclusion perpetua* to death and a fine ranging from five hundred thousand pesos (P500,000.00) to ten million pesos (P10,000,000.00) shall be imposed upon any person or group of persons who shall maintain a den, dive or resort where any prohibited drug is used in any form or where such prohibited drugs, in quantities specified in Section 20, Paragraph 1 of this Act, are found.

Notwithstanding the provisions of Section 20 of this Act to the contrary, the maximum of the penalty shall be imposed in every case where a prohibited drug is <u>administered, delivered or sold to a minor who is allowed to use the same</u> in such place. [*Underscoring supplied.*]

Should a prohibited drug be the proximate cause of the death of a person using the same in such den, dive or resort, the maximum penalty herein provided shall be imposed on the maintainer, notwithstanding the provisions of Section 20 of this Act to the contrary.

x x x

Sec. 15.   Sale, Administration, Dispensation, Delivery,   Transportation   and   Distribution   of Regulated Drugs. -- The penalty of *reclusion perpetua* to death and a fine ranging from five hundred thousand pesos (P500,000.00) to ten million pesos (P10,000,000.00) shall be imposed upon any person who, unless authorized by law, shall sell, dispense, deliver, transport or distribute any regulated drug.

Notwithstanding the provisions of Section 20 of this Act to the contrary, <u>if the victim of the offense is a minor,</u> or should a regulated drug involved in any offense under this Section be the proximate cause of the death of a victim thereof, the maximum penalty herein provided shall be imposed. [*Underscoring supplied.*]

Sec. 15-a. Maintenance of a Den, Dive or Resort for Regulated Drug Users. - The penalty of *reclusion perpetua* to death and a fine ranging from five hundred thousand pesos (P500,000.00) to ten million pesos (P10,000,000.00) shall be imposed upon any person or group of persons who shall maintain a den, dive or resort where any regulated drug is used in any form, or where such regulated drugs in quantities specified in Section 20, paragraph 1 of this Act are found.

Notwithstanding the provisions of Section 20 of this Act to the contrary, the maximum penalty herein provided shall be imposed in every case where a regulated drug is <u>administered, delivered or sold to a minor who is allowed to use the same</u> in such place. [*Underscoring supplied.*]

Should a regulated drug be the proximate cause of the death of a person using the same in such den, dive or resort, the maximum penalty herein provided shall be imposed on the maintainer notwithstanding the provisions of Section 20 of this Act to the contrary.

K. ORDINANCES ON CHILD LABOR AND CHILD PROSTITUTION

1. SP Resolution -192-96 (Butuan City)

Republic of the Philippines
TANGGAPAN NO SANGGUNIANO PANLUNGSOD
LUNGSOD NO BUTUAN

A RESOLUTION CREATING AN INTER-AGENCY
"BANTAY-BATA" TASK FORCE WHICH SHALL BE
TASKED TO INSPECT ESTABLISHMENTS
EMPLOYING MINORS IN KTV BARS AND OTHER
RELATED ESTABLISHMENTS; AND OTHER
VIOLATIONS THEREOF, OF THE EXISTING YOUTH
RELATED ORDINANCES/POLICIES AND FOR
OTHER PURPOSES

WHEREAS, KTV Bars and other related establishments have been flourishing in Butuan City;

WHEREAS, it has been observed that these establishments attract job opportunities to youths and minors who are supposed to be protected against exploitation and improper influences or hazards prejudicial to his/her development;

WHEREAS, to ensure their safety, a task force shall be created with the following compositions:

Three [3] SP Members/Committee on Youth and Sports and Committee on Police

PNP Child and Youth Welfare Division

Representative from the City Health Office

Representative from the DSWD

Representative from the DOLE

Presidents of Students' Union

Vice President of High School and College Students Organizations

City Administrator

The City Administrator will be heading the Task Force and shall provide the needs of the team in relation to the accomplishment of the task and responsibility.

WHEREAS, that after the inspection within a number of days sufficient to finish the task, the team through the head shall submit a comprehensive report as soon as possible to the Sangguniang Panlungsod through the Committee on Youth and Sports for proper action and in aid of legislation].

NOW, THEREFORE, upon motion of Honorable Angelo S. Cab, jointly seconded by Honorable Jaime M. Cembrano, Jr., and Honorable Apolinario M. Asis, be it -

RESOLVED, AS IT IS HEREBY RESOLVED, to create an Inter-Agency "Bantay-Bata" Task Force which shall be tasked to inspect establishments employing minors in KTV Bars and other related establishments; and other violations thereof of the existing youth related ordinances/policies.

RESOLVED FURTHER, that in the implementation of this Resolution, the same shall be coordinated with the Program Implementation Committee of the Child Labor Program of the City Government of Butuan.

RESOLVED FINALLY, to furnish a copy of this Resolution to all concerned for their information and appropriate action.

UNANIMOUSLY APPROVED.

ENACTED: March 8, 1996

APPROVED: March 28, 1996

ATTESTED: APPROVED:

REMEDIOS H. GONZALES   LEOVIGILDO B. BANAAG
City Gov't Dept. Head III   Vice-Mayor
City Secretary   Presiding Officer

2. Resolution No. 4 (Region VIII)

REPUBLIC OF THE PHILIPPINES
REGIONAL SUB-COMMITTEE
FOR THE WELFARE OF CHILDREN
REGION VIII

RESOLUTION NO.4
Series of 1994

RESOLUTION REQUESTING ALL LOCAL
GOVERNMENT UNITS IN REGION VIII TO ENACT
OMNIBUS ORDNANCE PROHIBITING CHILDREN
BELOW 15 YEARS OLD TO DRIVE PEDICABS.

WHEREAS, the State ensures the protection, health safety, morals and normal development of the child;

WHEREAS, Republic Act 7658 prohibits the employment of children below 15 years old in hazardous and deleterious occupation;

WHEREAS, children below 15 years old is allowed to work under the sole responsibility of their parents or legal guardian provided that the parents or the legal guardian provides him with the primary and secondary education,

WHEREAS, it is observed that a great number of children below 15 years old are driving pedicabs;

WHEREAS, children of this age should be in school and not in the streets driving pedicabs;

WHEREAS, driving pedicabs by children below 15 is considered as hazardous and deleterious occupations, thereby endangers the health and safety of these children; NOW THEREFORE BE IT,

RESOLVED AS IT IS HEREBY RESOLVED, by the Regional Council for the Welfare of Children (RSCWC) in a meeting assembled, to request all LGUs in the region to enact an omnibus ordinance prohibiting children below 15 years old to drive pedicabs.

RESOLVED FURTHER, that a copy of this resolution be forwarded to all Governors, City/Municipal Mayors, Sangguniang Panlalawigan / Bayan. Regional Director, PNP Region VIII/City Municipal Station Commanders-Region VIII and the Regional Peace and Order Council.

Approved upon the motion of Hon. Rebecca C. Pacanan and duly seconded by Mrs. Gabina L. Raagas on October 12, 1993.

Done in the City of Tacloban this 12"' day of October in the year of our Lord nineteen hundred and ninety four.

DIR. ROSARIO P. NOVIZA
Chairman, RSCWC VIII
Field Office
Department of Social Welfare
and Development

3. Ordinance No. 06 (Municipality of Hinigaran, Negros Occidental)

Republic of the Philippines
PROVINCE OF NEGROS OCCIDENTAL
MUNICIPALITY OF HINIGARAN
Office of the Secretary

ORDINANCE NO.06
Series of 1994

AN ORDINANCE PRESCRIBING RULES AND
REGULATION IN THE EMPLOYMENT OF CHILDREN
FROM 15 TO 18 YEARS OLD IN THE
MANUFACTURING OF PYROTECHNICS AND
FIRECRACKERS WITHIN THE TERRITORIAL
JURISDICTION OF THE MUNICIPALITY OF
HINIGARAN, PROVINCE OF NEGROS OCCIDENTAL,
AND PROVIDING PENALTY FOR THE VIOLATION
THEREOF.

xxx

Now Therefore:

Sec. 1 - No children below 15 years old shall be employed by any person, group, or organization or company during weekends, holidays and whenever there are no classes;

Sec. 2 - Every person, group, or organization or company shall keep m detail a record of the following:
Section A.   A registry of all children employed by him indicating the dates of their birth;
Section B.   A separate file for the written consent of their parents or guardians to their employment;
Section C.   A separate file for their education and medical certificates;

Sec. 3 - Children 15 to 18 years old, may be employed in the pyrotechnics provided, the following are observed:

Section A.   The employer shall ensure the protection of health and safety of the child;

Section B.   The employer shall institute measure to prevent exploitation or discrimination, taking into account the system and level of remuneration and duration and arrangement of working time;

Section C.   Employer shall formulate and implement a continues program and training and skills acquisition of the child

xxx

Sec. 5 - Work Practices

Section A.   A child worker shall be restricted only to non-hazardous operation such as wrapping of wick, drying and collection of finished product and packing to designated work places segregated from hazardous processes;

Section B.   Young workers shall be equipped with a suitable protective equipment;

Section C.   Open flames and sources of sparks shall be prohibited near or within the vicinity of the production site;

Section D.   Strict control in all phases of work shall be observed and fire extinguishers shall be provided in case of fire emergencies

xxx

Sec. 7. Health Control and Supervision

Section A. Child workers should wear masks at all times when working;

Section B. They should wash their hands and face thoroughly before, eating, drinking or before leaving the premises;

Section C. Introduction, preparation and consumption of food and drinks in the work room shall be prohibited;

Section D.   There should be periodic physical and annual medical examination of children working in pyrotechnics such as X-ray and laboratory examination;

Section E.   Physical complaint and injury suffered in the course of work should be reported promptly to owner and operators;

xxx

Sec. 11 - Penalty

Any person or group of persons who violate this ordinance shall upon conviction by the court, be fined in an amount of not less than One Thousand (P1,000.00) pesos and a maximum of not exceeding Two Thousand (P2,000.00) pesos or an imprisonment of not less than One (1) month but not exceeding Two (2) months or both fine and imprisonment at the discretion of the court and in addition to the cancellation of her/his license and business permit.

Sec. 12 - Effectivity - This ordinance shall take effect upon the approval of the Sangguniang Panlalawigan of Negros Occidental.

Sponsored by: KAGAWAD TERESITA B. JOB
Seconded by: KAGAWAD JOSE NADIE P. ARCEO AND
              KAGAWAD ROY GUANZON

APPROVED: August 16, 1994

I hereby certify to the correctness of the above quoted ordinance.

CAROLL Y. GUANCO, Vice Mayor, Presiding

ATTESTED:

TERESITA B. ABLAO, Acting Secretary to the Sangguniang Bayan

APPROVED:

HERNILO L. AGUILAR, Municipal Mayor

4. SP Ordinance No. 1025-94 (Butuan City)

Republika ng Pilipinas
TANGGAPAN NG SANGGUNIANG PANLUNGSOD
Lungsod ng Butuan

AN ORDINANCE BANNING PERSONS WHO ARE
LESS THAN 18 YEARS OF AGE FROM LOITERING,
ENTERING OR WORKING IN THE PREMISES OF A
MASSAGE AND SAUNA BATH PARLORS, BEER
HOUSES, BEER GARDENS, HOTELS, MOTELS OR
LODGING HOUSES AND PROVIDING PENALTIES
THEREFOR AND FOR OTHER PURPOSES

Be it ordained by the Sangguniang Panlungsod ng Butuan in its session assembled, That:

Sec. 1. All persons who are less than 18 years of age are banned from loitering, entering or working in the premises of massage parlor and/or sauna, beer houses, beer gardens, hotels, motels or lodging houses within the City or Butuan.

Sec. 2. Exceptions. The provision of Section 1 hereof shall not apply to minors who on a legitimate or licit purpose enter the premises of the hotels or lodging houses in the company of their parents, guardians, chaperons or person exercising substitute parental authority.

Sec. 3. Definition. For the purpose of this Ordinance the following terms are defined, to wit:

1. *Hotel* - is an establishment that provides lodging and meals, entertainment, and various personal services for the public.
2. *Motel* - is an establishment which provides lodging and parking and in which the rooms are used accessible from an out door parking area,
3. *Lodging House* - is a place where one is living for a time.
4. *Massage Parlor* - is an establishment that provides massage treatment.

5.   *Sauna* - is a finish steam bath in which, the steam is provided by water thrown on hot stones; also a bathhouse or room used fir such bath.

Sec. 4. Any minor and/or owner or manager of the establishment who violates the provisions of Section 1 hereof shall be punished as follows, to wit:

1st Offense -   P 100.00 for the minors
                 500.00 for the establishment
2nd Offense -   P 300.00 for the minors
                 1,000.00 for the establishment
3rd Offense -   P 1,000.00 and one [I] day
                 imprisonment for the minors
                 2,000.00 for the establishment
                 and suspension or cancellation
                 of the Mayor's Permit.

A Citation Ticket will be issued to the offenders and the establishment by the Children and Youth Relation Section and the corresponding payment will be paid at the City Treasurer's Office.

Sec. 5. The revenues earned in the enforcement of this Ordinance will be used for the operation of the Children and Youth Relation Section.

Sec. 6. All Ordinances shall take effect for [10] days after a copy of it is posted at the Bulletin Board of the City Hall and in two [2] other conspicuous places in the City of Butuan, and after the salient features thereof are published in a newspaper of general circulation in the City of Butuan.

UNANIMOUSLY APPROVED.

ENACTED: July 15, 1994
APPROVED: July 29, 1994
APPROVED: LEO VIGILDO B. BANAAG
         SP Member
         Acting Presiding Officer

ATTESTED:

REMEDIOS H. GONZALES   LEOVIGILDO B. BANAAG
City Gov't Dept. Head III   SP Member
(City Treasurer)   Acting Presiding Officer

5. Ordinance No. 201 (Lapu-Lapu City)

SANGGUNIANG PANLUNGSOD
RESOLUTION NO. 1983-94

AN ORDINANCE PROHIBITING THE HIRING OR
MINORS AS WAITRESSES, ENTERTAINERS,
HOSPITALITY GIRLS OR COMMERCIAL SEX
WORKERS IN ANY LOCAL RESTAURANT,
BEERHOUSES, PUB, KARAOKE, CLUB AND
SIMILAR ESTABLISHMENT WITHIN THE CITY OF
LAPU-LAPU.

PREPARATORY STATEMENTS:

WHEREAS, it seeks to give more teeth to
Republic Act No. 7610, otherwise known as "The
Special Protection of Children Against Child Abuse,
Exploitation and Discrimination Act" which was
passed in 1992;

WHEREAS, it aimed at curbing child abuse
and exploitation of minors and promoting children's
rights and welfare; and therefore, it stressed that
minors in such establishments are exposed to risks
and conditions detrimental to their health and
mental development.

Be it ordained by the Sangguniang
Panlungsod of the City of LapuLapu, that;

Sec. 1. The hiring of minors, who are below 18
years old, as waitresses, entertainers, hospitality
girls or commercial sex workers in any local
restaurant, beerhouse, pub, karaoke, club and
similar establishments within the City of Lapu-Lapu
shall be prohibited.

Sec. 2. Any person, operator or
owner/managers of any restaurant, beerhouse, pub,
karaoke, club or similar establishment who shall

violate the provisions of Section 1 hereof shall be prohibited.

Upon filling of the said offense, the business establishment shall be deemed closed, thereof, revoking the business or mayor's permit covering therein.

Sec. 3. This ordinance shall take effect fifteen (15) days from its approval and publication in the newspaper of general circulation in the Province of Cities of Cebu.

ENACTED: May 20, 1994.
APPROVED: May 30, 1994.

I hereby certify to the correctness of the above-quoted ordinance.

RODULFO S. YMBONG
City Secretary

ATTESTED:

ARTURO   O.   LALDAZA   ROBIN   E.   DIMATIGA
Vice Mayor & Presiding   Secretary to the Mayor
Officer

APPROVED:

ERNEST H. WEIGEL, JR.
City Mayor

6. Ordinance No. 7780 (City of Manila)

AN ORDINANCE PROHIBITING AND PENALIZING THE
PRINTING, PUBLICATION, SALE, DISTRIBUTION AND
EXHIBITION OF OBSCENE AND PORNOGRAPHIC ACTS
AND MATERIALS, AND THE PRODUCTION, RENTAL,
PUBLIC SHOWING AND VIEWING OF INDECENT AND
IMMORAL MOVIES, TELEVISION SHOWS, MUSIC
RECORDS, VIDEO AND VHS TAPES, LASER DISCS,
THEATRICAL OR STAGE AND OTHER LIVE
PERFORMANCES, EXCEPT THOSE REVIEWED BY THE
MOVIE, TELEVISION REVIEW AND CLASSIFICATION
BOARD (MTRCB).

Be it ordained by the City Council of Manila, THAT:

Sec. 1. Title: This ordinance shall be known as
the   ANTI-OBSCENITY   AND   PORNOGRAPHY
ordinance of the City of Manila.

Sec. 2. Definition of Terms: As used in this
ordinance, the terms:

a. *"Obscene"* shall refer to any material or act
that is indecent, erotic, lewd or offensive, or contrary
to morals, good customs or religious belief, principles
or doctrines, or to any material or act that tends to
corrupt or deprive the, human mind, or is calculated
to excite impure imagination or arouse prurient
interest, or is unfit to be seen or heard, or which
violates the proprieties of language or behavior,
regardless of the motive of the printer, publisher,
seller, distributor, performer or author of such act or
material, such as but not limited to:

1. printing, showing, depicting or describing
sexual acts;
2. printing, showing, depicting or describing
children in sexual acts;
3. printing, showing, depicting or describing
completely nude human bodies, and
4. printing, showing, depicting or describing the

human sexual organs or the female breasts.

b. *"Pornographic or pornography"* shall refer to such objects or subjects of photography, movies, music records, video and VHS tapes, laser discs, billboards, television, magazines, newspapers, tabloids, comics and live shows calculated to excite or stimulate sexual drive or impure imagination, regardless of the motive of the author thereof, such as, but not limited to the following:

1. performing live sexual ads in whatever form;
2. those other than live performances showing, depicting or describing sexual acts;
3. those showing, depicting or describing children in sexual acts;
4. those showing, depicting, or describing completely nude human bodies, or showing, depicting or describing the human sexual organs or the female breasts.

c. *"Materials"* shall refer to magazines, newspapers, tabloids, comics, writings, photographs, drawings, paintings, billboards, decals, movies, music records, video and VHS tapes, laser discs, and similar matters.

Sec. 3. Prohibited Acts: The printing, publishing, distribution, circulation, sale and exhibition of obscene and pornographic acts and materials and the production, public showing and viewing of video and VHS tapes, laser discs, theatrical or stage and other live performances and private showing for public consumption, whether for free or for a fee, of pornographic pictures as herein defined are hereby prohibited within the City of Manila and accordingly penalized as provided herein.

Sec. 4. Penalty Clause: Any person violating this ordinance shall be punished as follows:

1. for printing, publishing, distribution or circulation of obscene or pornographic materials; the production or showing of obscene movies, television shows, stage and other live performances; for producing or renting obscene video and VHS tapes, laser discs, for viewing obscene movies, television shows, video and VHS tapes, and laser discs or stage and other live performances; and for performing obscene acts on stage and other live performances -imprisonment of one (1) year or fine of five thousand (P5,000.00) pesos, or both, at the discretion of the court.

2. for the selling of obscene or pornographic materials -imprisonment of not less than six (6) months nor more than one (1) year or a fine of not less than one thousand (P1,000.00) pesos, nor more than three thousand (P3,000.00) pesos.
Provided, that in case the offender is a juridical person, the President and the members of the board of directors, shall be held criminally liable; Provided, further, that in case of conviction, all pertinent permits and licenses issued by the City Government to the offender shall automatically be revoked and the obscene or pornographic materials shall be confiscated in favor of the City Government for destruction; Provided, furthermore, that in case the offender is a minor and unemancipated and unable to pay the fine, his parents or guardian shall be liable to pay such fine; Provided finally, that this ordinance shall not apply to materials printed, distributed, exhibited, sold, filmed, rented, viewed or produced by reason of or in connection with or in furtherance of science and scientific research and medical or medically related, art, profession, and for educational purposes.

Sec. 5. Repealing Clause: All ordinances, rules and regulations or parts thereof in conflict or inconsistent with the provisions of this ordinance are hereby repealed, amended or modified accordingly.

Sec. 6. Separability Clause: If any provision of this ordinance is declared void, the provisions not affected thereby shall remain in full force and effect.

Sec. 7. Effectivity: This ordinance shall take effect thirty (30) days after publication in a newspaper of general circulation in the City of Manila.

Enacted by the City Council of Manila at its regular session today, January 28, 1993.

Approved by His Honor, the Mayor on February 19, 1993.

APPROVED:

ALFREDO S. LIM   JOSE L. ATIENZA, JR.
Mayor   Vice-Mayor and Presiding Officer
City of Manila   City Council, Manila

ATTESTED:

RAFAELITO M. GARAYBLAS
Secretary to the Mayor

EMMANUEL R. SISON
Secretary to the City Council

7. Ordinance No. 7791 (City of Manila)

AN ORDINANCE PROHIBITING SEXUAL RELATIONS WITH, AND SOLICITATION OR PROCUREMENT OF, PROSTITUTES AND OTHER RELATED ACTS, PROVIDING PENALTIES THEREFOR.

Be it ordained by the City Council of Manila, THAT:

Sec. 1. Declaration of Policy - It is hereby declared the policy of the City of Manila that prostitution is a social menace that destroys the moral integrity of a person and which causes irreparable damage to the image of both the City and the Filipino nation and must be stopped at all cost.

Sec. 2. Prohibited Acts - Pursuant to the above declared policy, it shall be unlawful for any person:

a. to have sexual relations with a prostitute for some consideration including payment but not limited to sums of money;

b.   to solicit, procure, pimp or pander; and

c. to act as a middle person or go-between for a third person and a prostitute in any place in the City of Manila for purposes of prostitution.

Sec. 3. Definition of Terms - as used in this ordinance, the following words shall have their corresponding meanings, to wit:

a. PROSTITUTE - is a person who habitually engages in sexual relations with another person for profit, gain or fee.

b. PROSTITUTION - refers to the act of habitually engaging in sexual relations with persons for certain considerations including payment but not limited to sums of money.

c. SOLICITOR, PROCURER., PANDER OR PIMP - is a person who secures or engages the services of a prostitute for sexual relations or who otherwise acts as middle person or go-between for a third person and a prostitute for purposes of facilitating prostitution whether or not sexual relation is actually performed or consummated.

d. SEXUAL RELATION - any act committed for sexual gratification to include sexual intercourse, touching, manipulation, acts of lasciviousness and other similar conduct.

Sec. 4. Penal Clause - Violation of this Ordinance shall be punishable by a fine of Five thousand (P5,000.00) pesos or imprisonment of one (1) year, or both such fine and imprisonment at the discretion of the court, Provided that:

a. if the violator is a foreigner, he/she shall in addition to penalties prescribed herein, be subject to deportation as may be determined by the proper authorities.

b. in case the violator is between the ages of 10 to 17 years, he/she shall pay a fine of not more than Two thousand five hundred (P2,500.00) pesos or suffer imprisonment of not more than six months, or both such fine and imprisonment, at the discretion of the court.

Sec. 5. Repealing Clause - Any Ordinance or portions thereof, which are inconsistent or contrary to this Ordinance or portions hereof are hereby deemed repealed or modified accordingly.

Sec. 6. Separability Clause - If for any reason any provision of this Ordinance is declared invalid or unconstitutional, the remaining provisions that are not affected thereby shall continue to be in full force and effect

Sec. 7. Effectivity Clause - This Ordinance shall take effect on and after the twentieth day following its publication.

Enacted by the City Council of Manila at its regular session today, June 3, 1993.

Approved by His Honor, the Mayor on June ll, 1993.

APPROVED:

ALFREDO S. LIM	JOSE L. ATIENZA
Mayor	Vice-Mayor and Presiding Officer
City of Manila	City of Manila

ATTESTED:

RAFAELITO M. GARAYBLAS	EMMANUEL R. SISON
Secretary to the Mayor	Secretary to the City Council

8. Ordinance No. 92-012 (Zamboanga City)

REPUBLIC OF THE PHILIPPINES
SANGGUN1ANG PANLUNGSOD
City of Zamboanga

AN ORDINANCE REGULATING THE OPERATION OF
PEDICAB IN THE CITY OF ZAMBOANGA
AND PROVIDING PENALTY
FOR VIOLATIONS THEREFOR.

xxx

ARTICLE IV - PEDICAB DRIVER

Sec. 1. - No person shall be allowed to drive a pedicab either for public or private use, unless he is issued a license to drive a pedicab by the Office of the City Mayor upon payment of a free of TWENTY FIVE (P 25.00) PESOS and upon submission of the following requirements:

1. Two (2) copies of I x I pictures
2. Birth Certificate or Voter's Affidavit
3. Medical Certificate issued by a government physician
4. Police Clearance
5. Fiscal Clearance
6. Barangay Clearance

Sec. 2. - No person shall be issued a license to drive a pedicab unless he is Eighteen (I 8) years of age, and has passed the examination conducted by the Office of the City Mayor. The Office of the City Mayor shall require attendance to a similar or traffic rules and regulations to be conducted by the Traffic Division of the Police District concerned or any agency designated by the Office of the City Mayor before a license can be issued or renewed.

Sec. 3. - No public utility/commercial use pedicab driver shall be allowed to drive with slippers, wearing short pants, sleeveless clothes and smoking while driving.

xxx

ARTICLE X - EFFECTIVITY

Sec. 1. - This Ordinance shall take effect in accordance with the provisions of the New Local Government Code of 1991.

ENACTED: DECEMBER 28, 1992.

ROBERTO W. S. KO
City Vice Mayor III
Presiding Officer

9. MMC Ordinance No. 85-04 (Metro Manila)

METROPOLITAN MANILA COMMISSION

PROVIDING PENALTIES FOR PROSTITUTION
AND/OR SEXUAL EXPLOITATION OF MINORS AND
FOR OTHER PURPOSES

WHEREAS, recently published reports concerning cases of prostitution and/or sexual exploitation of minors in many places of our country, particularly the Metro Manila area, have alarmed both the government and concerned private citizens group;

WHEREAS, it is felt that existing penal laws and local ordinances on various crimes/offenses against public morals and child welfare do not adequately cover such cases of prostitution and/or sexual exploitation of minors;

WHEREAS, it is the duty of the government to provide measures for the promotion of the welfare of children and to protect them against exploitation, improper influence, hazards, and other conditions or circumstances prejudicial to their physical, mental, emotional, social and moral development;

NOW, THEREFORE, be it ordained by the Metropolitan Manila Commission, acting through its Chairman and Governor of Metropolitan Manila, pursuant to Presidential Decree No. 824, as amended that:

Sec. 1. Definition of Terms - Whenever used in this ordinance, the following terms or phrases shall be taken and understood in the sense indicated hereunder, unless the context otherwise requires:

a. *Minor* - shall refer to any person under eighteen (18) years of age.

b. *Prostitution* - shall mean the act of sexual intercourse or lascivious conduct with another person of the same or opposite sex, for monetary or other consideration.

c. *Sexual Exploitation* - shall pertain to the satisfaction of lust by any act other than sexual intercourse, such as manipulation of sex organs, masturbation, oral sex, anal sex, or the employment, use, persuasion, enticement, or coercion of any minor to engage in, or of a minor to assist any other minor to indulge in any sexual conduct, or engaging minors to perform sexual acts, and/or similar acts, for monetary or other consideration.

d. *Relative* - shall include the parents, adopting parents, step-parent, grandparent, foster parent or guardian, uncle, aunt, granduncle, grandaunt, or any other relative by consanguinity (whether full or half-blood) or by affinity, within the sixth civil degree.

Sec. 2. Prostitution and/or Sexual Exploitation of Minors - Any person who shall avail of the service of a minor for prostitution and/or sexual exploitation shall suffer the penalty of imprisonment of not less than one (I) year nor more than four (4) years or a fine of not less than Two thousand pesos (P2,000.00) but not exceeding Eight thousand pesos (P8,000.00) or both such fine and imprisonment at the discretion of the court. The offender shall in addition pay Ten thousand pesos (P10,000.00) which shall form part of the fluids for the rehabilitation of the offended minor.

Sec. 3. Legal Presumption - The following persons are presumed to engage in the prostitution/sexual exploitation of minors:

a. Any person who, not being a relative of a minor, is found alone under suspicious circumstances with the said minor inside the room and/or cubicle Of an inn, hotel, motel, pension house. apartelle or other similar establishments.

b. Any person who, in the company of a minor not related to him, is found showing/exhibiting pornographic films, photographs and other similar materials to such minors.

c. Any person receiving services from a minor in a sauna parlor or bath, massage clinic, health club and other similar establishments.

Sec. 4. Corruption of Minors - Any person who shall promote, facilitate or induce the prostitution and/or sexual exploitation of minors through coercion, deceits or other means for his or her benefit shall suffer the same penalty provided in Section 2 hereof.

Sec. 5. Liability of Owner, Operator, Manager, Administrator, Caretaker or Tender of any Hotel, Motel, Apartelle, Pension House, Inn, as well as Bars or Baths, Massage Clinics, Lounges, Disco Clubs, Sauna Parlors or Baths, Massage Clinics, Health Clubs and Other Similar Establishments. - Any owner, operator, manager, administrator, caretaker or tender of any hotel, motel, apartelle, pension house, inn, as well as bars, nightclubs, cocktail lounges, disco clubs, sauna parlors or baths, massage clinics, health clubs and other similar establishments who admits, allows, permits or otherwise neglects to prevent the entry and stay of a minor into said place to facilitate the commission of the acts penalized under Section 2 hereof shall be liable for imprisonment of not less than six (6) months nor more than (2) years or a fine of not less than One thousand pesos (P 1,000.00) but not more than Four thousand pesos (P4,000.00) or both such fire and imprisonment at the discretion of the court. The offender shall in addition pay Five thousand pesos (P5,000.00) which shall form part of the funds for the rehabilitation of the offended minor

Sec. 6. *Neglect/Failure to Report to Authorities* - Any person who knows of the sexual exploitation or prostitution of a minor but fails, refuses or neglects to denounce, report or inform the proper authorities of said exploitation or prostitution, shall suffer the penalty of imprisonment of not more than (1) year or a fine not exceeding Two thousand pesos (P2,000.00) or both such fine and imprisonment at the discretion of the court.

Sec. 7. *Offense/s Committed by Relatives* - If the person committing any of the offense/s provided in Sections 2, 4, and 6 hereof be a relative of the minor, the penalty shall be imposed in its maximum period.

For purposes of this Ordinance, a public officer, guardian, teacher, or any person, charged with the care and/or custody of the minor shall be considered a relative of the minor,

Sec. 8. *Rehabilitation of Minors* - The minor shall not be criminally prosecuted but shall be placed under the rehabilitation or reformation and committed to the care of his or her parents, relatives or family friend, or to the Ministry of Social Services Development (MSSD), subject to such condition as the court may impose.

The funds mentioned in Sections 2 and 5 hereof shall be administered by the Metropolitan

Manila Commission (MMC) as a trust fund and disbursed for the rehabilitation of offended minors under this ordinance.

Sec. 9. Role of the Committee on Justice - It shall be the responsibility of the Metro Manila Committee on Justice to monitor the status/progress of cases filed with the Fiscal's Office or the court under this ordinance.

Sec. 10. Responsibility of Mayors and Police Authorities- It shall be the responsibility of the Mayors in coordination with the police authorities to strictly enforce the provisions of this Ordinance within their respective areas or jurisdiction.

Sec. 11. Effectivity -This Ordinance shall take effect thirty (30) days after its approval.

Done in Quezon City, this 30th day of October in the Year of Our Lord, Nineteen Hundred and Eighty Five.

IMELDA ROMUALDEZ MARCOS
Governor

by: ISMAEL A. MATHAY, JR.
Vice-Governor

L. LIABILITIES OF HOTEL/MOTEL OWNERS

1. Department of Tourism Administrative Order No. 95-17

ADMINISTRATIVE ORDER NO. 95-17
Series of 1995

Pursuant to the provisions of Executive Order No. 120 and the Rules and Regulations governing accommodation establishments, all accredited hotels, resorts, tourist inns, motels, apartelles and pension houses are hereby enjoined to observe and/or comply with Section 40, Chapter X of the Rules which provides the following, to wit:

"Managers or operators of hotels, resorts, tourist inns, motels, apartels and pension houses shall exert all possible efforts not to permit any person, whom they know or have reason to believe to be either a prostitute, a pedophile or of questionable character, to occupy a room or to enter the premises of the establishment. To accomplish this end, they shall immediately report to the nearest police station or to the Tourist Security Division personnel of the Department of Tourism the presence of any such person in the premises."

Any violation of the above-mentioned provision may be a valid ground for the cancellation of the establishment's accreditation with this Department without prejudice to the filing of the appropriate case against the errant establishment.

For strict compliance.
26 July 1995

EDUARDO P. PILAPIL
Secretary

2. Bureau of Tourism Services

Circular No. 11
(Series of 1982)

To: All Managers or Operators of Hotels, Motels Resorts, Inns, Pension Houses and Lodging Houses.

Pursuant to the authority of the Ministry of Tourism under Presidential Decree 1463 and in line with the concerted effort of concerned government agencies to curb the growing problem of corruption and prostitution of children and minors, the following guidelines are hereby promulgated:

1. No Minors, below 15 years of age, male or female, shall be allowed to be registered, to rent room or otherwise allowed to stay, in the room of any hotel, motel, resort, tourist inn, pension house or lodging house unless he or she i~ in the company of his or her parent(s) or immediate close adult relative, which relationship the managers or registering employee shall ascertain;

2. No minor as defined above shall be allowed to visit or be brought inside the room of any guest in any of the above lodging facilities unless the guest is established to be a close adult relative; and

3. The managers/operators shall take steps and proper measures to discourage and prohibit the unnecessary loitering of non-guest minors within the premises of their establishments.

Any of the above enumerated establishments and/or their officers or employees that violate the provisions of this circular shall be subject to a penalty in the form of administrative fine of Ten thousand pesos (P 10,000.00) and/or revocation of the license of the establishment depending on the circumstances attending the violation or termination of employment in the case of the officers or employees.

Imposition of the above administrative sanction shall be based on the findings of the Ministry or on the investigation reports of local military/police authorities who are hereby enlisted, pursuant to Sec. 4, par.(m) of PD. 1463 to implement and enforce this circular.

Promulgated on the 7th day of December 1982.
By Authority of the Tourism Minister

IRINEO T. AGUIRRE, JR.
Director

PART THREE

LEGAL PROCEDURES FOR THE ENFORCEMENT OF RIGHTS

The procedures for the protection of children's rights encompass different levels and categories of interventions. The procedures outlined in this book are divided into several major parts: 1) detection and reporting; 2) information verification; 3) removal and rescue; 4) custody and rehabilitation; 5) recovery of wages and other monetary benefits; 6) administrative sanctions; and 7) criminal prosecution.

I. DETECTION AND REPORTING

*Detection of child workers relies heavily on the participation of the **community**. Since most child workers are hidden, it is hard for the government, given its limited resources, to track down all of them for possible intervention. Many concerned citizens and non-governmental organizations conduct their own investigations or undercover operations to detect and monitor the presence of child workers.*

*Anyone with sufficient knowledge of any violation committed against a child worker may **report** the same to any of the following agencies, organizations, or groups:*

1. *DOLE, Child Labor Program Committee*
2. *DSWD, Bureau of Child and Youth Welfare*
3. *Local/Barangay Council for the Protection of Children*
4. *Philippine National Police, Child and Youth Relations Unit/Officer*
5. *National Bureau of Investigation*

6. *Commission on Human Rights, Child Rights Center*
7. *Department of Justice, Task Force on Child Protection*
8. *City/Provincial Fiscals/Prosecutors*
9. *Social Services Department of Hospitals or Clinics*
10. *School Authorities*
11. *Church Officials & Community Groups*
12. *Non-Governmental Organizations*

A. SPECIAL AGENCIES AND COMMITTEES

Presented below are some of the laws and executive and administrative orders creating special agencies, committees, or units specifically mandated to respond to the needs of child workers.

1. Local Council For The Protection Of Children

CHILD AND YOUTH WELFARE CODE (P.D. 603)

Art. 87. Council for the Protection of Children -- Every barangay council shall encourage the organization of a local Council for the Protection of Children and shall coordinate with the Council for the Welfare of Children and Youth in drawing and implementing plans for the promotion of child and youth welfare. Membership shall be taken from responsible members of the community including a representative of the youth, as well as representatives of government and private agencies concerned with the welfare of children and youth whose area of assignment includes the particular barangay and shall be on a purely voluntary basis.

Said Council shall:

(1) Foster the education of every child in the barangay;
(2) Encourage the proper performance of the duties of parents and provide learning opportunities on the adequate rearing of children and on positive parent-child relationship;

(3) Protect and assist abandoned or maltreated children and dependents;

(4) Take steps to prevent juvenile delinquency and assist parents of children with behavioral problems so they can get expert advice;

(5) Adopt measures for the health of children;

(6) Promote the opening and maintenance of playgrounds and day-care centers and other services that are necessary for child and youth welfare;

(7) Coordinate the activities of organizations devoted to the welfare of children and secure their cooperation;

(8) Promote wholesome entertainment in the community, especially in movie houses; and

(9) Assist parents, whenever necessary, in securing expert guidance counselling from the proper governmental or private welfare agency.

In addition, it shall hold classes and seminars on the proper rearing of the children. It shall distribute to parents available literature and other information on child guidance. The Council shall assist parents, with behavioral problems whenever necessary, in securing expert guidance counselling from the proper governmental or private welfare agency.

2. Committee For The Special Protection Of Children

Malacañang
Manila
By The President Of The Philippines

EXECUTIVE ORDER NO. 275
CREATING A COMMITTEE FOR THE SPECIAL
PROTECTION OF CHILDREN FROM ALL FORMS OF
NEGLECT, ABUSE, CRUELTY, EXPLOITATION,
DISCRIMINATION AND OTHER CONDITIONS
PREJUDICIAL TO THEIR DEVELOPMENT

WHEREAS, the Constitution provides that the natural and primary right and duty of parents in the rearing of the youth for civic efficiency and the development of moral character shall receive the support of the government;

WHEREAS, the State shall defend the right of children to assistance, including proper care and nutrition and special protection from all forms of neglect, abuse, cruelty, exploitation and discrimination, and other conditions prejudicial to their development;

WHEREAS, there is a need to consolidate in one body the assessment, monitoring and implementation of the aforecited policy on a continuing bases;

NOW, THEREFORE, I, FIDEL V. RAMOS, President of the Republic of the Philippines, by virtue of the powers vested in me by law, do hereby order: ·

Sec. 1. There is hereby created a Special Committee for Children to be composed of:

1. The Secretary of Justice – *Chairman*
2. The Secretary of Social Welfare and Development - *Co-Chairman*
3. The Chairman of the Commission on Human Rights – *Member*
4. Commissioner of the Bureau of Immigration - *Member*

A representative with a rank not lower than undersecretary from the following:

5. Department of Labor and Employment – *Member*
6. Department of Tourism – *Member*
7. Department of the Interior and Local Government – *Member*
8. Department of Foreign Affairs – *Member*
9. Three representatives of private organizations to be nominated by said groups and appointed by the President - *Members*

Sec. 2. The Committee shall exercise the following functions and duties:

a. To report to the President actions taken to address specific issues on child abuse and exploitation brought to the Committee's attention;

b. To direct other agencies to immediately respond to the problems brought to their attention and to report to the Committee on action taken; and

c. To perform such other functions and duties as may be necessary to meet the objectives of the Committee.

Sec. 3. The Council for the Welfare of Children shall act as the Secretariat of the Committee.

Sec. 4. The initial amount of ₱10,000,000.00 is hereby authorized to be released from the Presidential Social Fund.

Sec. 5. This Executive Order shall take effect immediately.

DONE in the City of Manila, this 14th day of September, in the year of Our Lord, Nineteen Hundred and Ninety-Five.

By the President:
RUBEN D. TORRES
Executive Secretary

3. Child Labor Project Management Team

Republic of the Philippines
DEPARTMENT OF LABOR AND EMPLOYMENT
Manila
ADMINISTRATIVE ORDER NO. 2
(Series of 1992)

In line with the mandate of the Department of Labor and Employment on workers' protection and welfare and in order to facilitate implementation of the UNICEF-assisted project "Breaking Ground for

Community Action on Child Labor," a Child Labor Project Management Team is hereby constituted to be responsible for planning, implementation, monitoring and evaluation of all child labor program activities falling within the area of responsibility of the Department under the project.

The Child Labor Project Management Team (CLPMT) shall be under the direct supervision of the Undersecretary for Workers' Protection and Welfare, Chairman of the National Child Labor Program Committee (NCLPC).

The CLPMT shall be composed of a Project Director, an Asst. Project Director and technical personnel who shall be selected from the bureaus and agencies of the Department as indicated in attached organizational and functional structure.

Moreover, in line with the government's decentralization policy and to ensure the efficient and effective implementation of project activities in the pilot and expansion areas, all concerned Regional Offices shall assign full-time coordinators for the project.

Funds for operational and other requirements of the CLPMT shall be drawn from the existing project funds including the government counterpart (GOP), subject to the project's approved Work and Financial Plan for 1992-1993.

All bureaus, offices and attached agencies of the Department are enjoined to extend assistance to the NCLPC and the CLPMT whenever necessary.

For strict compliance.

RUBEN D. TORRES
Secretary

02 January 1992

4. Agencies To Investigate Sex Tours

Malacañang
Manila
By The President Of The Philippines

MEMORANDUM ORDER NO. 287

DIRECTING THE INVESTIGATION OF THE ALLEGED
OPERATION OF SEX TOURS IN THE COUNTRY BY
FOREIGN NATIONALS

WHEREAS, the participants in the recent Conference on Sexual Exploitation that met in Quezon City had examined the alleged involvement of foreigners in sex trafficking and prostitution of Filipino women and children, particularly in Angeles City;

WHEREAS, certain foreign nationals allegedly own and operate numerous bars and hotels which cater to foreigners on sex tours in the country;

WHEREAS, it is imperative to strengthen the ethical and spiritual values of victims of said sex tours and to devise viable economic alternatives to wean them away from prostitution.

NOW, THEREFORE, I, FIDEL V. RAMOS, President of the Republic of the Philippines, by virtue of the powers vested in me by law, do hereby direct the following government agencies, to wit:

1. The Department of Foreign Affairs (DFA) - to coordinate efforts with the foreign Governments concerned to curtail these nefarious activities of foreign nationals in the country.

2. The Department of Social Welfare and Development - to extend all possible assistance to victims of sexual trafficking and prostitution and their eventual rehabilitation.

3. All concerned Local Government Units (LGUs) - to exercise their authority/power to clamp down on prostitution within their jurisdiction and to close establishments being used in sex tours or as fronts of prostitution.

4. The Philippine National Police (PNP) - to immediately investigate and apprehend any Filipino and/or foreign nationals involved in said sex tours.

Done in the City of Manila, this 5th day of July, in the year of Our Lord, nineteen hundred and ninety-five.

By the President:

RUBEN D. TORRES
Executive Secretary

5. *"Sagip Batang Manggagawa"* - Inter-Agency Quick Action Team On The Handling Of Exploitative/Hazardous Child Labor Cases

The Department of Labor and Employment entered into an agreement with various government and non-government agencies in 1994, delineating the roles of each of the parties in responding to the most pressing situations of child laborers.

SAGIP BATANG MANGGAGAWA
[Child Labor Project Management Team Files]

"Sagip Batang Manggagawa", an Inter-Agency Quick Action Program, aims to respond to cases of child laborers in extremely abject conditions. An Inter-Agency Quick Action Team (QAT) shall be involved in detecting, monitoring and responding to the most hazardous forms of child labor. The program activities include monitoring and reporting cases to proper authorities who can either refer cases to appropriate institutions or provide assistance directly such as rescuing the child laborers from factories or other places of employment and, when necessary, imposing sanctions on the illegal employer/recruiter; provision of psycho-social services to child labor victims; and rendering assistance in the prosecution of civil and/or criminal cases against violators of child labor laws.

x x x

"[S]agip Batang Manggagawa" shall pursue the following objectives:

1. establishment of community-based mechanisms for detecting, monitoring and reporting most hazardous forms of child labor to proper authorities who can either refer cases to appropriate institutions or provide assistance directly;
2. establishment of 24-hour Quick Action Team Centers and Network to respond to immediate/serious child labor cases;
3. effectuation of immediate relief for child laborers in hazardous/exploitative conditions through conduct of search and rescue operations and other appropriate interventions;
4. provision of appropriate physical, psycho-social, and other needed services for the rescued child labor victims;
5. imposing administrative sanctions and filing criminal cases against violators of child labor laws;
6. provision of technical assistance for the prosecution of civil and/or criminal cases filed against employers and employment agencies violating laws and standards relative to child labor;
7. facilitation of the return of child laborers to parents/guardians or appropriate custodian; and
8. upgrading of capabilities of implementors in coming up with child-friendly procedures in protecting children.

[T]he following are the general roles and responsibilities of the members of the implementation machinery:

a. The *Department of Labor and Employment* (DOLE) shall lead the program implementation. It shall be the overall coordinator of activities under the QAT, like standards setting, particularly in the improvement of conditions of work of children; banning of child employment in hazardous occupations; and enforcement of laws, standards and policies under the mandate of the Department.

b.   The *Department of Social Welfare and Development* (DSWD) shall provide appropriate psycho-social services to child labor victims. When necessary, the child laborers shall be placed under the protective custody of the DSWD, which shall notify the parents or guardians of the children of their whereabouts. It shall also facilitate the return of the children to their parents/guardians or place of origin, unless such is against the best interests of the children. Its Crisis Intervention Centers shall serve as the 24-hour QAT network Center which will receive reports of exploitative/hazardous child labor and will refer reports to the operations team which will be led by the DOLE, for immediate/appropriate action/response.

c.   The *Department of Health* (DOH) shall provide appropriate medical and other related services for the child labor victims. If necessary, it shall also facilitate the admission and care of victims in state clinics/hospitals.

The Child and Youth Health Unit shall be the focal point for the provision of necessary medical interventions. The National Center for Mental Health shall also provide services for the psychological/psychiatric needs of the child labor victims.

d.   The role of the *Department of Education, Culture and Sports* (DECS) includes provision of special educational assistance to the rescued child laborers. It shall determine the educational needs of the victims and shall provide appropriate interventions such as specialized tutorial classes. Once the children are taken back to their parents/guardian, it shall extend assistance for the return of the children to school and shall monitor the progress of the children's education.

e. The role of the *Philippine Information Agency* (PIA) is the provision of technical assistance in the conduct of information, education and communication efforts focusing on activities aimed at strengthening the system for banning employment of children in working conditions that are hazardous/exploitative. It shall take the lead in the implementation of the QAT's advocacy and social mobilization activities.

f. The role of the *Department of Justice* (DOJ) includes rendering of legal assistance to child laborers. It shall give priority to the preliminary investigation of complaints filed or inquest cases referred by the National Bureau of Investigation and the Philippine National Police relating to violations of the law, rules and regulations pertaining to child labor and, if warranted by the evidence, of their prosecution in the courts of competent jurisdiction. Whenever necessary and in extreme cases, it shall place informants/witnesses under the Witness Protection, Security and Benefit Program (WPSB) in accordance with the provisions of Republic Act No. 6981.

The Task Force on Protection of Children Against Abuse, Exploitation and Discrimination of the National Prosecution Service shall be the focal point for the criminal prosecution of child labor cases to ensure immediate and appropriate response to such.

g. The *National Bureau of Investigation* (NBI) and the Department of the Interior and Local Government (DILG) through the Philippine National Police (PNP) shall assist in the conduct of search and rescue operations and other appropriate interventions. Said agencies shall also render technical assistance in the prosecution of civil and/or criminal cases filed in relation to violation of laws and policies relative to child labor.

h. The *Department of the Interior and Local Government* (DILG) shall also develop and strengthen the capabilities of the Local Government Units (LGUs) for effective detection, monitoring and response to child labor cases. It shall also help the LGUs in the establishment of local *"Sagip Batang Manggagawa"* networks.

i. The role of the *Child Rights Center of the Commission on Human Rights* (CHR-CRC) includes provision of assistance to the child labor victims in terms of the investigation of human rights violations against children. It shall initiate legal action for and in behalf of the child victims, and shall look into and report on violations of civil rights and freedoms (Articles 12, 13, 14, 15 and 16), as well as the special protection provisions (Articles 19, 38, 39 and 40) of the Convention on the Rights of the Child.

j. The *Trade Union Congress of the Philippines* (TUCP), the Labor and Advisory Consultative Council (LACC), the Employers Confederation of the Philippines (ECOP), the National Council of Social Development Foundation of the Philippines, Inc. (NCSD), the Kamalayan Development Center (KDC), and other NGOs/POs shall be the key cooperators for the implementation of the project. Said institutions shall develop among their ranks, mechanisms of surveillance and detection of child labor cases both in the formal and the informal work situations. Such institutions shall also participate in the establishment and manning of community-based 24-hour network centers in different localities.

x x x

6. Department Of Justice - Task Force On The Protection Of Children

DEPARTMENT OF JUSTICE
TASK FORCE ON PROTECTION OF CHILDREN
AGAINST ABUSE, EXPLOITATION AND
DISCRIMINATION
DEPARTMENT ORDER NO. 19

January 10, 1994

SUBJECT: DESIGNATION OF PERSONNEL

In the interest of the public service and pursuant to the provisions of existing laws, the Task Force on Protection of Children Against Abuse, Exploitation and Discrimination is hereby constituted composed of the following:

1.   xxx
2.   xxx
3.   xxx
4.   xxx
5.   xxx
6.   xxx

The prosecutors herein designated shall constitute the Secretariat, which shall be tasked with the preparation of all necessary documents for the creation of a Presidential Committee for the Protection of Children. They shall also perform alt other related functions thereto apart from the primary task of conducting preliminary investigation and the prosecution, if warranted by the evidence, of cases in violation of R.A. 7610 and other related laws in courts of competent jurisdiction.

This Order takes effect immediately and shall remain in force unless sooner revoked.

FRANKLIN M. DRILON
Secretary

HISTORY OF THE TASK FORCE
ON PROTECTION OF CHILDREN
AGAINST ABUSE,
EXPLOITATION AND DISCRIMINATION

The birth of the Task Force on the Protection of Children against abuse. Exploitation and Discrimination was the result of the passage of Republic Act 7610 wherein Department Order No. 19 dated January 10, 1994 was issued. Said Department Order designated six (6) prosecutors, chaired by Senior State Prosecutor Aurora S. Lagman, with the primary function of conducting preliminary investigation and the prosecution of cases in violation of RA 7610 and other related laws. Moreover, they shall constitute a Secretariat with the task of preparing all necessary documents for the creation of Presidential Committee for the Protection of Children.

Presently, there are thirteen (13) prosecutors under the task~ force who are handling more than sixty (60) cases all over the country.

7. National Bureau Of Investigation- VAWCD

PROFILE OF VAWCD

The VIOLENCE AGAINST WOMEN AND CHILDREN DIVISION (VAWCD) is one of the investigative commands of the NBI based in Manila. It was formerly named as Anti-Child Abuse Discrimination and Exploitation Division (ACADED) as a response of the Bureau to curb the growing menace of child abuse in the country. Created on August 6, 1996 under the administration of the late Director Santiago Y. Toledo; ACADED was renamed Violence Against Women and Children Division (VAWCD) by the late Director Federico M. Opinion, JR by virtue of a Special Order dated August 10, 2000.

MISSION

To provide total quality service by discharging its duties and responsibilities with UTMOST DISPATCH through a ONE-stop-shop (among others) with updated services to keep in step with the times protecting the victims in the process from the rigors and trauma of their experiences and providing all the needed investigative, legal, medical, psychological and rehabilitation/aftercare services. The VAWCD is committed to take a "WHOLISTIC" APPROACH to every case it handles, earnestly showing concern in all areas of needs of the victims.

VISION

A Filipino nation that is God centered with women and children living and breathing, moving and growing in a free, non-violent peace-loving environment that will provide self-dignity, self-worth, wholeness and completeness of person – as guided by and in line with the Bureau's mission.

8. Commission On Human Rights - Child Rights Center

Malacañang
Manila
By The President Of The Philippines

MEMORANDUM ORDER NO. 257

CONTINUING THE CHILD RIGHTS CENTER IN THE COMMISSION ON HUMAN RIGHTS AND APPROPRIATING FUNDS THEREFOR

WHEREAS, the Memorandum of Undertaking - Pledge of Commitment to the Rights of Filipino Children (MOD) dated 18 April 1994 urgently tasked the Commission on Human Rights to operate a Child Rights Center (CRC) that will spearhead the investigation and initiate legal action for and in behalf of child victims of human rights violations and monitor government's compliance with specific provisions of the Convention on the Rights of the Child (Convention);

WHEREAS, the MOU also tasks the CRC to coordinate the national network of special prosecutors and pan-legal volunteers, develop training programs on children's rights, and serve as a clearing house for government agencies and NGOs;

WHEREAS, the "Progress Towards the Mid-Decade Goals" of the Philippine Plan of Action for Children by Year 2000 reports the establishment of the Child Rights Center and underscores the need to update the legislative agenda fir children, continue public education and advocacy for sustaining community-based initiatives on protecting children's rights, and develop a national system for monitoring implementation of the Convention.

WHEREAS, the same Progress Report underscores the need for capacity-building on integrating the Convention in advocacy, programming and monitoring across sectors in all levels;

WHEREAS, Executive Order No. 163 dated 5 May 1987 shrouds the Commission on Human Rights with powers and functions to include monitoring Government compliance with international treaty obligations on human rights, investigation of all forms of human rights violations, and establishment of continuing programs of research education and information to enhance respect for primary of human rights,

NOW, THEREFORE, I FIDEL V. RAMOS, President of the Republic of the Philippines do hereby order.

Sec. 1. Continuance of the Child Rights Center in the Commission on Human Rights. In order to facilitate and expedite the national implementation of the Philippine Plan of Action for Children by Year

2000, especially with regard to the commitments vis-à-vis the Philippine ratification of the Convention on the Rights of the Child, the organization and operations of the Child Rights Center under the Office of the Chairman in the Commission on Human Rights is hereby continued.

Sec. 2. Inter-agency Support. The CRC shall continue to enjoy the support of key agencies as follows:

a. The Department of Social Welfare and Development shall provide protection custody, treatment and rehabilitative services to the child victims and their families.

b. The Armed Forces of the Philippines and the Philippine National Police shall promote child rights advocacy in their respective organizations and designate Child and Youth Relations Officers in all field offices.

c The Department of Justice shall facilitate the prosecution of child rights cases by appointing special prosecutors for children's cases in every region and deputize lawyers attached to the Child Rights Center to handle specific cases. It shall also coordinate with the CRC on Witness Protection and the referral of cases involving youthful offenders.

d. The Department of Education, Culture and Sports shall include the teaching of children's rights in all levels of the educational system.

e. The Department of Interior and Local Government shall mobilize support from local governments for the implementation of the Convention on the Rights of the Child.

Sec. 3. Technical and Secretariat Support Focused towards National Monitoring. The CRC continue to have an Executive Director IV and a Deputy Executive Director who shall provide technical and secretariat support to the CRC, respectively. The support shall be especially focused to setting up a national system for monitoring the implementation of the Convention on the Rights of the Child.

Sec. 4. Funding Support. The amount of TWO MILLION PESOS from the President's CY 1995 Contingent Fund shall be allocated for
the CRC, particularly its Technical and Secretariat Support for the National System for Monitoring the Convention's implementation, for February to December *1995,* after which funding support in succeeding year shall come from the fund of the Commission on Human Rights.

Sec. 5. This Memorandum Order shall take effect immediately.

Done in the City of Manila, this 7th of February in the year of Our Lord, Nineteen Hundred and Ninety Five.

By the President:

TEOFISTO T. GUINGONA, JR.
Executive Secretary

THE CHR'S CHILD RIGHTS CENTER

The rearing of the Filipino child cannot be done alone nor by just a few. The future of the nation lies in the hands of all members of society. Everyone must do their/his/her share.

For its part, the Commission on Human Rights has created a Child Rights Center tasked to perform the following functions consistent with the Commission's constitutional mandate:

1. Investigate human rights violation against children;
2. Initiate legal action for and in their behalf;
3. Monitor and report on government compliance

other human rights instruments pertaining to
children;

4. Coordinate with GOs and NGOs in the
promotion of child rights and protection of the
welfare of children; and

5. Develop and implement awareness programs
on children's rights.

In pursuit of its goals, the Center has linked
up with government agencies and NGOs involved in
child welfare such as:

1. The Department of Justice;
2. The Department of Social and Welfare and
Development;
3. The Department of Interior and Local
Government;
4. Children's Christian Fund;
5. Stop Trafficking of Pilipinos (STOP);
6. Adhikain para sa Karapatang Pantao of the
Ateneo Human Rights Center;
7. Center for Child Advocacy; and
8. Phil. Action for Youth Offenders (PAYO).

ACTIVITIES

INVESTIGATION

There are complaints desks found at the
CHR's Central Office and in all of its regional offices
manned by trained investigators and lawyers who
attend to all cases, with or without a complainant.
The CRC's complaints desk are a part of a two-way
referral monitoring network involving government
agencies and non-government organizations working
on child rights cases, to provide specialized services
to the victims.

INTERNAL AND EXTERNAL LIAISING

The internal and external liaising activity
enables the Center to develop, implement and
participate in national and international fora on

child tights promotion and protection. This activity also involves organizing consultative meetings, study groups and symposia, and initiates statements, position papers and opinions on current issues on the rights of children.

MONITORING

The Center's monitoring activities include working with the Council for the Welfare of Children, the Department of Justice and other concerned government agencies as well as NGOs to monitor the incidence of violations of the civil rights and freedoms of children and guarantees for their special protection.

RESEARCH AND SPECIAL STUDIES

The Center prepares studies on alternative strategies and approaches as well as pro-active papers on preventive measures and collaborative undertakings with the five pillars of the justice system. It endeavors to publish these studies with the view of informing the public on child rights and issues. It draws up performance indicators for monitoring the government's compliance with provisions in the Convention on the Rights of the Child on civil rights and freedoms and special protection measures, and prepares corresponding reports.

B.   DUTY TO REPORT

CHILD AND YOUTH WELFARE CODE

Art. 166.   Report of Maltreated or Abused Child. -- All hospitals, clinics and other institutions as well as private physicians providing treatment shall, within forty-eight hours from knowledge of the case, report in writing to the city or provincial fiscal or to the Local Council for the Protection of Children or to the nearest unit of the Department of Social

Welfare, any case of a maltreated or abused child, or exploitation of an employed child contrary to the provisions of labor laws. It shall be the duty of the Council for the Protection of Children or the unit of the Department of Social Welfare to whom such a report is made to forward the same to the provincial or city fiscal.

In cases of sexual abuse, the records pertaining to the case shall be kept strictly confidential and no information relating thereto shall be disclosed except in connection with any court official proceeding based on such report.

Any person disclosing confidential information in violation of this provision shall be punished by a fine of not less than two thousand pesos or by imprisonment of not more than one year or both such fine and imprisonment, at the discretion of the court.

Art. 167. *Freedom from Liability of Reporting Person or Institution.* -- Persons, organizations, physicians, nurses, hospitals, clinics and other entities which shall in good faith report cases of child abuse, neglect, maltreatment or abandonment or exposure to moral danger, shall be free from any civil or criminal liability arising therefrom.

C. PROCEDURES IN REPORTING AND INVESTIGATION

RULES AND REGULATIONS ON THE
REPORTING AND INVESTIGATION OF
CHILD ABUSE CASES

Pursuant to Section 32 of Republic Act No.7610 ("*An Act Providing For Stronger Deterrence and Special Protection Against Child Abuse, Exploitation and Discrimination, Providing Penalties For Its Violation and For Other Purposes*"), the following Rules and Regulations are hereby promulgated concerning the reporting and investigation of child abuse cases:

Sec. 1. Objectives. These Rules and Regulations seek to encourage the reporting of cases of physical or psychological injury, sexual abuse or exploitation, or negligent treatment of children and to ensure the early and effective investigation of cases of child abuse towards the prosecution of the offender consistent with the need to promote the best interests of the child victim.

Sec. 2. Definition of Terms. -- As used in these Rules, unless the context requires otherwise--

a) *"Child"* shall refer to a person below (18) years of age or one over said age and who, upon evaluation of a qualified physician, psychologist or psychiatrist, is found to be incapable of taking care of himself fully because of a physical or mental disability or condition or of protecting himself from abuse;

b) *"Child abuse"* refers to the infliction of physical or psychological injury, cruelty to, or neglect, sexual abuse or exploitation of a child;

c) *"Cruelty"* refers to any act, word or deed which debases, degrades or demeans the intrinsic worth and dignity of a child as a human being. Discipline administered by a parent or legal guardian to a child does not constitute cruelty provided it is reasonable in manner and moderate in degree and does not constitute physical or psychological injury as defined herein;

d) *"Physical injury"* includes but is not limited to lacerations, fractured bones, burns, internal injuries, severe injury or serious bodily harm suffered by a child;

e) *"Psychological injury"* means harm to a child's psychological or intellectual functioning which may be exhibited by severe anxiety, depression, withdrawal or outward aggressive behavior, or a combination of said behaviours, which may be demonstrated by a change in behavior, emotional response or cognition;

f) *"Neglect"* means failure to provide, for reasons other than poverty, adequate food, clothing, shelter, basic education or medical care so as to seriously endanger the physical, mental, social and emotional growth and development of the child;

g) *"Sexual abuse"* includes the employment, use, persuasion, inducement, enticement or coercion of a child to engage in, or assist another person to engage in, sexual intercourse or lascivious conduct or the molestation, prostitution, or incest with children;

h) *"Lascivious conduct"* means the intentional touching, either directly or through clothing, of the genitalia, anus, breast, inner thigh, or buttocks, or the introduction of any object into the genitalia, anus or mouth, of any person, whether of the same or opposite sex, with an intent to abuse, humiliate, harass, degrade, or arouse or gratify the sexual desire of any person, bestiality, masturbation, lascivious exhibition of the genitals or pubic area of a person;

i) *"Exploitation"* means the hiring, employment, persuasion, inducement, or coercion of a child to perform in obscene exhibitions and indecent shows, whether live or in video or film, or to pose or act as a model in obscene publications or pornographic materials, or to sell or distribute said materials; and

j) "Department" shall refer to a duly authorized officer or social worker of the Department of Social Welfare and Development or similar agency of a local government unit.

Sec. 3. Reporting. -- A person who learns of facts or circumstances that give rise to the belief that a child has suffered abuse may report the same, either orally or in writing, to the Department, to the police or other law enforcement agency or to a Barangay Council for the Protection of Children.

Sec. 4. Mandatory Reporting.-- The head of any public or private hospital, medical clinic and similar institution, as well as the attending physician and nurse, shall report, either orally or in writing, to the Department the examination and/or treatment of a child who appears to have suffered abuse within forty-eight (48) hours from knowledge of the same;

Sec. 5. Duty of Government Workers to Report. -- It shall be the duty of all teachers and administrators in public schools, probation officers, government lawyers, law enforcement officers, barangay officials, corrections officers and other government officials and employees whose work involves dealing with children to report all incidents of possible child abuse to the Department.

Sec. 6. Failure to Report.-- Failure of the individuals mentioned in Section 4 above and the administrator of the hospital, clinic or similar institution concerned to report a possible case of child abuse shall be punishable with a fine of not more than two thousand pesos (P2,000.00).

Sec. 7. Immunity for Reporting. -- A person who, acting in good faith, shall report a case of child abuse shall be free from any civil or administrative liability arising therefrom. There shall be a presumption that any such person acted in good faith.

Sec. 8. Investigation. -- Not later than forty-eight (48) hours after receipt of a report on a possible incident of child abuse, the Department shall immediately proceed to the home or establishment where the alleged child victim is found and interview said child to determine whether an abuse was committed, the identity of the perpetrator and the need of removing the child from his home or the establishment where he may be found or placing him under protective custody pursuant to Section 9 of these Rules.

Whenever practicable, the Department shall conduct the interview jointly with the police and/or a barangay official.

To minimize the number of interviews of the child victim, his statement shall be transcribed or recorded on voice or videotape.

Sec. 9.   Protective Custody. -- If the investigation discloses sexual abuse, serious physical injury or life-threatening neglect of the child, the duly authorized officer or social worker of the Department shall immediately remove the child from his home or the establishment where he was found and place him under protective custody to ensure his safety.

Sec. 10.   Immunity of Officer Taking the Child under Protective Custody. -- The duly authorized officer or social worker of the Department and the assisting police officer or barangay official, if any, who shall take a child under protective custody shall be exempt from civil, criminal and administrative liability therefor.

Sec. 11.   Notification of Police. -- The Department shall inform the police or other law enforcement agency whenever a child victim is placed under protective custody.

Sec. 12.   Physical Examination; Interview. -- The Department shall refer the child who is placed under protective custody to a government medical or health officer for a physical/mental examination and/or medical treatment.   Thereafter, the Department shall determine the rehabilitation or treatment program which the child may require and to gather data relevant to the filing of criminal charges against the abuser.

Sec. 13.   Involuntary Commitment. -- The Department shall file a petition for the involuntary commitment of the child victim under the provisions of Presidential Decree No. 603, as amended, if the investigation confirms the commission of child abuse.

Sec. 14. Suspension or Deprivation of Parental Authority.-- The Department shall ask the Court to suspend the parental authority of the parent or lawful guardian who abused the child victim, Provided, that in cases of sexual abuse, the Department shall ask for the permanent deprivation of parental authority of the offending parent or lawful guardian.

Sec. 15. Transfer of Parental Authority. -- The Department shall, in case of suspension or deprivation of parental authority and if the child victim cannot be placed under the care of a next kin, ask the proper Court to transfer said authority over the child victim to the Department or to the head of a duly accredited children's home, orphanage or similar institution.

Sec. 16.   Who May File a Complaint. -- A complaint against a person who abused a child may be filed by the-
    a. offended party;
    b. parent or legal guardian;
    c. ascendant or collateral relative of the child within the third degree of consanguinity;
    d. duly authorized officer or social worker of the Department;
    e. officer, social worker or representative of a licensed child caring institution;
    f. barangay chairman; or
    g at least three (3) concerned responsible citizens of the community where the abuse took place who have personal knowledge of the offense committed.

Sec. 17.   Filing of Criminal Case. -- The investigation report of the Department and/or of the police or other law enforcement agency on the abuse of a child, together with the results of the physical/mental examination and/or medical treatment and other relevant evidence, shall be immediately forwarded to the provincial or city prosecutor concerned for the preparation and filing of the appropriate criminal charge against the person who allegedly committed the abuse.

Sec. 18.   Closure of Establishments. -- The Department shall immediately close the establishment or enterprise found to have promoted, facilitated or conducted activities constituting child abuse. The closure shall be for a period of not less than one (1) year.   Upon said closure, the Department shall post signs with the words "OFF LIMITS" in conspicuous places outside the premises of the closed establishments or enterprise.   The unauthorized removal of said sign shall be punishable by *prision correccional.*

The Department shall seek the assistance of the local government unit concerned or the police or other law enforcement agency in the closure of an offending establishment or enterprise.

The Department shall file the appropriate criminal complaint against the owner or manager of the closed establishment or enterprise under the provisions of R.A. 7610, the Revised Penal Code, as amended, or special laws.

An establishment or enterprise shall be presumed to promote or facilitate child abuse if the acts constituting the same occur within its premises. An establishment such as a sauna parlor, travel agency, or recruitment agency which promotes acts of child sexual abuse as part of a tour program; exhibits children in a lewd or indecent show; provides child masseurs or masseuses for adults of the same or opposite sex and includes any lascivious conduct as part of the services constituting sexual abuse, shall be deemed to have promoted or facilitated child abuse.

Sec. 19. Guardian Ad Litem. -- Upon the filing of the criminal complaint for child abuse, the Department shall ask the appropriate court to appoint a guardian *ad litem* to represent the best interests of the child.

The guardian *ad litem* shall --

a. explain to the child the legal proceedings in which the child will be involved;
b. advise the judge, when appropriate, and as a friend of the court, regarding the child's ability to understand the proceedings and questions propounded therein;
c. advise the prosecutor concerning the ability of the child to cooperate as a witness for the prosecution;
d. attend all investigations, hearings and trial proceedings in which the child   is a participant; and

e. monitor and coordinate concurrent administrative and court actions.

Sec. 20.   Confidentiality of Identity of Victim.-- At the request of the victim or his representative, the name of the child   shall be withheld by the Department until the court has acquired jurisdiction over his case.

Sec. 21.   Speedy Trial of Child Abuse Cases. -- The trial of child abuse cases shall take precedence over all other cases before the courts, except election and habeas corpus cases.   The trial in said cases shall commence within three (3) days from the date the accused is arraigned and no postponement of the initial hearing shall be granted except on account of the illness of the accused or other grounds beyond his control.

Sec. 22.   Protection of Victim From   Undue Publicity.--   The prosecutor in a child abuse case shall,   taking   into   consideration   the   age, psychological maturity and understanding of the child victim, the nature of the unlawful acts committed, the desire of the victim and the interests of the child's family, take the necessary steps to exclude the public during the giving of testimony of the child victim; to limit the publication of information, photographs or artistic renderings that may identify the victim; and to prevent the undue and sensationalized publicity of the case.

Sec. 23. Confidentiality of Records. -- All records pertaining to cases of sexual abuse shall be strictly confidential and no information relating thereto shall de disclosed except in connection with any court or official proceeding based thereon.

The unauthorized disclosure of the aforementioned records shall be punishable by a fine of not more than two thousand four hundred pesos (P2,400.00) or by imprisonment of not more than one (1) year or such fine and imprisonment.

Sec. 24. Effectivity. -- These Rules shall take effect upon the approval of the Secretary of Justice and fifteen (15) days after its publication in two (2) national newspapers of general circulation.

Done in the City of Manila this _____ day of October 1993.

FRANKLIN M. DRILON
Secretary of Justice
CONFORME:

CORAZON ALMA DE LEON
Secretary of Social Welfare and
Development

II. INFORMATION VERIFICATION

Reports of child labor cases reaching the different agencies are eventually reported to two key government agencies which take the lead role in responding to cases of child labor and in coordinating the efforts of all concerned agencies and organizations. These are the:

> *1) DOLE, Child Labor Program Committee - for children working in the formal sector; and,*

> *2) DSWD, Bureau of Child and Youth Welfare - for children working in the informal sector such as the street children and prostituted children.*

Upon receipt of reports, the DOLE and/or the DSWD shall proceed to **validate the report** *in order to identify the appropriate intervention that should be made. Specific interventions are effected depending on the assessment of the case. The DOLE and the DSWD may seek the assistance of the PNP or the NBI in conducting inspection and surveillance.*

A. VISITORIAL AND INSPECTION POWERS OF THE DOLE

In formal work establishments, the DOLE may make use of its visitorial and inspection powers to confirm reports received regarding employer violations. This power is contained in the Labor Code, which provides that:

> *Art. 128. Visitorial and Enforcement Power. --*
> a. The Secretary of Labor or his duly authorized representatives, including labor regulation officers, shall have access to employers records and premises at any time of the day or night whenever work is being undertaken therein, and the right to copy therefrom, to question any employee and investigate any fact, condition or matter which

may be necessary to determine violations or which may aid in the enforcement of this Code and of any labor law, wage order or rules and regulations issued pursuant thereto.

B. INSPECTION PRIORITIES

Since 1993, establishments suspected of employing child workers have been among the top of the list of priorities for inspection of the Department of Labor and Employment. In 1995, child labor was again made a **priority for inspection** *by Administrative Order No. 100.*

Republic of the Philippines
DEPARTMENT OF LABOR AND EMPLOYMENT
Manila
ADMINISTRATIVE ORDER NO. 100
Series of 1995

In the interest of the service and, to further improve the effectiveness and efficiency of the labor standards enforcement machinery of the Department of Labor and Employment (DOLE), the following guidelines are hereby prescribed:

Sec. 1. Inspection Priorities. - The following shall be the priorities for inspection in 1995:
    1.1 Establishments in Export Processing Zones and similar special industrial areas
    1.2 Establishments Employing
        1.2.1 Child Labor
        1.2.2 Women Workers
    1.3 Security Agencies
    1.4 The Shipping Industry
    1.5 Homeworkers
    1.6 Other establishments classified as hazardous or high risk. [*Underscoring supplied.*]

Sec. 2. Inclusion for Inspection Coverage. -
The labor inspectors shall include in their findings compliance or non-compliance with remittances of social security contributions. The Regional Offices shall refer these findings to the Social Security System (SSS) for appropriate action.

x x x

For strict compliance.

06 February 1995

MA. NIEVES R. CONFESSOR
Secretary

C.   INVESTIGATION BY THE DEPARTMENT OF SOCIAL WELFARE AND DEVELOPMENT

For children working in the informal sector (e.g., street children and prostituted children) the DSWD is mandated by law to investigate reports on child abuse. Under Section 8 of the Rules and Regulations in the Reporting and Investigation of Child Abuse Cases, presented earlier, the DSWD shall, not later than 48 hours, immediately proceed to the place where the alleged child victim is found and interview said child to determine whether an abuse was committed, the identity of the perpetrator and whether or not there is a need to remove the child from his home or the establishment where he/she may be found. Whenever practicable, the DSWD shall conduct the interview jointly with the police and/or barangay official.

III. REMOVAL AND RESCUE

Once enough evidence is gathered confirming reports of child abuse and exploitation, there is a need to determine whether or not it is for the child's best interest to be removed from the home or establishment where the child is found. Negotiations with the child's employer must necessarily follow for the smooth, safe and non-traumatic removal of the child. Nevertheless, if the negotiation is deemed futile from the start because of the hostile atmosphere between the parties, a rescue operation is undertaken, with the objectives of rescuing the child worker, arresting the violator, and seizing objects or documents which may be used as evidence against the latter.

A. Application For Warrants Of Arrest, Search And Seizure

Before the actual rescue, a search warrant and/or warrant of arrest must first be secured from the courts in compliance with legal processes. Otherwise, any articles or documents obtained from such illegal search and seizure may not be used as evidence in prosecuting the offender. At the same time, the persons conducting the illegal search and seizure and/or arrest may be held criminally liable under the Revised Penal Code.

1. Who Issues The Warrant

Although the Secretary of Labor possesses visitorial and enforcement powers over work establishments, and although the Secretary of Social Welfare and Development possesses powers of investigation over cases of child abuse and exploitation, both do not have the power to issue warrants of arrest, search and seizure. This is because under Article 3, Section 2 of the Philippine Constitution, only judges and no other, may issue warrants of arrest and search. This does not mean, however, that the Secretary of Labor and the Secretary of Social Welfare and Development, or their duly authorized representatives, cannot cause the search of *suspected establishments, the seizure of documents therein, or the arrest of offenders. They may still cause the same to be made by virtue of a warrant issued by a judge.*

A search warrant may be issued at any time by a judge of any trial court with jurisdiction over the property to be searched. A warrant of arrest, on the other hand, may only be issued by the judge of the Municipal Trial Court or Regional Trial Court which has proper jurisdiction over the offense charged, upon the filing of a criminal information with the said courts by the investigating fiscal who conducted the preliminary investigation. However, where the Municipal Trial Court judge is the one conducting the preliminary investigation, in the instances allowed by law, such investigating judge may already issue a warrant of arrest even before it files an information with the Regional Trial Court which has jurisdiction over the offense charged.

2. Requisites For A Valid Search Warrant And/Or Warrant Of Arrest

Before a warrant may be issued by a judge, the following requisites must first be met:[87]

1. It must be issued based on *probable cause* or such circumstances which would lead a reasonably prudent man to believe that:
   a. an offense has been committed; and
   b. the offense has been committed by the person(s) sought to be arrested (in the case of a warrant of arrest); or
   the objects sought in connection with the offense are in the place to be searched (in the case of a search warrant).

2. Probable cause must be *determined personally by the judge*.

---

[87] Pursuant to the Philippine Constitution, Art. 3, Sec. 2, and the Revised Rules of Court, Secs. 3 and 4.

3.   The determination must be made *after examination* under oath or affirmation of the complainant and the witnesses he/she may produce.

4.   The complainant or witnesses must have *personal knowledge* of said probable cause.

5.   The warrant must *particularly describe* the place to be searched and/or the persons or things to be seized.

6.   The warrant must be issued only *for one specific offense*.

3. When Warrant Is Not Needed

Despite the above legal requisites, an arrest, search and seizure may nevertheless be made even without a warrant in the instances presented below.

3.1 Lawful Arrest Without Warrant

A person accused of committing a crime may be arrested even without a warrant, by a peace officer or even by a private person, in the following instances: [88]

a. When, in his presence, the person to be arrested has committed, is actually committing, or is attempting to commit an offense;

b.   When an offense has in fact just been committed, and he has personal knowledge of facts indicating that the person to be arrested has committed it; and

c.   When the person to be arrested is an escaped prisoner.

---

[88]   Revised Rules of Court, Rule 113, Sec. 5.

3.2. Lawful Search And Seizure Without Warrant

Searches and seizures may be made even without a warrant under any of the following conditions:

a.   When the individual concerned _knowingly consents_ to the search or when there is a valid waiver of the right.[89]

b.   When the _search is incidental to a lawful arrest._ The search should be made simultaneous to the arrest and should be limited to the person of the suspect and the immediate area of arrest where accused may reach for arms or destroy evidence. The "officer making the arrest may take from the person arrested any money or property found upon his person which was used in the commission of the crime or was the fruit of the crime, or which might furnish the prisoner with the means of committing violence or escaping, or which may be used in evidence in the trial of the case..."[90]

c.   When the articles to be seized are _in plain view_ of the officer, meaning, its discovery was inadvertent or merely stumbled upon.[91]

B. Assembly Of Rescue Team

A rescue team is assembled by the DOLE, composed of labor inspectors of the DOLE, social workers of the DSWD, members of the Philippine National Police (PNP) and/or National Bureau of Investigation (NBI), a lawyer, and representatives of NGOs if possible to brief them regarding the facts of the case and the strategies to be taken in the rescue operation.

---

[89]   De Garcia vs. Locsin, 65 Phil 689.
[90]   Moreno vs. Ago Chi, 12 Phil 439, 442.
[91]   Harris vs. United States, 390 U.S. 234.

C. Rescue

After a series of briefings and armed with the requisite warrants, the rescue team proceeds to conduct the actual rescue operation. Once inside the premises, the team first looks for the child workers who are at once turned-over to the social workers present during the rescue. Together, the labor inspectors and other law enforcers within the team proceed to search the premises for evidence which may be used against the employer/offender and to seize the same. If the offender is present, then an arrest is simultaneously made. The conduct of the arrest and search is again subject to certain legal procedures as follows:

REVISED RULES OF COURT
RULE 113
ARREST

Sec. 7. Method of arrest by officer by virtue of warrant. -- When making an arrest by virtue of a warrant the officer shall inform the person to be arrested of the cause of the arrest and of the fact that a warrant has been issued for his arrest, except when he flees or forcibly resists before the officer has opportunity so to inform him or when the giving of such information will imperil the arrest. The officer need not have the warrant in his possession at the time of the arrest but after the arrest, if the person arrested so requires, the warrant shall be shown to him as soon as practicable.

RULE 126
SEARCH AND SEIZURE

x x x

Sec. 6. Right to break door or window to effect search. -- The officer, if refused admittance to the place of directed search after giving notice of his purpose and authority, may break open any outer or inner door or window of a house or any part of a house or anything therein to execute the warrant or liberate himself or any person lawfully aiding him when unlawfully detained therein.

Sec. 7. Search of a house, room, or premise, to be made in presence of two witnesses. -- No search of a house, room, or any other premise shall be made except in the presence of the lawful occupant thereof, or any member of his family or in the absence of the latter, in the presence of two witnesses of sufficient age and discretion residing in the same locality.

x x x

Sec. 10. Receipt for the property seized. -- The officer seizing property under the warrant must give a detailed receipt for the same to the lawful occupant of the premises in whose presence the search and seizure were made, or in the absence of such occupant, must, in the presence of at least two witnesses of sufficient age and discretion residing in the same locality, leave a receipt in the place in which he found the seized property.

Sec. 11.   Delivery of property and inventory thereof to court. -- The officer must forthwith deliver the property seized to the judge who issued the warrant, together with a true inventory thereof duly verified under oath.

IV. CUSTODY AND REHABILITATION

Since rescue operations often lead to dislocation of the child workers, **protective custody** *is immediately given to the children by the DSWD, through its centers for children such as the Marillac Hills for girls and the Nayon ng Kabataan for boys, or through other licensed institutions which have facilities for temporary shelter.*

The DSWD shall give the children **intake and medical evaluations, counselling, psychological services and other rehabilitative services** *to help them deal with probable trauma and emotional disturbance.   Child laborers needing more specialized medical or psychological services are referred to the Department of Health.*

The parents, relatives or guardians of the children are then contacted for the eventual **return of the children to their families,** *except if it is found out that the parents or guardians themselves are responsible for the abuse and exploitation of their children.   In the latter case,* **petitions for commitment** *of the children to the DSWD or any licensed child placement agency, and also petitions for the* **suspension or termination of parental authority,** *are filed in court by the DSWD in order to secure prolonged custody over the children.*

Below are the pertinent laws regarding the custody and rehabilitation of children.

A.   R.A. 7610 (Section 28)

[See page 319.]

B.   RULES AND REGULATIONS IN THE INVESTIGATION AND REPORTING OF CHILD ABUSE CASES (Sections 9-15)

[See pages 371-379.]

C.   EXECUTIVE ORDER NO. 56

The Revised Penal Code, under Article 202 punishes vagrancy and prostitution whether committed by minor or not. By virtue of Executive Order No. 56, a minor who is apprehended or taken into custody for engaging in prostitution or other illicit conduct must be delivered to the Department of Social Welfare and Development (DSWD) for protective custody. Sections 1 provides that the DSWD shall be responsible for the appearance of the minor under its protective custody in court or any administrative agency whenever required. Section 2 on the other hand states that the DSWD shall also provide suitable programs for the full rehabilitation of the minors under its custody which shall, among others, include the appreciation of proper moral values, psychological or psychiatric treatment, education in the probable physical ailment or disease which they may contract or the dangers of unwanted pregnancy, and appropriate training for work-skills to prepare them for a decent living.

[See pages 165-167]

D. LEGAL PROCEDURES FOR THE CUSTODY OF DEPENDENT, ABANDONED, NEGLECTED CHILDREN

Protective custody ends when the child worker is reunited with his/her family. However, in cases where the child has no parents or guardian, or where the child's own parents or guardian have abandoned, abused or neglected the child, legal steps must be taken for the permanent custody of the child by the DSWD or a licensed child placement agency. The following are the relevant provisions of the Child and Youth Welfare Code with respect to the custody of dependent, abandoned and neglected children.

CHILD AND YOUTH WELFARE CODE

Art. 141. Definition of Terms. -- As used in this Chapter:

1. A dependent child is one who is without a parent, guardian, or custodian; or one whose parents, guardian or other custodian for good cause desires to be relieved of his care custody; and is dependent upon the public for support.

2. An abandoned child is one who has no proper parental care or guardianship, or whose parents or guardians have deserted him for a period of at least six continuous months.

3. A neglected child is one whose basic needs have been deliberately unattended or inadequately attended. Neglect may occur in two ways:

a. There is physical neglect when the child is malnourished ill-clad and without proper shelter.

A child is unattended when left by himself without provisions for his needs and/or without proper supervision.

b. Emotional neglect exists: When children are maltreated, raped or seduced; when children are exploited, overworked or made to work under conditions not conducive to good health; or are made to beg in the streets or public places, or when children are in moral danger, or exposed to gambling, prostitution and other vices. [*Underscoring supplied.*]

4. Commitment or surrender of a child is the legal act of entrusting a child to the care of the Department of Social Welfare or any duly licensed child placement agency or individual.

Commitment may be done in the following manner:

a. Involuntary commitment, in case of a dependent child, or through the termination of parental or guardianship rights by reason of abandonment, substantial and continuous or repeated neglect and/or parental incompetence to discharge parental responsibilities, and in   the manner, form and procedure hereinafter prescribed.

      b.   Voluntary commitment through the relinquishment of parental or guardianship rights in the manner and form hereinafter prescribed.

      Art. 142.   Petition for Involuntary Commitment of a Child: Venue.--   The Department of Social Welfare Secretary or his authorized representative or any duly licensed child placement agency having knowledge of a child who appears to be dependent, abandoned or neglected, may file a verified petition for involuntary commitment of said child to the care of any duly licensed placement agency or individual.

      The petition shall be filed with the Juvenile and Domestic Relations Court, if any, or with the Court of First Instance of the province or City Court in which the parents or guardian reside or the child is found.

      Art. 143. Contents of Petition: Verification. -- The petition for commitment must state so far as known to the petitioner:

      1. The facts showing that the child is dependent, abandoned, or neglected;

      2. The names of the parent or parents, if known, and their residence.   If the child has no parent or parents living, then the name and residence of the guardian, if any; and

      3. The name of the duly licensed child placement agency or individual to whose care the commitment of the child is sought.

      The petition shall be verified and shall be sufficient if based upon the information and belief of the petitioner.

Art. 144. Court to Set Time for Hearing: Summons. - When a petition for commitment is filed, the court shall fix a date for the hearing thereof. If it appears from the petition that one or both parents of the child, or the guardian, resides in province or city, the clerk of court shall immediately issue summons, together with a copy of the petition, which shall be served on such parent or guardian not less than two days before the time fixed for the hearing. Such summons shall require them to appear before the court on the date mentioned.

Art. 145. When Summons Shall Not be Issued. -- The summons provided for in the next preceding article shall not be issued and the court shall thereupon proceed with the hearing of the case if it appears from the petition that both parents of the child are dead or that neither parent can be found in the province or city and that the child has no guardian residing therein.

Art. 146. Representation of Child. -- If it appears that neither of the parents nor the guardian of the child can be found in the province or city, it shall be the duty of the court to appoint some suitable person to represent him.

Art 147. Duty of Fiscal. -- The provincial or city fiscal shall appear for the State, seeing to it there has been due notice to all parties concerned and that there is justification for the declaration of dependency, abandonment or neglect.

Art. 148. Hearing. -- During the hearing of the petition the child shall be brought before the court, which shall investigate the facts and ascertain whether he is dependent, abandoned, or neglected, and, if so, the cause and circumstances of such condition. In such hearing the court shall not be bound by the technical rules of evidence.

Failure to provide for the child's support for a period of six months shall be presumptive evidence of the intent to abandon.

Art. 149. Commitment of Child. -- If after the hearing, the child is found to be dependent, abandoned, or neglected, an order shall be entered committing him to the care and custody of the Department of Social Welfare or any duly licensed child placement agency or individual.

Art. 150. When Child may Stay in his Own Home.-- If in the court's opinion the cases of the abandonment or neglect of any child may be remedied, it may permit the child to stay in his own home and under the care and control of his own parents or guardian, subject to supervision and direction of the Department of Social Welfare.

When it appears to the court that it is no longer for the best interests of such child to remain with his parents or guardian, it may commit the child in accordance with the next preceding article.

Art. 151. Termination of Rights of Parents. -- When a child shall have been committed to the Department of Social Welfare or any duly licensed child placement agency or individual pursuant to an order of the court, his parents or guardian shall thereafter exercise no authority over him except upon such conditions   as the court may impose.

Art. 152. Authority of Person, Agency or Institution. -- The Department of Social Welfare or any duly licensed placement agency or individual receiving a child pursuant to an order of the court shall be the legal guardian and entitled to his legal custody and control, be responsible for his support as defined by law, and when proper, shall have authority to give consent to his placement, guardianship and/or adoption.

Art. 153. Change of Custody. -- The Department of Social Welfare shall have the authority to change the custody of a child committed to any duly licensed child placement agency or individual if it appears that such change is for the best interests of the child. However, when conflicting interests arise among child placement agencies the court shall order the change of commitment of the child.

Art. 154. Voluntary Commitment of a Child to an Institution. -- The parent or guardian of a dependent, abandoned or neglected child may voluntarily commit him to the Department of Social Welfare or any duly licensed child placement agency or individual subject to the provisions of the next succeeding articles.

Art. 155. Commitment must be in Writing. -- No child shall be committed pursuant to the preceding article unless he is surrendered in writing by his parents or guardian to the care and custody of the Department of Social Welfare or duly licensed child placement agency. In case of the death or legal incapacity of either parent or abandonment of the child for a period of at least one year, the other parent alone shall have the authority to make the commitment. The Department of Social Welfare, or any proper and duly licensed child placement agency or individual shall have the authority to receive, train, educate, care for or arrange appropriate placement of such child.

Art. 156. Legal Custody. -- When any child shall have been committed in accordance with the preceding article and such child shall have been accepted by the Department of Social Welfare or any duly licensed child placement agency or individual, the rights of his natural parents, guardian, or other custodian to exercise parental authority over him shall cease. Such agency or individual shall be entitled to the custody and control of such child during his minority, and shall have authority to care for, educate, train and place him out temporarily or for custody and care in a duly licensed child placement agency. Such agency or individual may intervene in adoption proceedings in such manner as shall best inure to the child's welfare.

x x x

Art. 159. Temporary Custody of Child. -- Subject to regulation by the Department of Social Welfare and with the permission of the court in case of judicial commitment, the competent authorities of any duly licensed child placement agency or individual to which a child has been committed may place him in the care of any suitable person, at the latter's request, for a period not exceeding one month at a time.

The temporary custody of the child shall be discontinued if it appears that he is not being given proper care, or at his own request, or at the instance of the agency or person receiving him.

Art. 160. Prohibited Acts. -- It shall be unlawful for any child to leave the person or institution to which he has been judicially or voluntarily committed or the person under whose custody he has been placed in accordance with the next preceding article, or for any person to induce him to leave such person or institution, except in case of grave physical or moral danger, actual or imminent, to the child.

Any violation of this article shall be punishable by an imprisonment of not more than one year or by a fine of not more than two thousand pesos, or both such fine and imprisonment at the discretion of the court: Provided, That if the violation is committed by a foreigner, he shall also be subject to deportation.

If the violation is committed by a parent or legal guardian of the child, such fact shall aggravate or mitigate the offense as circumstances shall warrant.

x x x

Art. 163. Restoration of Child After Involuntary Commitment.-- The parents or guardian of a child committed to the care of a person, agency or institution by judicial order may petition the proper court for the restoration of his rights over the child: Provided , That the child in the meantime, has not been priorily given away in adoption nor has left the country with the adopting parents or the guardian. The petition shall be verified and shall state that the petitioner is now able to take proper care and custody of said child.

Upon receiving the petition, the court shall fix the time for hearing the questions raised thereby and cause reasonable notice thereof to be sent to the petitioner and to the person, agency or institution to which the child has been committed. At the trial, any person may be allowed, at the discretion of the court, to contest the right to relief demanded, and witnesses may be called and examined by the parties or by the court *motu propio*. If it is found that the cause for the commitment of the child no longer exists and that the petitioner is already able to take proper care and custody of the child, the court, after taking into consideration the best interests and the welfare of the child, shall render judgment restoring parental authority to the petitioner.

Art. 164.   Restoration after Voluntary Commitment. -- Upon petition filed with the Department of Social Welfare the parent or parents or guardian who voluntarily committed a child may recover legal custody and parental authority over him from the agency, individual or institution to which such child was voluntarily committed when it is shown to the satisfaction of the Department of Social Welfare that the parent, parents, or guardian is in a position to adequately provide for the needs of the child: Provided, That the petition for restoration is filed within six months after the surrender.

In all cases, the person, agency or institution having legal custody of the child shall be furnished with a copy of the petition and shall be given the opportunity to be heard.

Art. 165. Removal of Custody. -- A petition to transfer custody of a child may be filed against a person or child welfare agency to whose custody a child has been committed by the court based on neglect of such child as defined in Article 141 (3). If the court, after notice and hearing, is satisfied that the allegations of the petition are true and that it is for the best interest and welfare of the child, the court shall issue an order taking him from the custody of the person or agency, as the case may be, and committing him to the custody of another duly licensed child placement agency or individual.

The license of the agency or individual found guilty of such neglect may be suspended or revoked, as the court may deem proper, in the same proceeding.

E. SUSPENSION/ TERMINATION OF PARENTAL AUTHORITY - FAMILY CODE (Arts. 230-232)

[See pages 304-306.]

V. RECOVERY OF WAGES AND OTHER MONETARY BENEFITS

After the child workers are rescued and given protective custody, cases for the enforcement of their rights or for the redress of their grievances necessarily follow. For children working in the formal sector where an employer-employee relationship is present, cases for the recovery of wages and other monetary benefits may be brought against the employer. The children need not be physically present in the hearing of their claims in case they wish to go back to their homes. Instead, they may execute "powers of attorney" to ensure that the complaints are pursued and that due compensation are given them.

Claims for work-related injury and welfare benefits are filed with the Social Security System. On the other hand, recovery of wages, rates of pay, hours of work and other terms and conditions of employment are filed either with the Regional Director or the Labor Arbiter in accordance with the following guidelines.

A. PERIOD WITHIN WHICH TO FILE

LABOR CODE

Art. 291.   All money claims arising from employer-employee relations accruing during the effectivity of this Code shall be filed within three (3) years from the time the cause of action accrued; otherwise they shall be forever barred.

B. WHERE TO FILE/ JURISDICTION

1. DOLE Regional Director

Jurisdiction: Complaints for recovery of wages and other monetary claims and benefits, including legal interest, not exceeding P5,000.00 and provided the complaint does not include a claim for reinstatement. [92]

---

[92] Pursuant to Article 129 of the Labor Code.

2. Labor Arbiters And The National Labor Relations Commission (NLRC)

Jurisdiction:

1. Complaints for recovery of wages, rates of pay, hours of work and other terms and conditions of employment, if total amount exceeds Five thousand pesos (P5,000.00), OR if accompanied with a claim for reinstatement (even if below P5,000).

2. Claims for actual, moral, exemplary and other forms of damages arising from the employer-employee relations.[93]

C. PROCEDURES WITH THE DOLE REGIONAL DIRECTOR[94]

1. *Filing of Complaint*

2. *Hearing*

3. *Decision:* The Regional Director or hearing officer shall decide the complaint within 30 calendar days from the date of filing.

4. *Appeal to NLRC:* The decision may be appealed to the National Labor Relations Commission (NLRC) within 5 calendar days from receipt of a copy of the decision.

5. *Resolution of NLRC:* The NLRC shall resolve the appeal within 10 calendar days from the submission of the last pleading allowed under its rules.

---

[93] Pursuant to Articl 217 of the Labor Code.
[94] Condensed from Article 129 of the Labor Code.

6. *Payment:* The Secretary of Labor and Employment or his duly authorized representatives may supervise the payment of unpaid wages and other monetary claims and benefits, including legal interest, found owing to any employee or househelper. Any sum thus recovered on behalf of any employee or househelper shall be held in a special deposit account by, and shall be paid on order of, the Secretary of Labor and Employment or the regional director directly to the employee or househelper concerned. Any such sum not paid to the employee or househelper, because he cannot be located after diligent and reasonable effort within a period of 3 years, shall be held as a special fund of the DOLE to be used exclusively for the amelioration and benefit of workers.

D. PROCEDURES WITH THE LABOR ARBITERS AND THE NATIONAL LABOR RELATIONS COMMISSION [95]

1. *Filing of Complaint*

2. *Hearing*

3. *Decision of Labor Arbiter:* The Labor Arbiter shall decide within 30 calendar days from submission of the case by the parties for decision.

4. *Appeal:* Appeal to NLRC within 10 calendar days from receipt of decision. In case of a judgment granting a monetary award, an appeal by the employer may be perfected only upon the posting of a cash bond or surety bond in an amount equivalent to the monetary award.

---

[95] Condensed from Article 223 of the Labor Code.

5. *Decision of NLRC:* The NLRC shall decide within 20 calendar days from receipt of answer of the appellee. The decision of NLRC shall be final and executory after 10 calendar days from receipt thereof by the parties.

6. *Execution of decisions or awards:* A writ of execution on a judgment may be issued by the Secretary, the Regional Director, the Labor Arbiter or the Commission, within 5 years from the date it becomes final and executory, requiring a sheriff or a duly deputized officer to execute or enforce the final decision.

E. AMICABLE SETTLEMENT/ COMPROMISES

The technical rules of evidence used in courts of law are not binding in labor cases where prior resort to amicable settlement or compromises between the employers and employees is encouraged to arrive at a speedy resolution of disputes.

LABOR CODE

Art. 221. Technical rules not binding and prior resort to amicable settlement. -- In any proceeding before the Commission or any of the Labor Arbiters, the rules of evidence prevailing in courts of law or equity shall not be controlling and it is the spirit and intention of this Code that the Commission and its members and the Labor Arbiters shall use every and all reasonable means to ascertain the facts in each case speedily and objectively and without regard to technicalities of law or procedure, all in the interest of due process.

x x x

Art. 227.   Compromise agreements. -- Any compromise settlement, including those involving labor standards laws, voluntarily agreed upon by the parties with the assistance of the [National Conciliation and Mediation Board] or the regional office of the Department of Labor, shall be final and binding upon the parties.   The National Labor Relations Commission or any court shall not assume jurisdiction over issues involved therein except in case of non-compliance thereof or if there is prima facie evidence that the settlement was obtained through fraud, misrepresentation, or coercion.

VI.   ADMINISTRATIVE SANCTIONS

A.   DEPARTMENT OF LABOR AND EMPLOYMENT

After appropriate inspection and investigation, the Department of Labor and Employment shall evaluate the degree of exploitation and other violations committed by a work establishment or recruitment agency.   Based on its findings, after appropriate hearing, it may order the stoppage of work or the suspension of the operations of the work establishment, and the cancellation of the license of the recruitment agency. [See the enforcement powers of the Secretary of Labor on page 167.] *Moreover, under the implementing rules of R.A. 7658 or the Child Labor Law, in case of repeated violations by the employer of the provisions of such law, the offender's license to operate shall be revoked. [See* page 108.]

B.   DEPARTMENT OF SOCIAL WELFARE AND DEVELOPMENT

In cases where the establishment or workplace is engaged in hospitality service, child trafficking, obscene publications and/or indecent shows, the DSWD may cause the immediate closure of the said establishments, and the cancellation of their authority or license to operate, by virtue of Section 11 of R.A. 7610 and Section 18 of its implementing rules and regulations.   The assistance of local government units and other law enforcement agencies may be sought by the DSWD for this purpose.

[See pages 316 and 317.]

C. LOCAL GOVERNMENT UNITS

Local government units, by virtue of their "general welfare" powers over their respective territorial jurisdictions may also cause the closure of establishments which exploit children therein or the cancellation of their licenses to operate.   This power is contained in the Local Government Code which grants to local government units all powers essential to the promotion of the general welfare of their inhabitants including the preservation and enrichment of culture, the promotion of health and safety, the improvement of public morals, and the preservation of the comfort and convenience of their inhabitants, among others.[95] Moreover, the regulatory powers of local government units over business enterprises within their respective jurisdictions, necessarily give them the power to revoke licenses which they themselves have issued. Under the Local Government Code, cities and municipalities, through their mayors and "Sanggunian" members, have the following specific powers among others.

LOCAL GOVERNMENT CODE

1. "to issue licenses and permits [to business enterprises within] and to suspend or revoke the same for any violation of the conditions upon which said licenses or permits had been issued, pursuant to law or ordinance";[96]

2. "to regulate any business...within the city/municipality and the conditions under which the license for said business...may be issued or revoked";[97] and

3. "to regulate the establishment, operation and maintenance of cafes, restaurants, beerhouses, hotels, motels, inns, pension houses, lodging houses, and other similar establishments..." and of "entertainment or amusement facilities, including...sauna baths, massage parlors and other places of entertainment or amusement;...particularly those which tend to disturb the community or annoy the inhabitants; or require the suspension or suppression of the same; or prohibit certain forms of

---

[96] The Local Government Code of 1991, Sec. 15.
[97] Local Government Code of 1991, Sec. 444 b. 3) (iv), and Sec. 455 b. 3) (iv).
[98] *Id.*, at Sec. 446 b. 3) (ii), and Sec. 458 a. 3) (ii).

amusement or entertainment in order to protect the
social and moral welfare of the community.[98]

D. DEPARTMENT OF TOURISM

*If the offending establishment is a hotel, motel, resort, tourist
inn, apartelle, pension house, or other accommodation
establishment, the establishment's accreditation with the
Department of Tourism may also be cancelled pursuant to
Administrative Order No. 95-17.*

[See page 348-349.]

---

[99] *Id.,* at Sec. 447 a. 4) (iv) & (vii), and Sec. 458 a. 4) (iv) & (vii).

VII. CRIMINAL PROSECUTION

Protection of the rights of child workers will not be complete without the attainment of justice. For the attainment of justice, conviction of the offenders must be ensured through the cooperation of the different members of the criminal justice system beginning with the law enforcement pillar. Thus, immediately after a rescue operation, or upon receipt of reports, the law enforcement agencies should secure the individual sworn statements of the child workers and gather other vital evidence for the filing of appropriate criminal charges. They shall then coordinate with concerned agencies such as the Child Rights Center of the Commission on Human Rights and the Task Force on Child Protection of the Department of Justice regarding the extension of legal assistance. Such agencies, together with the social workers of DSWD, shall properly orient the children regarding the prosecution of their cases and adequately prepare them as witnesses. Illustrated hereunder are the step-by-step procedures in the prosecution of criminal cases.

A. JURISDICTION OVER CRIMINAL CASES

1. Katarungang Pambarangay

Offenses punishable by <u>imprisonment of one year or less</u>, and a <u>fine of P5,000.00 or less</u>, shall be brought for amicable settlement before the Katarungang Pambarangay (Barangay Justice System) if the parties actually <u>reside in the same city or municipality</u>. [98]

However, even if the parties reside in different cities or municipalities, if their respective barangays adjoin each other, the parties may still opt to bring the dispute before the Katarungang Pambarangay provided that the penalty for the offense is still within its jurisdiction as stated above.[99]

---

[100] The Local Government Code of 1991. Chapter 7 - Katarungang Pambarangay, Sec. 408.
[101] *Id.*

2. Family Courts

On October 28, 1997, Republic Act No. 8369 otherwise known as "Family Courts Act of 1997" was signed into law. Under the new law, the Family Courts shall be given exclusive jurisdiction over all cases which involve children. Pending the establishment of such Family Courts, the Supreme Court shall designate from among the branches of the Regional Trial Courts at least one Family Court in the cities enumerated under Section 17 of the Family Courts Act and in such other places as the Supreme Court may deem necessary. The rules of procedure governing the Regional Trial Courts shall govern the Family Courts insofar as it is not inconsistent with the special rules of procedure that the Supreme Court may promulgate for the disposition of children and family cases.

AN ACT ESTABLISHING FAMILY COURTS,
GRANTING THEM EXCLUSIVE ORIGINAL
JURISDICTION OVER CHILD AND FAMILY CASES,
AMENDING BATAS PAMBANSA BILANG 129, AS
AMENDED, OTHERWISE KNOWN AS THE
JUDICIARY REORGANIZATION ACT OF 1980,
APPROPRIATING FUNDS THEREFOR AND FOR
OTHER PURPOSES

Sec. 1. Title. — This Act shall be known as the "Family Courts Act of 1997."

Sec. 2. State and National Policies. — The State shall protect the rights and promote the welfare of children in keeping with the mandate of the Constitution and the precepts of the United Nations Convention on the Rights of the Child. The State shall provide a system of adjudication for youthful offenders which takes into account their peculiar circumstances.

The State recognizes the sanctity of family life and shall protect and strengthen the family as a basic autonomous social institution. The courts shall preserve the solidarity of the family, provide procedures for the reconciliation of spouses and the amicable settlement of family controversy.

Sec. 3.Establishment of Family Courts. — There shall be established a Family Court in every province and city in the country. In case where the city is the capital of the province, the Family Court shall be established in the municipality which has the highest population.

Sec. 4. Qualification and Training of Family Court Judges. — Section 15 of Batas Pambansa Blg. 129, as amended, is hereby further amended to read as follows:

"*Sec. 15.* (a) Qualification. — No person shall be appointed Regional Trial Judge or Presiding Judge of the Family Court unless he is a natural-born citizen of the Philippines, at least thirty-five (35) years of age, and, for at least ten (10) years, has been engaged in the practice of law in the Philippines or has held a public office in the Philippines requiring admission to the practice of law as an indispensable requisite.
"(b) Training of Family Court Judges. — The Presiding Judge, as well as the court personnel of the Family Courts, shall undergo training and must have the experience and demonstrated ability in dealing with child and family cases.

"The Supreme Court shall provide a continuing education program on child and family laws, procedure and other related disciplines to judges and personnel of such courts."

Sec. 5.Jurisdiction of Family Courts. — The Family Courts shall have exclusive original jurisdiction to hear and decide the following cases:

a) <u>Criminal cases where one or more of the accused is below eighteen (18) years of age but not less than nine (9) years of age, or where one or more of the victims is a minor at the time of the commission of the offense</u>: Provided, That if the minor is found guilty, the court shall promulgate sentence and ascertain any civil liability which the accused may have incurred. The sentence, however, shall be suspended without need of application pursuant to Presidential Decree No. 603, otherwise known as the "Child and Youth Welfare Code"; *[Underscoring supplied]*

b) Petitions for guardianship, custody of children, habeas corpus in relation to the latter;

c) Petitions for adoption of children and the revocation thereof;

d) Complaints for annulment of marriage, declaration of nullity of marriage and those relating to marital status and property relations of husband and wife or those living together under different status and agreements, and petitions for dissolution of conjugal partnership of gains;

e) Petitions for support and/or acknowledgment;

f) Summary judicial proceedings brought under the provisions of Executive Order No. 209, otherwise known as the "Family Code of the Philippines";

g) Petitions for declaration of status of children as abandoned, dependent or neglected children, petitions for voluntary or involuntary commitment of children; the suspension, termination, or restoration of parental authority and other cases cognizable under Presidential Decree No. 603, Executive Order No. 56, (Series of 1986), and other related laws;

h) Petitions for the constitution of the family home;

i) Cases against minors cognizable under the Dangerous Drugs Act, as amended;

j) Violations of Republic Act No. 7610, otherwise known as the "Special Protection of Children Against Child Abuse, Exploitation and Discrimination Act," as amended by Republic Act No. 7658; and

k) Cases of domestic violence against:

(1) Women — which are acts of gender based violence that results, or are likely to result in physical, sexual or psychological harm or suffering to women; and other forms of physical abuse such as battering or threats and coercion which violate a woman's personhood, integrity and freedom of movement; and

(2) Children — which include the commission of all forms of abuse, neglect, cruelty, exploitation, violence, and discrimination and all other conditions prejudicial to their development.

If an act constitutes a criminal offense, the accused or batterer shall be subject to criminal proceedings and the corresponding penalties.

If any question involving any of the above matters should arise as an incident in any case pending in the regular courts, said incident shall be determined in that court.

x x x

Sec. 7. Special Provisional Remedies. — In cases of violence among immediate family members living in the same domicile or household, the Family Court may issue a restraining order against the accused or defendant upon a verified application by the complainant or the victim for relief from abuse.

The court may order the temporary custody of children in all civil actions for their custody. The court may also order support *pendente lite*, including deduction from the salary and use of conjugal home and other properties in all civil actions for support.

x x x

Sec. 9. Social Services and Counseling Divisions. - The Social Services and Counselling Division (SSCD) shall be established in each judicial region as the Supreme Court shall deem necessary based on the number of juvenile and family cases existing in such jurisdiction. It shall provide appropriate social services to all juvenile and family cases filed with the court and recommend the proper social action. It shall also develop programs, formulate uniform policies and procedures, and provide technical supervision and monitoring of all SSCD in coordination with the judge.

Sec. 10. Social Services and Counseling Division Staff — The SSCD shall have a staff composed of qualified social workers and other personnel with academic preparation in behavioral sciences to carry out the duties of conducting intake assessment, social case studies, casework and counseling, and other social services that may be needed in connection with cases filed with the court: Provided, however, That in adoption cases and in petitions for declaration of abandonment, the case studies may be prepared by social workers of duly licensed child caring or child placement agencies, or the DSWD. When warranted, the division shall recommend that the court avail itself of consultative services of psychiatrists, psychologists, and other qualified specialists presently employed in other departments of the government in connection with its cases.

The position of Social Work Adviser shall be created under the Office of the Court Administrator, who shall monitor and supervise the SSCD of the Regional Trial Court.

Sec. 11. *Alternative Social Services.* — In accordance with Section 17 of this Act, in areas where no Family Court has been established or no Regional Trial Court was designated by the Supreme Court due to the limited number of cases, the DSWD shall designate and assign qualified, trained, and DSWD accredited social workers of the local government units to handle juvenile and family cases filed in the designated Regional Trial Court of the place.

Sec. 12. *Privacy and Confidentiality of Proceedings.* — All hearings and conciliation of the child and family cases shall be treated in a manner consistent with the promotion of the child's and family's dignity and worth, and shall respect their privacy at all stages of the proceedings. Records of the cases shall be dealt with utmost confidentiality and the identity of parties shall not be divulged unless necessary and with authority of the judge.

Sec. 13. *Special Rules of Procedure.* — The Supreme Court shall promulgate special rules of procedure for the transfer of cases to the new courts during the transition period and for the disposition of family cases with the best interests of the child and the protection of the family as primary consideration taking into account the United Nations Convention on the Rights of the Child.

x x x

Sec. 17. *Transitory Provisions.* — Pending the establishment of such Family Courts, the Supreme Court shall designate from among the branches of the Regional Trial Court at least one Family Court in each of the cities of Manila, Quezon, Pasay, Caloocan, Makati, Pasig, Mandaluyong, Muntinlupa, Laoag, Baguio, Santiago, Dagupan, Olongapo, Cabanatuan, San Jose, Angeles, Cavite, Batangas, Lucena, Naga, Iriga, Legazpi, Roxas, Iloilo, Bacolod, Dumaguete, Tacloban, Cebu, Mandaue, Tagbilaran, Surigao, Butuan, Cagayan de Oro, Davao, General Santos, Oroquieta, Ozamis, Dipolog, Zamboanga, Pagadian, Iligan, and in such other places as the Supreme Court may deem necessary.

Additional cases other than those provided in Section 5 may be assigned to the Family Courts when their dockets permit: Provided, That such additional cases shall not be heard on the same day family cases are heard.

In areas where there are no Family Courts, the cases referred to in Section 5 of this Act shall be adjudicated by the Regional Trial Court.

B. WHO MAY FILE COMPLAINT

A complaint is a sworn written statement charging a person with an offense, subscribed by the offended party, any peace officer or other public officer charged with the enforcement of the law violated.[100]

1. Crimes Under R.A. 7610

The following may file a complaint for crimes under R.A. 7610:[101]

a. offended party;
b. parent or legal guardian;

---

[102] Revised Rules of Court, Rule 110, Sec. 3.
[103] R.A. 7610, Sec. 27.

   c. ascendant or collateral relative of the child within the third degree of consanguinity;

   d. a duly authorized officer or social worker of the Department;

   e. officer, social worker or representative of a licensed child-caring institution;

   f. Barangay Chairman; or

   g. at least (3) concerned, responsible citizens where the violation occurred.

2. Crimes Under The RPC And Other Criminal Laws

The following may file a complaint for crimes under the RPC and other criminal laws, unless otherwise stated in such laws:

1. Any peace officer or other public officer charged with the enforcement of the law violated.

2. The crimes of seduction, abduction, or acts of lasciviousness shall not be prosecuted except upon a complaint filed by the following persons:
   a. offended minor;
   b. parents;
   c. grandparents; or
   d. legal guardian.

In case the minor fails to file the complaint, the right to file the action granted to parents, grandparents or guardian shall be exclusive of all other persons and shall be exercised successively in the order provided. If the offended party dies or becomes incapacitated before she can file a complaint, and she has no known parents, grandparents or guardian, the State shall initiate the criminal action in her behalf. If the offender has been expressly pardoned by any of the above-named persons the crime cannot anymore be prosecuted. [104]

C. WHERE TO FILE COMPLAINT

---

[104] Revised Rules of Courts, Rule 110, Sec. 5.

C. WHERE TO FILE COMPLAINT

1. Offenses Subject To The Katarungang Pambarangay[105]

a. Disputes between persons residing in the same barangay shall be brought for amicable settlement before the lupon of said barangay.

b. Those involving actual residents of different barangays within the same city or municipality shall be brought in the barangay where the respondent(s) actually reside.

2. Offenses Under The Jurisdiction Of The Regional Trial Courts or Family Courts[106]

For offenses falling under the jurisdiction of the Regional Trial Courts or Family Courts, the complaint shall be filed for preliminary investigation before the office of the provincial or city fiscal or the national or regional state prosecutor. The preliminary investigation may also be conducted by the judges of the Municipal Trial Courts or the Municipal Circuit Trial Courts. The foregoing persons shall, thereafter, file the corresponding information in the Regional Trail Courts or Family Courts, if their findings so warrant.

2.1 Compromise Agreements/Affidavits of Desistance/Plea Bargaining

Criminal cases cognizable by the trial courts, as a policy, cannot be the subject of compromise agreements or amicable settlements, unlike in cases brought before the Katarungang Pambarangay or in labor cases filed with the DOLE wherein such settlements are even encouraged.

---

[105] The Local Government Code of 1991, Sec. 409.
[106] Revised Rules of Court, Rule 110, Sec. 1, and Rule 112, Sec. 2.

Accordingly, if the accused enters into an agreement with the minor victim or the latter's parents for the payment of money in exchange for the withdrawal of the complaint, such agreement is not binding or conclusive upon the prosecutors or the courts which may continue with the hearing or trial of the case as long as there are still other witnesses willing to testify against the accused. Nevertheless, if the child and/or his/her witnesses refuse to testify in the course of the proceedings, and very little evidence is left at hand, the case may eventually be dismissed for insufficiency of evidence to prove the guilt of the accused beyond reasonable doubt.

Compromise agreements with respect to criminal cases, however, should be distinguished from plea-bargaining and from execution of affidavits of desistance which are permitted by law. Plea-bargaining or a plea of guilty to a lesser offense, if accepted by the complainant, is allowed by law, in which case the accused may be convicted only for the lesser offense. An affidavit of desistance executed by the complainant is also admissible in court as evidence in favor of the accused. Although such does not necessarily result in the outright dismissal of the case, an affidavit of desistance usually weakens the case against the complainant/offended party and may eventually lead to the same result.

D. PROCEDURES IN KATARUNGANG PAMBARANGAY[105]

1. **Complaint** - Upon payment of the appropriate filing fee, the complainant shall complain orally or in writing to the Lupon Chairman (Barangay Captain) of the barangay.

2. **Summons** - The Lupon Chairman shall within the next working day summon the respondent with notice to the complainant and their witnesses, to appear before him for a mediation.

---

[107] Condensed from The Local Government Code of 1991, Chapter 7 - Katarungang Pambarangay.

3. **Mediation** - The Lupon Chairman has 15 days, from the first meeting of the parties before him, to settle the conflict. If he fails to settle within 15 days, he shall constitute the Pangkat Tagapagkasundo which must convene within 3 days.

4. **Hearing** - A hearing shall be conducted by the Pangkat in order to simplify issues, and explore all possibilities for **amicable settlement**. The Pangkat shall arrive at a settlement/resolution within 15 days from the day it convenes, extendible for another 15 days in meritorious cases.

    Proceedings shall be public and informal. Parties must appear in person without the assistance of lawyers or representatives, except for minors or incompetents who may be assisted by their next-of-kin who are not lawyers.

5. **Agreement to Submit to Arbitration** - The parties may, at any stage of the proceedings, agree in writing to submit the dispute for arbitration by the Lupon Chairman or the Pangkat, and that they shall abide by the arbitration award.

6. **Amicable Settlement/Arbitration Award** - An amicable settlement reached by the parties, or an arbitration award given by the Lupon Chairman or Pangkat Chairman shall be in writing, in a language or dialect known to the parties, and signed by them and the Lupon Chairman or Pangkat Chairman, as the case may be.

7. **Repudiation of Settlement or Agreement to Arbitrate** - In the case of settlement, any party may, within 10 days from the date of the settlement, repudiate the same on the ground of fraud, violence or intimidation, by filing with the Lupon Chairman or the Pangkat Chairman a sworn statement to such effect.

    In the case of an agreement to arbitrate, such agreement may be repudiated within 5 days from the date of such agreement, on the same grounds stated above. If no repudiation of the agreement is made within the said 5 days, the Lupon Chairman or Pangkat shall issue an arbitration award within 10 days thereafter.

8. **Finality of Settlement or Arbitration Award** - The amicable settlement and arbitration award shall have the force and effect of a final judgment of a court upon the expiration of 10 days from the date thereof, unless repudiation of the settlement has been made as described above, or a "petition to nullify" the arbitration award has been filed before the proper city or municipal court.

9. **Certification for Filing a Complaint in Court** - In case no settlement is reached, or in case the settlement is repudiated on time, the Lupon or Pangkat Chairman shall issue a certificate to such effect, which entitles the parties to file their case with the regular courts.

E. SUMMARY PROCEDURES IN THE FAMILY COURTS

In cases involving children, violations of municipal or city ordinances, as well as, all other criminal cases where the penalty prescribed for the offense is imprisonment not exceeding 6 months, or a fine not exceeding P1,000.00, or both, irrespective of other imposable penalties or civil liability arising therefrom shall be subject to summary procedure before the Family Courts. The Revised Rules on Summary Procedure for Municipal Trial Courts shall apply. [108]

1. **Complaint or Information** - A complaint or information shall be filed with the Municipal Trial judge together with the affidavits of the complainant and of his/her witnesses. The court may already dismiss the complaint outright for being patently without basis or merit and order the release of the accused if in custody.

---

[108] *See* Revised Rules on Summary Procedure in relation to Section 5(a) of the Family Courts Act.

2. **Counter-Affidavits** - If the case is commenced by an information filed by the fiscal/prosecutor, the accused may submit counter-affidavits and the affidavits of his witnesses as well as any evidence in his behalf within 10 days from receipt of such order.

3. **Reply Affidavits** - The prosecution may file reply affidavits within 10 days from receipt of the counter-affidavits of the defense.

4. **Dismissal or Setting for Arraignment** - The court upon consideration of the complaint or information and affidavits may either dismiss the case or set the case for arraignment and trial.

5. **Arraignment** - If the accused is in custody for the crime charged, he shall be immediately arraigned and if he enters a plea of guilty, the court shall forthwith pronounce its sentence.

6. **Preliminary Conference** - Before actual trial, the court shall call the parties to a preliminary conference for a stipulation of facts, plea bargaining or for clarification of issues to ensure a speedy disposition of the case.

7. **Trial** - The affidavits of witnesses shall already constitute their direct testimonies. However, they may be subjected to cross-examination, redirect or re-cross examination. No witnesses shall be allowed to testify unless their affidavits were previously submitted to the court.

8. **Arrest of Accused** - The court shall not order the arrest of the accused except for failure to appear whenever required. Release of the person arrested shall either be on bail or on recognizance by a responsible citizen acceptable to the court.

9. **Judgment.** - The judge must promulgate the judgment not later than 30 days after the termination of the trial.

10. **Appeal** - Only the accused may appeal to the Regional Trial Court within 15 days from receipt of decision. The decision of the Regional Trial Court may again be appealed by the accused to the Court of Appeals or to the Supreme Court within 15 days from receipt of such.

F. PROCEDURES IN PRELIMINARY INVESTIGATION BEFORE FISCALS OR PROSECUTORS [107]

A preliminary investigation is an inquiry or proceeding for the purpose of determining whether there is sufficient ground to engender a well-founded belief that a crime cognizable by the Regional Trial Court or Family Court has been committed and that the respondent is probably guilty thereof. It is conducted by a fiscal or state prosecutor, or by a Municipal Trial judge, before an information is filed in court.

However, if the accused is lawfully arrested without a warrant, for an offense cognizable by the Regional Trial Court or Family Court, the complaint or information may be filed by the offended party, peace officer or fiscal without a preliminary investigation having been first conducted, on the basis of the affidavit of the offended party or arresting officer. The accused may still ask for a preliminary investigation later, if he signs a waiver of the provisions of Article 125 of the Revised Penal Code governing the release of detained persons.

1. **Complaint** - The complainant shall file a complaint and submit the affidavits of his/her witnesses, which shall be sworn to before the fiscals/state prosecutors.

2. **Dismissal or Subpoena** - Within 10 days from filing of complaint, the investigating officer shall either dismiss the same if he finds no ground to continue with the inquiry, or issue a subpoena to the respondent, together with a copy of the complaint and affidavits.

---

[109] Condensed from the Revised Rules of Court, Rule 112.

3. **Counter-affidavits** - Respondent is given 10 days from receipt of subpoena, to submit counter-affidavits.

4. **Hearing** - If the investigating officer believes that there are matters to be clarified he <u>may</u> set a hearing to propound clarificatory questions to the parties or their witnesses.

5. **Resolution** - The investigating officer shall resolve the case within 10 days from the last clarificatory hearing or the date the case has been submitted by both parties for resolution.

6. **Forward Records to Provincial/City Fiscal or Chief State Prosecutor** - Within 5 days from resolution, the investigating fiscal shall forward the records of the case to the provincial/city fiscal or chief state prosecutor.

7. **Approval or Reversal of Findings** - The provincial or city fiscal or chief state prosecutor shall take appropriate action within 10 days from receipt of records.

8. **Appeal to Secretary of Justice** - Upon petition by any party, the Secretary of Justice may reverse the resolution of the provincial or city fiscal or chief state prosecutor.

9. **Dismissal of Case or Filing of Information in Court** - The case may either be dismissed or filed in court for trial. In the latter case, an **information** is prepared and subscribed by the fiscal/prosecutor, charging the accused with an offense, and filed in court.[108]

---

[110] Revised Rules of Court, Rule 100, Sec. 4.

G. ORDINARY PROCEDURES IN THE REGIONAL TRIAL COURTS OR FAMILY COURTS

1. Arrest Of Accused

Upon the filing of an information by the fiscal the trial court shall issue a warrant for the arrest of the accused unless the latter is already under detention.

(See requirements for the issuance of warrants and the procedures on arrest on pages 380-383)

2. Bail

After the arrest of the accused, he or she may apply for bail unless charged with a capital offense or heinous crime and the evidence against him is strong.

Bail is the security given for the release of a person in custody of the law, furnished by him/her or a bondsman, conditioned upon his/her appearance before any court as required.[109] Under the Philippine Constitution, all persons are entitled to bail by sufficient sureties or to be released on recognizance by a responsible citizen, except those charged with offenses punishable by *reclusion perpetua,* life imprisonment or death when the evidence of guilt is strong.[110] Thus, even if the accused is charged with a heinous crime punishable by *reclusion perpetua* or death, he or she may still be granted bail if no strong evidence of guilt is presented before the judge in a hearing called for the purpose.

---

[111] Revised Rules of Court, Rule 114, Sec.1.

[112] Philippine Constitution, Art. 3 - Bill of Rights, Sec. 13; and Revised Rules of Court, Rule 114, Sec.7.

3. Arraignment And Plea

Arraignment consists of reading the information to the accused and asking him or her, in open court whether or not he or she is guilty of the crime charged.

A plea of guilty to a lesser offense may be allowed by the trial court if the offended party and the fiscal consents to such. A conviction under this lesser plea will constitute a bar to another prosecution for the higher offense.

4. Trial

At the trial, the prosecution shall present all its evidence to prove the charge against the accused and also his or her civil liability. After the prosecution rests its case, the defense is then given the chance to present its own evidence to dispute the charges. The parties may, thereafter, present rebutting evidence.

After all evidence has been presented, the court may order the parties to submit their respective briefs or memoranda proving their respective claims. The case shall be deemed submitted for decision upon the filing of the last pleading or memorandum.

The following are the laws which specifically govern the trial of cases of child abuse and exploitation:

4.1. R.A. 7610

Under R.A. 7610 and its implementing rules,[113] the trial of child abuse cases shall take precedence over all other cases before the courts, except election and habeas corpus cases. The said law also mandates that the trial of child abuse cases shall commence within 3 days from arraignment of the accused. Furthermore, the law permits the exclusion of the public during the giving of the testimony of the child victim and mandates that proceedings be held in the chambers of the judge.

---

[113] R.A. 7610, Sec. 29-30; and Rules and Regulations in the Reporting and Investigation of Child Abuse Cases, Sec. 20-23.

4.2 Administrative Circular No. 23-95

In October 1995, the Supreme Court issued Administrative Circular No. 23-95 governing the speedy trial of child labor and other child abuse cases. The provisions of the circular are as follows:

Republic Of The Philippines
Supreme Court
Manila
ADMINISTRATIVE CIRCULAR NO. 23-95

TO   : PRESIDING JUDGE OF ALL TRIAL
                    COURTS

SUBJECT : SPEEDY DISPOSITION OF CASES
                    INVOLVING CHILDREN
All trial judges are enjoined to act with dispatch on all cases involving children, including but not limited to child labor cases under Rep. Act No. 7610, cases of child abuses and pedophilia.

It is directed that arraignments should be scheduled within a week after the accused is placed in the court's custody or upon filing of the bailbond and pre-trial/trial shall commence within three (3) days from arraignment.

Attention is called to Section 30 of Rep. Act. 7610 which provides that violations of this Act should be heard in the chambers of the RTC duly designated as Juvenile and Domestic Relations Courts.

October 11, 1995.

ANDRES R. NARVASA
Chief Justice

4.3 Rule On Examination Of A Child Witness

Sec. 1. Applicability of the Rule.- Unless otherwise provided, this Rule shall govern the examination of child witnesses who are victims of crime, accused of a crime, and witnesses to crime. It shall apply in all criminal proceedings and non-criminal proceedings involving child witnesses

Sec. 2. Objectives.- The objectives of this Rule are to create and maintain an environment that will allow children to give reliable and complete evidence, minimize trauma to children, encourage children to testify in legal proceedings, and facilitate the ascertainment of truth.

Sec. 3. Construction of the Rule. - This Rule shall be liberally construed to uphold the best interests of the child and to promote maximum accommodation of child witnesses without prejudice to the constitutional rights of the accused.

Sec. 4. Definitions.-
(a) A "child witness" is any person who at the time of giving testimony is below the age of eighteen (18) years. In child abuse cases, a child includes one over eighteen (18) years but is found by the court as unable to fully take care of himself or protect himself from abuse, neglect, cruelty, exploitation, or discrimination because of a physical or mental disability or condition.

(b) "Child abuse" means physical, psychological, or sexual abuse, and criminal neglect as defined in Republic Act No. 7610 and other related laws.

(c) "Facilitator" means a person appointed by the court to pose questions to a child.

(d) "Record regarding a child" or "record" means any photograph, videotape, audiotape, film, handwriting, typewriting, printing, electronic recording, computer data or printout, or other memorialization, including any court document, pleading, or any copy or reproduction of any of the foregoing, that contains the name, description, address, school, or any other personal identifying information about a child or his family and that is produced or maintained by a public agency, private agency, or individual.

(e) A "guardian *ad litem*" is a person appointed by the court where the case is pending for a child who is a victim of, accused *of,* or a witness to a crime to protect the best interests of the said child.

(f) A "support person" is a person chosen by the child to accompany him to testify at or attend a judicial proceeding or deposition to provide emotional support for him.

(g) "Best interests of the child" means the totality of the circumstances and conditions as are most congenial to the survival, protection, and feelings of security of the child and most encouraging to his physical, psychological, and emotional development. It also means the least detrimental available alternative for safeguarding the growth and development of the child.

(h) "Developmental level" refers to the specific growth phase in which most individuals are expected to behave and function in relation to the advancement of their physical, socio-emotional, cognitive, and moral abilities.

(i) "In-depth investigative interview" or "disclosure interview" is an inquiry or proceeding conducted by duly trained members of a multidisciplinary team or representatives of law enforcement or child protective services for the purpose of determining whether child abuse has been committed.

Sec. 5. Guardian ad litem.-

(a)   The Court may appoint a guardian ad litem for a child who is a victim of, accused of, or a witness to a crime to promote the best interests of the child. In making the appointment, the court shall consider the background of the guardian *ad litem* and his familiarity with the judicial process, social service programs, and child development, giving preference to the parents of the child, if qualified. The guardian *ad litem* may be a member of the Philippine Bar. A person who is a witness in any proceeding involving the child cannot be appointed as a guardian *ad litem.*

(b)   The guardian *ad litem:*

(1)   Shall attend all interviews, depositions, hearings, and trial proceedings in which a child participates;

(2)   Shall make recommendations to the court concerning the welfare of the child;

(3)   Shall have access to all reports, evaluations, and records necessary to effectively advocate for the child, except privileged communications;

(4)   Shall marshal and coordinate the delivery of resources and special services to the child;

(5)   Shall explain, in language understandable to the child, all legal proceedings, including police investigations, in which the child is involved;

(6)   Shall assist the child and his family in coping with the emotional effects of crime and subsequent criminal or non-criminal

proceedings in which the child is involved;

(7)   May remain with the child while the child waits to testify;

(8)   May interview witnesses; and

(9)   May request additional examinations by medical or mental health professionals if there is a compelling need therefor.

(c)   The guardian *ad litem* shall be notified of all proceedings but shall not participate in the trial. However, he may file motions pursuant to sections 9, 10, 25, 26, 27 and 31(c). If the guardian *ad litem* is a lawyer, he may object during trial that questions asked of the child are not appropriate to his developmental level.

(d)   The guardian *ad litem* may communicate concerns regarding the child to the court through an officer of the court designated for that purpose.

(e)   The guardian *ad litem* shall not testify in any proceeding concerning any information, statement, or opinion received from the child in the course of serving as a guardian *ad litem,* unless the court finds it necessary to promote the best interests of the child.

(f)   The guardian *ad litem* shall be presumed to have acted in good faith in compliance with his duties described in sub-section (b).

Sec. 6. Competency.- Every child is presumed qualified to be a witness. However, the court shall conduct a competency examination of a child, *motu proprio* or on motion of a party, when it finds that substantial doubt exists regarding the ability of the child to perceive, remember, communicate, distinguish truth from falsehood, or appreciate the duty to tell the truth in court.

(a)   *Proof of necessity.-* A party seeking a competency examination must present proof of necessity of competency examination. The age of the child by itself is not a sufficient basis for a competency examination.

(b)   *Burden of proof.-* To rebut the presumption of competence enjoyed by a child, the burden of proof lies on the party challenging his competence.

(c)   *Persons allowed at competency examination.-* Only the following are allowed to attend a competency examination:
   (1)   The judge and necessary court personnel;
   (2)   The counsel for the parties;
   (3) The guardian *ad litem;*
   (4)   One or more support persons for the child; and
   (5)   The defendant, unless the court determines that competence can be fully evaluated in his absence.

(d)   *Conduct of examination.-* Examination of a child as to his competence shall be conducted only by the judge. Counsel for the parties, however, can submit questions to the judge that he may, in his discretion, ask the child.

(e) *Developmentally appropriate questions.* - The questions asked at the competency examination shall be appropriate to the age and developmental level of the child; shall not be related to the issues at trial; and shall focus on the ability of the child to remember, communicate, distinguish between truth and falsehood, and appreciate the duty to testify truthfully.

(f) *Continuing duty to assess competence.* - The court has the duty of continuously assessing the competence of the child throughout his testimony.

Sec. 7. *Oath or affirmation.* - Before testifying, a child shall take an oath or affirmation to tell the truth.

Sec. 8. *Examination of a child witness.* - The examination of a child witness presented in a hearing or any proceeding shall be done in open court. Unless the witness is incapacitated to speak, or the question calls for a different mode of answer, the answers of the witness shall be given orally.

The party who presents a child witness or the guardian *ad litem* of such child witness may, however, move the court to allow him to testify in the manner provided in this Rule.

Sec. 9. *Interpreter for child.* -
(a)   When a child does not understand the English or Filipino language or is unable to communicate in said languages due to his developmental level, fear, shyness, disability, or other similar reason, an interpreter whom the child can understand and who understands the child may be appointed by the court, *motu proprio* or upon motion, to interpret for the child.

(b)   If a witness or member of the family of the child is the only person who can serve as an interpreter for the child, he shall not be disqualified and may serve as the interpreter of the child. The interpreter, however, who is also a witness, shall testify ahead of the child.

(c)   An interpreter shall take an oath or affirmation to make a true and accurate interpretation.

Sec. 10. Facilitator to pose questions to child. -

(a) The court may, *motu proprio* or upon motion, appoint a facilitator if it determines that the child is unable to understand or respond to questions asked. The facilitator may be a child psychologist, psychiatrist, social worker, guidance counselor, teacher, religious leader, parent, or relative.

(b) If the court appoints a facilitator, the respective counsels for the parties shall pose questions to the child only through the facilitator. The questions shall either be in the words used by counsel or, if the child is not likely to understand the same, in words that are comprehensible to the child and which convey the meaning intended by counsel.

(c) The facilitator shall take an oath or affirmation to pose questions to the child according to the meaning intended by counsel.

Sec. 11. Support persons. -

(a) A child testifying at a judicial proceeding or making a deposition shall have the right to be accompanied by one or two persons of his own choosing to provide him emotional support.

(1) Both support persons shall remain within the view of the child during his testimony.

(2) One of the support persons may accompany the child to the witness stand, provided the support person does not completely obscure the child from the view of the opposing party, judge, or hearing officer.

(3) The court may allow the support person to hold the hand of the child or take other appropriate steps to provide emotional support to the child in the course of the proceedings.

(4) The court shall instruct the support

persons not to prompt, sway, or influence the child during his testimony.

(b) If the support person chosen by the child is also a witness, the court may disapprove the choice if it is sufficiently established that the attendance of the support person during the testimony of the child would pose a substantial risk of influencing or affecting the content of the testimony of the child.

(c) If the support person who is also a witness is allowed by the court, his testimony shall be presented ahead of the testimony of the child.

Sec. 12. Waiting area for child witnesses.- The courts are encouraged to provide a waiting area for children that is separate from waiting areas used by other persons. The waiting area for children should be furnished so as to make a child comfortable.

Sec. 13. Courtroom environment.- To create a more comfortable environment for the child, the court may, in its discretion, direct and supervise the location, movement and deportment of all persons in the courtroom including the parties, their counsel, child, witnesses, support persons, guardian ad litem, facilitator, and court personnel. The child may be allowed to testify from a place other than the witness chair. The witness chair or other place from which the child testifies may be turned to facilitate his testimony but the opposing party and his counsel must have a frontal or profile view of the child during the testimony of the child. The witness chair or other place from which the child testifies may also be rearranged to allow the child to see the opposing party and his counsel, if he chooses to look at them, without turning his body or leaving the witness stand. The judge need not wear his judicial robe.

Nothing in this section or any other provision of law, except official in-court identification provisions, shall be construed to require a child to look at the accused.

Accommodations for the child under this section need not be supported by a finding of trauma to the child.

Sec. 14. Testimony during appropriate hours.- The court may order that the testimony of the child should be taken during a time of day when the child is well-rested.

Sec. 15. Recess during testimony. -The child may be allowed reasonable periods of relief while undergoing direct, cross, re-direct, and re-cross examinations as often as necessary depending on his developmental level.

Sec. 16. Testimonial aids.- The court shall permit a child to use dolls, anatomically-correct dolls, puppets, drawings, mannequins, or any other appropriate demonstrative device to assist him in his testimony.

Sec. 17. Emotional security item.- While testifying, a child shall be allowed to have an item of his own choosing such as a blanket, toy, or doll.

Sec. 18. Approaching the witness.- The court may prohibit a counsel from approaching a child if it appears that the child is fearful of or intimidated by the counsel.

Sec. 19. Mode of questioning.- The court shall exercise control over the questioning of children so as to (1) facilitate the ascertainment of the truth, (2) ensure that questions are stated in a form appropriate to the developmental level of the child,

(3) protect children from harassment or undue embarrassment, and (4) avoid waste of time.

The court may allow the child witness to testify in a narrative form.

Sec. 20. Leading questions.- The court may allow leading questions in all stages of examination of a child if the same will further the interests of justice.

Sec. 21. Objections to questions.- Objections to questions should be couched in a manner so as not to mislead, confuse, frighten, or intimidate the child.

Sec. 22. Corroboration.- Corroboration shall not be required of a testimony of a child. His testimony, if credible by itself, shall be sufficient to support a finding of fact, conclusion, or judgment subject to the standard of proof required in criminal and non-criminal cases.

Sec. 23. Excluding the public.- When a child testifies, the court may order the exclusion from the courtroom of all persons, including members of the press, who do not have a direct interest in the case. Such an order may be made to protect the right to privacy of the child or if the court determines on the record that requiring the child to testify in open court would cause psychological harm to him, hinder the ascertainment of truth, or result in his inability to effectively communicate due to embarrassment, fear, or timidity. In making its order, the court shall consider the developmental level of the child, the nature of the crime, the nature of his testimony regarding the crime, his relationship to the accused and to persons attending the trial, his desires, and the interests of his parents or legal guardian. The court may, *motu proprio,* exclude the public from the courtroom if the evidence to be produced during trial is of such character as to be offensive to decency or public morals. The court may also, on motion of the accused, exclude the public from trial, except court personnel and the counsel of the parties.

Sec. 24. Persons prohibited from entering and leaving courtroom.- The court may order that persons attending the trial shall not enter or leave the courtroom during the testimony of the child.

Sec. 25. Live-link television testimony in criminal cases where the child is a victim or a witness.

(a) The prosecutor, counsel or the guardian *ad litem* may apply for an order that the testimony of the child be taken in a room outside the courtroom and be televised to the courtroom by live-link television.

Before the guardian *ad litem* applies for an order under this section, he shall consult the prosecutor or counsel and shall defer to the judgment of the prosecutor or counsel regarding the necessity of applying for an order. In case the guardian *ad Itiem* is convinced that the decision of the prosecutor or counsel not to apply will cause the child serious emotional trauma, he himself may apply for the order.

The person seeking such an order shall apply at least five (5) days before the trial date, unless the court finds on the record that the need for such an order was not reasonably foreseeable.

(b) The court may *motu proprio* hear and determine, with notice to the parties, the need for taking the testimony of the child through live-link television.

(c) The judge may question the child in chambers, or in some comfortable place other than the courtroom, in the presence of the support person, guardian *ad litem,* prosecutor, and counsel for the parties. The questions of the judge shall not be related to the issues at trial but to the feelings of the child about testifying in the courtroom.

(d) The judge may exclude any person, including the accused, whose presence or conduct causes fear to the child.

(e) The court shall issue an order granting or denying the use of live-link television and stating the reasons therefor. It shall consider the following factors:

(1) The age and level of development of the child;
(2) His physical and mental health, including any mental or physical disability;
(3) Any physical, emotional, or psychological injury experienced by him;
(4) The nature of the alleged abuse;
(5) Any threats against the child;
(6) His relationship with the accused or adverse party;
(7) His reaction to any prior encounters with the accused in court or elsewhere;
(8) His reaction prior to trial when the topic of testifying was discussed with him by parents or professionals;
(9) Specific symptoms of stress exhibited by the child in the days prior to testifying;
(10) Testimony of expert or lay witnesses;
(11) The custodial situation of the child and the attitude of the members of his family regarding the events about which he will testify; and
(12) Other relevant factors, such as court atmosphere and formalities of court procedure.

(f) The court may order that the testimony of the child be taken by live-link television if there is a substantial likelihood that the child would suffer trauma from testifying in the presence of the accused, his counsel or the prosecutor as the case may be. The trauma must be of a kind which would impair the completeness or truthfulness of the testimony of the child.

(g)   If the court orders the taking of testimony by live-link television:

(1)   The child shall testify in a room separate from the courtroom in the presence of the guardian *ad litem;* one or both of his support persons; the facilitator and interpreter, if any; a court officer appointed by the court; persons necessary to operate the closed-circuit television equipment; and other persons whose presence are determined by the court to be necessary to the welfare and well-being of the child;

(2)   The judge, prosecutor, accused, and counsel for the parties shall be in the courtroom. The testimony of the child shall be transmitted by live-link television into the courtroom for viewing and hearing by the judge, prosecutor, counsel for the parties, accused, victim, and the public unless excluded.

(3)   If it is necessary for the child to identify the accused at trial, the court may allow the child to enter the courtroom for the limited purpose of identifying the accused, or the court may allow the child to identify the accused by observing the image of the latter on a television monitor.

(4)   The court may set other conditions and limitations on the taking of the testimony that it finds just and appropriate, taking into consideration the best interests of the child.

(h) The testimony of the child shall be preserved on videotape, digital disc, or other similar devices which shall be made part of the court record and shall be subject to a protective order as provided in section 31(b).

Sec. 26. Screens, one-way mirrors, and other devices to shield child from accused.-
(a)   The prosecutor or the guardian *ad litem* may apply for an order that the chair of the child or that a screen or other device be placed in the courtroom in such a manner that the child cannot see the accused while testifying. Before the guardian *ad litem* applies for an order under this section, he shall consult with the prosecutor or counsel subject to the second and third paragraphs of section *25(a)* of this Rule. The court shall issue an order stating the reasons and describing the approved courtroom arrangement.

(b)   If the court grants an application to shield the child from the accused while testifying in the courtroom, the courtroom shall be arranged to enable the accused to view the child.

Sec. 27. Videotaped deposition.-
(a)   The prosecutor, counsel, or guardian *ad litem* may apply for an order that a deposition be taken of the testimony of the child and that it be recorded and preserved on videotape. Before the guardian *ad litem* applies for an order under this section, he shall consult with the prosecutor or counsel subject to the second and third paragraphs of section 25(a).

(b)   If the court finds that the child will not be able to testify in open court at trial, it shall issue an order that the deposition of the child be taken and preserved by videotape.

(c)   The judge shall preside at the

videotaped deposition of a child. Objections to deposition testimony or evidence, or parts thereof, and the grounds for the objection shall be stated and shall be ruled upon at the time of the taking of the deposition. The other persons who may be permitted to be present at the proceeding are:

(1) The prosecutor;
(2) The defense counsel;
(3) The guardian *ad litem;*
(4) The accused, subject to sub-section (e);
(5) Other persons whose presence is determined by the court to be necessary to the welfare and well-being of the child;
(6) One or both of his support persons, the facilitator and interpreter, if any;
(7) The court stenographer; and
(8) Persons necessary to operate the videotape equipment.

(d) The rights of the accused during trial, especially the right to counsel and to confront and cross-examine the child, shall not be violated during the deposition.

(e) If the order of the court is based on evidence that the child is unable to testify in the physical presence of the accused, the court may direct the latter to be excluded from the room in which the deposition is conducted. In case of exclusion of the accused, the court shall order that the testimony of the child be taken by live-link television in accordance with section 25 of this Rule. If the accused is excluded from the deposition, it is not necessary that the child be able to view an image of the accused.

(f) The videotaped deposition shall be preserved and stenographically recorded. The videotape and the stenographic notes shall be transmitted to the clerk of the court where the case is pending for safekeeping and shall be made a part of the record.

(g) The court may set other conditions on the taking of the deposition that it finds just and appropriate, taking into consideration the best interests of the child, the constitutional rights of the accused, and other relevant factors.

(h) The videotaped deposition and stenographic notes shall be subject to a protective order as provided in section 31(b).

(i) If, at the time of trial, the court finds that the child is unable to testify for a reason stated in section 25(f) of this Rule, or is unavailable for any reason described in section 4(c), Rule 23 of the 1997 Rules of Civil Procedure, the court may admit into evidence the videotaped deposition of the child in lieu of his testimony at the trial. The court shall issue an order stating the reasons therefor.

(j) After the original videotaping but before or during trial, any party may file any motion for additional videotaping on the ground of newly discovered evidence. The court may order an additional videotaped deposition to receive the newly discovered evidence.

Sec. 28. Hearsay exception in child abuse cases.- A statement made by a child describing any act or attempted act of child abuse, not otherwise admissible under the hearsay rule, may be admitted in evidence in any criminal or non-criminal proceeding subject to the following rules:

(a) Before such hearsay statement may be admitted, its proponent shall make known to the adverse party the intention to offer such statement and its particulars to provide him a fair opportunity to object. If the child is available, the court shall, upon motion of the adverse party, require the child to be present at the presentation of the hearsay statement for cross-examination by the adverse party. When the child is unavailable, the fact of such circumstance must be proved by the proponent.

(b)   In ruling on the admissibility of such hearsay statement, the court shall consider the time, content and circumstances thereof which provide sufficient indicia of reliability. It shall consider the following factors:

(1)   Whether there is a motive to lie;
(2)   The general character of the declarant child;
(3)   Whether more than one person heard the statement;
(4)   Whether   the   statement   was spontaneous;
(5)   The timing of the statement and the relationship between the declarant child and witness;
(6)   Cross-examination could not show the lack of knowledge of the dectarant child;
(7)   The possibility of faulty recollection of the declarant child is remote; and
(8)   The circumstances surrounding the statement are such that there is no reason to suppose the declarant~child misrepresented the involvement of the accused.

(c) The child witness shall be considered unavailable under the following situations:

(1)   Is deceased, suffers from physical infirmity, lack of memory, mental illness, or will be exposed to severe psychological injury; or
(2)   Is absent from the hearing and the proponent of his statement has been unable to

procure his attendance by process or other reasonable means.

(d) When the child witness is unavailable, his hearsay testimony shall be admitted only if corroborated by other admissible evidence.

Sec. 29. Admissibility of videotaped and audiotaped in-depth investigative or disclosure interviews in child abuse cases. - The court may admit videotape and audiotape in-depth investigative or disclosure interviews as evidence, under the following conditions:

(a) The child witness is unable to testify in court on grounds and under conditions established under section 28 (c).

(b) The interview of the child was conducted by duly trained members of a multidisciplinary team or representatives of law enforcement or child protective services in situations where child abuse is suspected so as to determine whether child abuse occurred.

(c) The party offering the videotape or audiotape must prove that:

> (1) the videotape or audiotape discloses the identity of all individuals present and at all times includes their images and voices;
> (2) the statement was not made in response to questioning calculated to lead the child to make a particular statement or is clearly shown to be the statement of the child and not the product of improper suggestion;
> (3) the videotape and audiotape machine or device was capable of recording testimony;
> (4) the person operating the device was competent to operate it;
> (5) the videotape or audiotape is authentic and correct; and
> (6) it has been duly preserved.

The individual conducting the interview of the child shall be available at trial for examination by any party. Before the videotape or audiotape is offered in evidence, all parties shall be afforded an opportunity to view or listen to it and shall be furnished a copy of a written transcript of the proceedings.

The fact that an investigative interview is not videotaped or audiotaped as required by this section shall not by itself constitute a basis to exclude from evidence out-of-court statements or testimony of th~ child. It may, however, be considered in determining the reliability of the statements of the child describing abuse.

Sec. 30. Sexual abuse shield rule. -

(a) *Inadmissible evidence.* - The following evidence is not admissible in any criminal proceeding involving alleged child sexual abuse:

(1) Evidence offered to prove that the alleged victim engaged in other sexual behavior; and
(2) Evidence offered to prove the sexual predisposition of the alleged victim.

(b) *Exception.* - Evidence of specific instances of sexual behavior by the alleged victim to prove that a person other than the accused was the source of semen, injury, or other physical evidence shall be admissible.

A party intending to offer such evidence must:
(1)   File a written motion at least fifteen (15) days before trial, specifically describing the evidence and stating the purpose for which it is offered, unless the court, for good cause, requires a different time for filing or permits filing during trial; and
(2)   Serve the motion on all parties and the guardian *ad litem* at least three (3) days before the hearing of the motion.

Before admitting such evidence, the court must conduct a hearing in chambers and afford the child, his guardian *ad litem,* the parties, and their counsel a right to attend and be heard. The motion and the record of the hearing must be sealed and remain under seal and protected by a protective order set forth in section 31(b). The child shall not be required to testify at the hearing in chambers except with his consent.

Sec. 31. *Protection of privacy and safety.* -

(a)   *Confidentiality of records.*- Any record regarding a child shall be confidential and kept under seal. Except upon written request and order of the court, a record shall only be released to the following:

(1)   Members of the court staff for administrative use;
(2)   The prosecuting attorney;
(3)   Defense counsel;
(4)   The guardian *ad litem;*
(5)   Agents of investigating law enforcement agencies; and
(6)   Other persons as determined by the court.

(b)   *Protective order.* - Any videotape or audiotape of a child that is part of the court record shall be under a protective order that provides as follows:

(1)   Tapes may be viewed only by parties, their counsel, their expert witness, and the guardian *ad litem.*
(2)   No tape, or any portion thereof, shall be divulged by any person mentioned in subsection (a) to any other person, except as necessary for the trial.
(3)   No person shall be granted access to the tape, its transcription or any part thereof

unless he signs a written affirmation that he has received and read a copy of the protective order; that he submits to the jurisdiction of the court with respect to the protective order; and that in case of violation thereof, he will be subject to the contempt power of the court.

(4) Each of the tape cassettes and transcripts thereof made available to the parties, their counsel, and respective agents shall bear the following cautionary notice:

> *"This object or document and the contents thereof are subject to a protective order issued by the court in (case title), (case number). They shall not be examined, inspected, read, viewed, or copied by any person, or disclosed to any person, except as provided in the protective order. No additional copies of the tape or any of its portion shall be made, given, sold, or shown to any person without prior court order. Any person violating such protective order is subject to the contempt power of the court and other penalties prescribed by law."*

(5) No tape shall be given, loaned, sold, or shown to any person except as ordered by the court.

(6) Within thirty (30) days from receipt, all copies of the tape and any transcripts thereof shall be returned to the clerk of court for safekeeping unless the period is extended by the court on motion of a party.

(7) This protective order shall remain in full force and effect until further order of the court.

(c) *Additional protective orders.* - The court may, *motu proprio* or on motion of any party, the child, his parents, legal guardian, or the guardian *ad litem,* issue additional orders to protect the privacy of the child.

(d) *Publication of identity contemptuous.*- Whoever publishes or causes to be published in any format the name, address, telephone number, school, or other identifying information of a child who is or is alleged to be a victim or accused of a crime or a witness thereof, or an immediate family of the child shall be liable to the contempt power of the court.

(e) *Physical safety of child; exclusion of evidence.* - A child has a right at any court proceeding not to testify regarding personal identifying information, including his name, address, telephone number, school, and other information that could endanger his physical safety or his family. The court may, however, require the child to testify regarding personal identifying information in the interest of justice.

(f) *Destruction of videotapes and audiotapes.* - Any videotape or audiotape of a child produced under the provisions of this Rule or otherwise made part of the court record shall be destroyed after five (5) years have elapsed from the date of entry of judgment.

(g) *Records of youthful offender.*- Where a youthful offender has been charged before any city or provincial prosecutor or before any municipal judge and the charges have been ordered dropped, all the records of the case shall be considered as privileged and may not be disclosed directly or indirectly to anyone for any purpose whatsoever.

Where a youthful offender has been charged and the court acquits him, or dismisses the case or commits him to an institution and subsequently releases him pursuant to Chapter 3 of P. D. No.603, all the records of his case shall also be considered as privileged and may not be disclosed directly or indirectly to anyone except to determine if a defendant may have his sentence suspended under Article 192 of P. D. No.603 or if he may be granted probation under the provisions of P. D. No.968 or to enforce hi~ civil liability, if said liability has been imposed in the criminal action. The youthful offender concerned shall not be held under any provision of law to be guilty of perjury or of concealment or misrepresentation by reason of his failure to acknowledge the case or recite any fact related thereto in response to any inquiry made to him for any purpose.

"Records" within the meaning of this sub-section shall include those which may be in the files of the National Bureau of Investigation and with any police department or government agency which may have been involved in the case. (Art. 200, P. D. No.603)

Sec. 32. *Applicability of ordinary rules.*- The provisions of the Rules of Court on deposition, conditional examination of witnesses, and evidence shall be applied in a suppletory character.

Sec. 33. *Effectivity.*- This Rule shall take effect on December 15, 2000 following its publication in two (2) newspapers of general circulation.

5. Judgment

Judgment is the adjudication by the court that the accused is guilty or not guilty of the offense charged, and the imposition of the proper penalty and civil liability provided for by law on the accused.[112]

Under the Philippine Constitution, all cases must be decided or resolved by all trial courts within 3 months from the date of submission. However, despite the expiration of this period,

---

[114] Revised Rules of Court, Rule 120, Sec. 1.

the court, without prejudice to such responsibilities as it may have incurred thereof, shall decide the case without further delay.[113]

6. Motion For Reconsideration/ New Trial/ Appeal

If the trial court acquits the accused or dismisses the case against him, the prosecution cannot appeal anymore. The right to appeal in criminal cases decided by the courts is only available to the accused, save in exceptional cases where there is failure of trial or gross ignorance of the law by the trial judge.

If the accused is convicted, he has 15 days to file a motion for new trial or reconsideration, or to file an appeal with the Court of Appeals or Supreme Court. Otherwise, the judgment becomes final and executory, after which he shall begin to serve his sentence.

Once a judgment becomes final, the complainant may not file another case against the accused for the same offense earlier charged or for any attempt to commit the same offense or frustration thereof. Nor may the complainant file another case for an offense which necessarily includes or is necessarily included in the offense earlier charged. If an act is punished by a law and an ordinance, conviction or acquittal under either shall also constitute a bar to another prosecution for the same act. To allow the foregoing would constitute "double jeopardy" which is prohibited under the Philippine Constitution. Under the rule on "double jeopardy,"[114] when an accused has been convicted or acquitted, or the case against him dismissed without his express consent, by a court of competent jurisdiction, his conviction or acquittal or the dismissal of the case shall constitute a bar to another prosecution for the offense charged.

---

[115] Philippine Constitution, Art. 8, Sec. 15.
[116] Philippine Constitution, Article 3, Sec. 21; Revised Rules of Court, Rule 117, Sec. 7.

BIBLIOGRAPHY

264th Session of the Governing Body. Committee on Employment and Social Policy, ILO, International Labour Office, Geneva, November 1995.

Amparita Sta. Maria, Mary Jane Zantua, Rea Chiongson, *Internal Trafficking in Children for the Worst Forms of Child Labor: Final Report*, p. 10 citing Revised Penal Code by Luis Reyes, vol. 2 p. 557, citing P. v. Apolinar (CA) 62 OG 9044. (forthcoming 2002).

Attacking Child Labour in the Philippines. *An Indicative Framework for Philippine-IL 0 Action*. International Labour Office, Geneva, 1994.

Ballescas, Rosario, The Institutional Context of Child Labor, UP. Department of Sociology, Quezon City, 1987.

Bequele, Assefa, "Questions and Answers," in Child Labour: A Briefing Manual, ILO Geneva, 1986.

Bequele, Aseffa and Boyden Jo, Combating Child Labour, ILO Geneva, 1988.

Boyden Jo and Myers W., *Exploring Alternative Approaches to Child Labour: Case Studies from Developing Countries,*Innocenti Occasional Payers. Child Rights Series, Number 8, UNICEF, International Child Development Center, Florence, Italy, February, 1995.

Child Labour: A Briefing Manual, *Excerpt from the Report of the Director-GeneraL* ILO, Geneva, 1986.

"Child Labor Program. Questions and Answers", unpublished reports, Child Labor Project Management Team, Department of Labor and Employment.

Children in Especially Difficult Circumstances (CEDC-1), UNICEF, Thailand, January 1989.

Comprehensive Study on Child Labor in the Philippines, Institute for Labor Studies, DOLE, Intramuros, Manila, 1994

Cruz, T., *Pact Signed on Protection of Child Labor,* Philippine Times Journal, August 15 1992.

Datasets on Child Labour in the Philippines, ILO-IPEC, Makati, Philippines, 1995.

Del Rosario, Victoria, Child Labor Phenomenon in the Philippines: Problems and Policy Thrusts, Philippine Journal of Industrial Relations, UP., 1986.

Geneva NGO Group for the Convention on the Rights of the Child Sub-Group on Child Labour, *The New ILO Worst Forms of Child Labour Convention 1999,* (visited June 18, 2001) <http://www.antislavery.org/homepage/resources/ILOeng.pdf>.

Kebebew Ashagrie, International Labour Office, Geneva. First Published in 1997, revised April 1998, *Statistics on Working Children and Hazardous Child Labour in Brief,* (visited October 9, 2001) <http://www.ilo.org/public/english/standards/ipec/simpoc/stats/child/stats.htm>.

Longford, Michael, Seminar on Ways and Means of Achieving the Elimination of Child Labour in All Parts of the World, Geneva, Switzerland, 1985.

Mendelievich, Elias, Children at Work, ILO, Geneva, 1979.

Mnookin, Robert and Weisberg, D. Kelly, Child. Family and State: Problems and Materials on Children and the Law, Little Brown and Company, Canada, 1989.

Philippine National Monograph on Child Labor, Bureau of Women and Young Workers, DOLE, Manila, 1987.

Rialp, Victoria, *Children and Hazardous Work in the Philippines,.* ILO-Child Labour Collection, International Labour Office - ILO, Geneva, 1993.

Statistics:Revealing a Hidden Tragedy, (visited May 2001) <http"//www.ilo.org/publish/English/standards/ipec/ simpoc/stats/4stt.htm>.

Still So Far to Go: Child Labor in the World Today. International Labor Office Special Report on the Occasion of the 10th Anniversary of the International Year of the Child, ILO, Geneva, 1989.

The Convention on the Worst Forms of Child Labour (No. 182) Comes into Force: What Does this Mean? (Visited October 10, 2001) <http://www.ilo.org/public/english/standards/ ipec/about/factsheet/facts23pr.htm>.

www.ingramcontent.com/pod-product-compliance
Lightning Source LLC
Chambersburg PA
CBHW062149270326

41930CB00009B/1483